NEW

THI

There are more than one hundred and fifty
Rough Guide travel, phrasebook, and music titles,
covering destinations from Amsterdam to Zimbabwe,
languages from Czech to Thai, and musics from
World to Opera and Jazz

Forthcoming titles include

Dominican Republic • Jerusalem • Laos
Melbourne • Sydney

Rough Guides on the Internet

www.roughguides.com

Rough Guide Credits

Text editor: Judith Bamber
Series editor: Mark Ellingham
Typesetting: Justin Bailey and Helen Ostick
Cartography: Nichola Goodliffe

Publishing Information

This first edition published August 1999 by
Rough Guides Ltd, 62–70 Shorts Gardens, London, WC2H 9AB

Distributed by the Penguin Group:

Penguin Books Ltd, 27 Wrights Lane, London W8 5TZ
Penguin Books USA Inc., 375 Hudson Street, New York 10014, USA
Penguin Books Australia Ltd, 487 Maroondah Highway,
PO Box 257, Ringwood, Victoria 3134, Australia
Penguin Books Canada Ltd, 10 Alcorn Avenue,
Toronto, Ontario, Canada M4V 1E4
Penguin Books (NZ) Ltd, 182–190 Wairau Road,
Auckland 10, New Zealand

Typeset in Bembo and Helvetica to an original design by Henry Iles.
Printed in Spain by Graphy Cems.

© Samantha Cook 320pp, includes index
A catalogue record for this book is available from the British Library.
ISBN 1-85828-440-6

NEW ORLEANS

THE MINI ROUGH GUIDE

by Samantha Cook

We set out to do something different when the first Rough Guide was published in 1982. Mark Ellingham, just out of university, was travelling in Greece. He brought along the popular guides of the day, but found they were all lacking in some way. They were either strong on ruins and museums but went on for pages without mentioning a beach or taverna. Or they were so conscious of the need to save money that they lost sight of Greece's cultural and historical significance. Also, none of the books told him anything about Greece's contemporary life – its politics, its culture, its people, and how they lived.

So with no job in prospect, Mark decided to write his own guidebook, one which aimed to provide practical information that was second to none, detailing the best beaches and the hottest clubs and restaurants, while also giving hard-hitting accounts of every sight, both famous and obscure, and providing up-to-the-minute information on contemporary culture. It was a guide that encouraged independent travellers to find the best of Greece, and was a great success, getting shortlisted for the Thomas Cook travel guide award, and encouraging Mark, along with three friends, to expand the series.

The Rough Guide list grew rapidly and the letters flooded in, indicating a much broader readership than had been anticipated, but one which uniformly appreciated the Rough Guide mix of practical detail and humour, irreverence and enthusiasm. Things haven't changed. The same four friends who began the series are still the caretakers of the Rough Guide mission today: to provide the most reliable, up-to-date and entertaining information to independent-minded travellers of all ages, on all budgets.

We now publish more than 150 titles and have offices in London and New York. The travel guides are written and researched by a dedicated team of more than 100 authors, based in Britain, Europe, the USA and Australia. We have also created a unique series of phrasebooks to accompany the travel series, along with an acclaimed series of music guides, and a best-selling pocket guide to the Internet and World Wide Web. We also publish comprehensive travel information on our Web site: **www.roughguides.com**

Help Us Update

We've gone to a lot of effort to ensure that this first edition of The Mini *Rough Guide to New Orleans* is as up to date and accurate as possible. However, if you feel there are places we've underrated or over-praised, or find we've missed something good or covered something which has now gone, then please write: suggestions, comments or corrections are much appreciated.

We'll credit all contributions, and send a copy of the next edition (or any other Rough Guide if you prefer) for the best letters. Please mark letters: "Rough Guide New Orleans Update" and send to: Rough Guides, 62–70 Shorts Gardens, London, WC2H 9AB, or
Rough Guides, 375 Hudson St, New York NY 10014.
Or send email to: **mail@roughguides.co.uk**
Online updates about this book can be found on Rough Guides' Web site (see opposite).

The Author

Samantha Cook first visited New Orleans in 1990, fell in love with the place and has returned every year since. She has been involved with Rough Guides for ten years, starting out as an author on the Rough Guide to the USA and contributing to many other titles. For several years she worked in the office as an editor and managing editor, but left in 1998 to return to full-time writing.

Acknowledgements

In New Orleans, many thanks to Christine de Cuir, Sal Impastato, Paul Gustings, Larone Hudson, Kathy, Tzarine, Julie Kahn Valentine, Bonnie Warren, Rob Faust, Constantine Georges, Calvin and Monica Williams Mark McGrain, Cheryl Gerber and Ernie K-Doe. A big thank you also to the team at Rough Guides, especially Judith Bamber for her calm and committed editing, but also Nichola Goodliffe for her hard work on the maps, Justin Bailey and Helen Ostick for typesetting. Margaret Doyle for reading the proofs. Finally, love and thanks to Greg Ward for his unwavering encouragement, for his wisdom and for so enthusiastically sharing the adventure; to Jim Cook for the big lunches, great ideas and infectious passion for travel; to Bev Thomas and Annie Shaw who helped more than they know; and, of course, to the inspirational Pam Cook for her invaluable support and her daredevil spirit.

CONTENTS

Contexts

Introduction

As it enters its fourth century, **New Orleans** remains proudly apart from the rest of the United States. Intoxicating and addictive, the product of a dizzying jumble of cultures, peoples and influences, it's a place where people dance at funerals and hold parties during hurricanes, where some of the world's finest musicians make ends meet busking on street corners, and fabulous Creole cuisine is dished up in hole-in-the-wall dives. There's a wistfulness too, in the peeling, ice-cream toned façades of the old French Quarter – site of the original settlement – in the filigree cast-iron balconies overgrown with lush ferns and fragrant jasmine, and in the cemeteries, or "cities of the dead", lined with crumbling above-ground marble tombs. Doubtless New Orleans' melancholy air – and perhaps its joie de vivre, also – is due to the city's perilous geography. Set largely below sea level, and exposed to the devastating storms that career through the Gulf of Mexico, New Orleans could be washed or blasted away in an instant.

Founded by the French in 1718 on the swampy flood plain of the lower Mississippi River, and today spreading back as far as the enormous Lake Pontchartrain, New Orleans is almost entirely surrounded by water, which since its earliest days has both isolated it from the interior and connected it to the outside world. By the time the

Americans bought it, in the Louisiana Purchase of 1803, New Orleans was a many-textured city whose ethnically diverse population had mingled to create a distinctive Creole culture. In the nineteenth century its huge importance as a port of entry made the city the haunt of smugglers, gamblers, prostitutes and pirates that gave it the decadent "sin city" notoriety that it keeps today. Ever since then more and more visitors, among them an inordinate number of artists, writers and sundry bohemians, have poured in to see what the fuss was about; many found themselves staying, unable to shake the place out of their system.

New Orleans is a surprisingly small town, with its million or so residents spread across a patchwork of neighborhoods. Its compact size makes it a dream to visit; simple to get around and easy to get to know, it's one of the best places in the US to kick back and unwind for a few days. Above all, New Orleans is less a city of major sights than of sensual pleasures. With its subtropical climate, Latin-influenced architecture and black majority population, its voodoo worshippers and its long-held carnival traditions, it has been called the northernmost Caribbean city. The pace of life is slow here, while the sybaritic vices are relished – no more so than during the many festivals, especially, of course, the world-famous carnival of Mardi Gras, when real life is put on hold as businessmen and bus-boys alike are swept along by an increasingly frenzied season of parties, street parades and masquerade balls. Whatever time of year you come, you'll slip easily into the indolent way of life, rejecting an itinerary of museum-hopping in favor of a stroll around the French Quarter, where the bohemian street life and crumbling buildings provide endless feasts for the eye; a leisurely steamboat cruise on the Mississippi; or simply a long cool drink in a hidden courtyard. Heading out to the Garden District on the slow-moving old streetcar takes you to a residential district where dark green shrubs weighed down by fat magnolia blossoms squat in the shadow of centuries-old Live Oaks – evergreen oak trees – tangled with ragged gray streamers of Spanish moss.

Though many of the city's most lingering pleasures come after dark, when the streets fill with people eating in the hundreds of superb restaurants, drinking at its many characterful bars, and enjoying a live music scene to rival any in the world, there's a whole lot more to New Orleans – the "Big Easy", the "city that care forgot" – than its fame as a non-stop party town. Ravaged by the Civil War and trailing in the wake of its more dynamic Southern rivals, today New Orleans depends heavily upon the cash brought by the millions of tourists seduced by the allure of authentic jazz, fine food, and free-flowing alcohol. While having enormous amounts of fun here, you're always liable to be pulled up short by the divisions between rich and poor (and, more explicitly, between white and black). Just foot-steps away from the feted French Quarter and Garden District – themselves touched by decrepitude and decay – lie woefully neglected housing projects and poverty-scarred neighborhoods.

Perversely, New Orleans' second-league status, in com-mercial terms, has protected it from the modernization that has ripped out the old hearts of wealthier cities, and allowed it to hold on to its distinctive character. And this sense of historic continuity is not limited to architecture. From the devout celebration of Catholic saints' days and the offerings left at voodoo shrines, to the local street parades, in which umbrella-twirling dancers and blasting brass bands lead crowds of thousands through poor black neighbor-hoods just as they have done for centuries, much of the city's vitality and its sheer panache comes from a heartfelt belief that what has gone before is worth keeping. The melange of cultures and races that built New Orleans still gives it its heart; not "easy", exactly, but quite unlike anywhere else in the States – or in the world.

When to visit

New Orleans has a subtropical **climate**, with warm temperatures, high humidity and heavy rainfall. Thanks to its busy convention calendar, heavy weekend tourist traffic and a seemingly endless stream of festivals, the city stays pretty full year round, but the peak **tourist seasons** are Mardi Gras – which starts on Twelfth Night and builds up in intensity until Mardi Gras itself, the day before Ash Wednesday – and JazzFest, which spreads across a fortnight at the end of April and the start of May. Both, along with the increasingly popular French Quarter festival, occur in **spring**, which is a pleasant, sunny time to visit. However, the humidity is already building up by then, and JazzFest especially can be plagued by heavy rain.

The torpid months between May and September, when the blistering heat and intense humidity prove debilitating in the extreme, count as **off-season**; prices may be lower and crowds thinner at this time, but for good reason. From May to November the city is at risk from the **hurricanes** that sweep through the Gulf of Mexico. Even if it doesn't get a direct hit, New Orleans can be seriously affected by a tropical storm hitting land anywhere along the coast.

Climate-wise, **fall** is one of the best times to visit: October especially tends to be sunny, warm and relatively dry, though the nights can be chilly. Even in **winter** the days never get too cold; the nights, however, are another matter, cursed by the bone-bitingly damp air that creeps in from the river.

Plagued by heavy pollination, humidity and pollution, New Orleans is a year-round nightmare for **allergy** sufferers, and can bring on miserable symptoms even for those who have never experienced them before. Bring your own medication, or stock up when you arrive.

New Orleans' climate

	°F Average daily		°C Average daily		Rainfall Average monthly	
	max	min	max	min	in	mm
Jan	69	43	20	6	4.97	126
Feb	65	45	18	7	5.23	133
March	71	52	21	11	4.73	120
April	79	59	26	15	4.50	114
May	85	65	29	18	5.07	129
June	90	71	32	21	4.63	118
July	91	74	33	23	6.73	171
Aug	90	73	32	22	6.02	153
Sept	87	70	30	21	5.87	49
Oct	79	59	26	15	2.66	67
Nov	70	50	21	10	4.06	52
Dec	64	45	17	7	5.27	133

THE GUIDE

Introducing the city

One of New Orleans' many nicknames is "the **Crescent City**", because of the way it nestles between the southern shore of Lake Pontchartrain and a dramatic horseshoe bend in the Mississippi River. This unique location makes the city's layout confusing, with streets curving to follow the river and shooting off at odd angles to head inland. In the face of such dizzying geography, compass points are of little use – locals refer instead to **lakeside** (toward the lake) and **riverside** (toward the river), and, using Canal Street as the dividing line, **uptown** (or upriver) and **downtown** (downriver).

In a sense, everything begins at **Canal Street**, the broad commercial thoroughfare that sweeps from the river to the lake. Streets crossing Canal, which in the 1800s divided the old Creole city from the new American suburbs, change their names on either side of it – thus Royal Street in the French Quarter becomes St Charles uptown; Bourbon becomes Carondelet and so on, while any street name prefixed with "North" simply swaps it for "South" uptown. **Building numbers** also restart at 100 on either side of Canal.

Most tourists head first for the battered old **French Quarter** (or Vieux Carré), the compact, thirteen-block-long site of the original grid settlement. Centering on

Staying safe in New Orleans

New Orleans' high **crime** rate should be taken seriously. Widespread poverty and attendant drug problems mean that simply crossing the street can take you from a familiar environment into a bleak, potentially threatening neighborhood, where tourists tripping around with cameras and wallets full of dollars are easy prey. That said, visitors who use a modicum of common sense will probably be faced with nothing more threatening than the gangs of young **street hustlers** who accost tourists in the French Quarter (see p.31).

However, you do need to keep your wits about you. While it's safe enough to walk around the **French Quarter** during the day, you should be on your guard after dark in the quieter streets above Bourbon. You're approaching **Rampart Street** here, the border with the underprivileged neighborhood of Tremé – though you're not necessarily in any danger (the proximity of *Donna's* and *Funky Butt*, two of the city's best music clubs, helps matters), it can feel intimidating until you get your bearings. The **Garden District**, also, is safe enough during the day, and there's little reason to be there at night; parts of the **Lower Garden District**, however, including some run-down stretches of lower Magazine Street, can feel menacing at any time.

Wherever you are, if you feel nervous, trust your instincts, turn back, or call a **taxi**. Above all, *always* take a cab when traveling any distance outside the Quarter at night.

Parisian-style **Jackson Square**, a stone's throw from the Mississippi, the Quarter's combination of crumbling Creole architecture, fabulous restaurants and eccentric street life proves irresistible. Downriver, oak-shaded **Esplanade Avenue**, lined with crumbling Italianate mansions, separates the Quarter from the funky **Faubourg Marigny**, a low-rent district of ramshackle Creole cottages. Though predominantly residential, the Faubourg, as it is known, features a host of excellent bars, clubs and restaurants, especially along **Frenchmen Street**, which shoots off at an angle from Esplanade. The Quarter's lakeside boundary, **Rampart Street**, marks the beginning of the historic African-American neighborhood of **Tremé**. Here, Congo Square, site of Sunday slave gatherings in the 1700s, stands in today's run-down **Louis Armstrong Park**, while a handful of neighborhood bars and clubs feature the city's best brass bands.

On the other side of the Quarter, across **Canal Street**, the **CBD** (Central Business District), bounded by the river and I-10, spreads upriver to the elevated Pontchartrain Expressway. This was the early "American sector", settled by Anglo-Americans after the Louisiana Purchase in 1803. Today, dominated by offices, hotels and banks, it also incorporates the revitalizing **Warehouse District** and, toward the lake, the gargantuan **Superdome**. A short ferry ride across the river from the foot of Canal Street takes you from the bustle of downtown to the suburban west bank, where peaceful old **Algiers**, set on a dramatic bend in the Mississippi, features the city's best Mardi Gras museum.

Back on the east bank, it's an easy journey upriver from the CBD to the rarefied **Garden District**, an area of gorgeous old mansions – some highly restored, others derelict – covering the sixteen or so blocks between Jackson and Louisiana avenues. (Don't confuse it with the **Lower Garden District**; creeping between the expressway and Jackson, this is quite a different creature, its run-down old houses filling with impoverished artists and musicians.) The best way to get to the Garden District is on the historic streetcar, which clangs its way along swanky **St Charles Avenue**, the district's lakeside boundary; you can also approach it from **Magazine Street**, a six-mile stretch of hip galleries and antique stores that runs parallel to St Charles riverside. Entering the Garden District, you cross the official boundary into **Uptown**, which spreads upriver to encompass **Audubon Park and Zoo**, Loyola and Tulane **universities**, and, where the streetcar takes a sharp turn inland, the studenty **Riverbend** district.

If you're here for JazzFest, you'll be spending a lot of time in **Mid-City**, the huge swathe of land fanning out beyond Tremé up to Lake Pontchartrain. In addition to the Fair Grounds racetrack, site of the annual festival, Mid-City incorporates **Esplanade Ridge**, where Victorian houses and a handful of good restaurants hug both sides of Esplanade Avenue. Esplanade slices through the heart of the district, ending up at **City Park** with its impressive Museum of Art.

....
The telephone area code for New Orleans is ©504.
....

ARRIVAL

By air

New Orleans International Airport, twelve miles northwest of downtown on I-10, is relatively small and easy to handle. The **information booth** (daily 8am–9pm) in the baggage claim area has leaflets and maps.

The best way to get into town is by **taxi**. Flat-rate fares to downtown – a twenty- to thirty-minute journey – are $21 for up to two people, or $8 each for three or more. Simply join the line outside baggage claim and wait for the controller to usher you into a cab. If you're traveling alone, it's cheaper to take the **airport shuttle** (every 10min; $10 to downtown hotels; ☎522-3500), but because it stops frequently to drop people off, the journey time can be as much as an hour. Tickets are available in the baggage claim area or from the driver.

There's also a **public bus** from the airport to Tulane Avenue in the CBD (daily 6am–5.30pm; every 15–25min; $1.50), but it takes carry-on luggage only and you'd have to be in dire financial straits to battle with this when you've just stumbled off a plane.

By car

New Orleans is traversed by **I-10**, which runs east–west between Florida and California. You can get onto it from I-59 (east of the city) and I-55 (west). Taking I-12, which runs east–west north of the lake, hooks you up with the **Lake Pontchartrain Causeway** – at 23 miles, the longest bridge in the world – which enters the city from the northwest and connects with I-10.

Approaching from either direction on I-10 you're confronted with the usual bewildering choice of lanes and lack of signs: make sure not to stray onto I-610, which bypasses downtown altogether. For the **CBD** take exit 234C, following signs for the Superdome; for the **French Quarter** take 235A, following signs for Vieux Carré, and for the **Garden District** take the St Charles Street exit.

By bus or train

Greyhound **buses** (☎1-800/231-2222) and Amtrak **trains** (☎1-800/872-7245), from LA, New York and Chicago, stop at the Union Passenger Terminal, Loyola Ave, near the Superdome (☎528-1610). This area, in the no-man's land beneath the Pontchartrain Expressway, is dangerous at night; take a cab to your hotel.

ARRIVAL: BY CAR, BUS OR TRAIN

MAPS AND INFORMATION

Before you leave home it can be worth contacting the **New Orleans CVB** (©1-800/672-6124, *www.nawlins.com*), who mail out stacks of glossy brochures. Once you've arrived, for detailed information on the city, self-guided walking tours and a variety of discount vouchers, drop in at the **New Orleans Welcome Center**, in the French Quarter at 529 St Ann St, on Jackson Square (daily 9am–5pm; ©566-5031). Their free **maps** are adequate, but for more detail – and if you're driving – you'd do better to buy the Dolph *Street Map of New Orleans* ($2.95) or the *MapEasy Guidemap*, a glossy, user-friendly publication marking restaurants, bars, stores and attractions.

Accommodation reviews begin on p.131.

THE MEDIA

Though New Orleans' **media** can be astoundingly parochial, there's no better way to get a sense of what drives this quirky, individualistic city than by reading its papers. The city **daily** is the *Times-Picayune* (a *picayune* being the Creole term for a small coin), which costs 50¢, $1 on Sunday. Heavily geared toward local news, it has a couple of strong columnists, and on Friday it includes a useful **entertainment supplement**, *Lagniappe* (another Creole term, meaning a little extra, a treat). Readings and literary events are listed in the books pages of the Sunday edition.

New Orleans also has a host of good **free papers**, available from cafés, bars and stores. The excellent **weekly** *Gambit* leans slightly more to the left than the *Times-Picayune*, with opinionated editorials and local news. Its *24/7* pages are a good source of **entertainment information** – though the

New Orleans on the Internet

www.annerice.com Author Anne Rice's official site, with more than 100 pages, including transcripts of her weekly voice-mail messages (✆522-8634; see p.80), question-and-answer sessions, and an occasional newsletter, *Commotion Strange*. The site also includes an ordering service for a range of Anne Rice-related merchandise.

www.bestofneworleans.com Online version of *Gambit Weekly* (see opposite), with an extensive archive of back issues.

www.nolalive.com Clearly laid out news, entertainment and community site, run by the *Times-Picayune* (see opposite). It features the Bourbocam, a 24-hour video-surveillance camera pointed on Bourbon Street, along with restaurant reviews and a range of lively forums.

www.offbeat.com Online version of the monthly music paper *Offbeat* (see p.10), with updates on festivals and local music events, a copious messageboard, and a marketplace for ordering CDs. Good links to other music- and tourism-related sites.

www.satchmo.com Excellent, definitive music site, featuring listings, hundreds of links to homepages of local musicians, bands and clubs, a music news archive, concert line, and CD- and video-ordering service.

www.yatcom.com Very useful list of more than ninety links of local interest, ranging from sites devoted to weather, cookery, Mardi Gras krewes and the like, to homepages put out by local families and businesses.

For a **gay Web site**, see p.235.

music listings, organized by genre, can be difficult to find your way around – and its useful cuisine section reviews restaurants and details upcoming foodie events. A sister publication, the magazine-format *Gambit Native's Guide*, is geared toward visitors who want to discover "the real New Orleans". Though useful for pulling together listings information, it doesn't reveal quite as many insiders' tips as it likes to imply: reviews are simply drawn from the weekly paper, and the articles tend to be uncritical puff pieces.

For gay publications in New Orleans see p.234.

Star among the city's publications, however, *Offbeat* is a superb **music monthly**, filled with articles, interviews, news, gossip, reviews and extensive listings. Though it's an essential read for anyone interested in the city's live music scene, by the end of the month the **listings** can be less reliable; if you're in town at that time call individual venues to check – the bi-hourly listings announcements made on WWOZ radio (see below) are simply drawn from *Offbeat*. Newer on the scene, the monthly entertainment paper *Where y'at* is still finding its feet; though not in the same class as *Offbeat*, it's worth a look for feature articles and record reviews.

Television and radio

You're not going to be spending a lot of time in front of the TV in New Orleans. However, the PBS station **WYES** is worth checking on Friday night for its mix of reviews and local news in *Steppin' Out* and *Informed Sources*. By far the best of the **radio stations**, the fabulous, non-profit **WWOZ** (90.7FM) calls itself a "jazz and heritage station". Playing roots New Orleans music – r'n'b, blues, brass, jazz, funk, gospel – along with world music and old time country, it also features jam sessions, poetry, and ticket competitions. Other stations worth tuning into are WODT (1280AM), for blues, and WQUE (93.3FM), for soul and r'n'b.

CITY TRANSPORT

Though New Orleans' most visited neighborhoods are a dream to **walk** around – the French Quarter and Garden District, in particular, are best enjoyed by a leisurely stroll – getting from one area to another is not always easy on foot. Other than the obligatory jaunt on the historic **St Charles streetcar**, however, you may find yourself getting limited mileage out of the city's **public transport** system – to make the most of your time, budget for a few **taxi** rides. And at **night**, of course, you shouldn't consider traveling outside the French Quarter in anything but a cab.

Buses and streetcars

The Regional Transit Authority (RTA) runs a network of **buses** across the city ($1–1.25; 24hr information ℂ248-3900). **Routes** are numbered and named; the most useful include "Canal" (#41), which runs along Canal Street; "Magazine" (#11) from the CBD to the Garden District; and "Esplanade" (#48) from the Quarter up to City Park.

....

VisiTour passes, available from major hotels,
give unlimited travel on all streetcars and buses
($4 per day, $8 for three consecutive days).

....

However, you're far more likely to use the handsome **St Charles streetcar** (a National Historic Monument, dating back around 100 years) that rumbles a thirteen-mile loop from Canal Street, along the "neutral ground" (median) of St Charles Avenue in the Garden District, past Audubon Park and the Riverbend, to Carrollton ($1 each way; 10¢ for transfers onto any connecting RTA line; exact fare required). The cars trundle along at an average speed of 9mph; it takes about 45 minutes for a full one-way trip.

Though the streetcar runs around the clock, services taper off after dark, when you're better off taking a cab (see below) than waiting around in an unfamiliar neighborhood. For more on the streetcar, see p.76.

....

Though you can drink a cocktail on the streets of New Orleans (see p.182), you can't carry it on the bus or the streetcar, nor can you eat or smoke on board.

....

There's a newer, tourist-targeted, streetcar line along the **riverfront**, where red trolleys make ten stops between the Convention Center and Esplanade Avenue (Mon–Fri 6am–midnight, Sat & Sun 8am–midnight; every 15min; $1.25; exact fare). However, as it's a total trip of less than two miles, and any hoped-for river views are limited by buildings and parking lots, there's little point using it unless you have trouble walking.

The only public transport within the French Quarter is the **Vieux Carré** shuttle (Mon–Fri 5am–5.30pm, Sat & Sun 8am–6pm; $1; exact fare) – little green buses done up to look like trolleys – but again, distances are so short that these are little use unless you're extremely tired or have difficulty walking.

Taxis

The easiest and most convenient way of traveling any distance in New Orleans is by **taxi** – and if you're going anywhere outside the Quarter after dark, they're essential. **United** is by far the best firm, with the most reliable drivers and the safest cars. You can call them (✆522-9771), hail them from the street (try along Canal or Decatur), or pick them up in the French Quarter outside the *Omni Royal Orleans Hotel* on St Louis St between Chartres and Royal, or the *Bourbon-Orleans* on Orleans Street.

Driving

It's not a particularly good idea to **drive** in New Orleans, especially around the French Quarter, where sections of the narrow, one-way streets are regularly closed off to create pedestrianized enclaves, plodding mule-drawn buggies cause traffic snarl-ups, and parking is all but impossible. Citywide, the brutal **parking** restrictions are something of a local joke, with a host of impenetrable regulations that lead to regular impoundments and steep fines. If you've arrived by car, your best bet is to stick it in the hotel parking lot – most French Quarter hotels charge for the privilege – and forget about it. You may, however, want to **rent a car** to make excursions out of the city (see p.115); though all the major national chains have booths at the airport, it may be cheaper to arrange rental from a branch in the city. Rates vary widely according to season, the day of the week and special deals.

SIGHTSEEING TOURS

There is a bewildering variety of **tours** of New Orleans, from whistlestop sightseeing jaunts in air-conditioned buses to preposterous moonlit ghost-hunts. **Walking tours** are especially popular – notwithstanding the possibility of showers and, especially in summer, debilitating heat and humidity. The list overleaf includes the best; the Welcome Center (see p.8) has racks of leaflets detailing many others.

Many people, especially first-timers or visitors with kids in tow, take a narrated trot through the Quarter in one of the **mule-drawn carriages** that wait in line behind Jackson Square on Decatur. These can be fun, though in most cases you should take the "historic" running commentary with a pinch of salt – and the sight of the mules, decked out in funny hats and sunglasses, puts some people off. Rates are generally negotiable, though you should expect to pay around $8–10 per person for thirty to forty-five minutes.

One romantic way to while away a few hours on a steamy afternoon is to take a narrated **cruise** along the Mississippi. For details of the authentic *Natchez* steamboat, and the *John James Audubon* riverboat, which travels between the aquarium and the zoo, see p.89.

....

Note that some of the tour operators listed below also venture further afield to the River Road plantations (see p.115).

....

Walking tours

Bienville Foundation ✆945-6789. Exemplary "alternative" French Quarter walking tours, emphasizing literary sites, women's history, jazz, the city's multicultural legacy, and its gay heritage (2hr–2hr 30min; $15–18; schedules vary with the season).

Friends of the Cabildo ✆523-3939. Reliable historical overviews, concentrating on the French Quarter. Tours set off from the 1850 House, 523 St Ann St on Jackson Square (Mon 1.30pm; Tues–Sun 10am & 1.30pm; 2hr; $10; no reservations required).

Jean Lafitte National Park Service ✆589-2636. Led by National Park rangers, these free daily tours include a history jaunt (10.30am; 1hr 30min) covering the French Quarter and giving an overview of the city; a Garden District walk (2.30pm; 1hr 30min; reservations required); and the changing "tour du jour" (11.30am; 1hr 30min). You should collect a pass, available from the NPS office, 419 Decatur St, after 9am on the day, to make sure of getting a place.

Le Monde Creole ✆568-1801. Run by the same people as the Laura Plantation on the River Road (see p.120), these superb French Quarter walking tours stop at sites that played a part in the true-life saga of a wealthy Creole family. They set off from their French Quarter store Le Monde Creole, 624 Royal St (Tues–Sun 10.30am & 2.30pm; 2hr; $16; includes entrance to the Pharmacy Museum, see p.38; reservations advised).

Save Our Cemeteries ✆525-3377. Non-profit organization that leads fascinating, culturally sensitive tours of Lafayette No. 1 (Mon, Wed & Fri 10.30am; $6 donation) and St Louis No. 1 (Sun 10am; $12 donation). Call for meeting points and to reserve.

Bus tours

Cukie's Travels ✆882-3058. Lively van tours led by native New Orleanians, visiting the Quarter, Garden District and the lakefront (3hr; $25); the cemeteries (3hr; $25); and Destrehan and San Francisco plantations (5hr; $45). They can also take you out to Honey Island swamp (5hr; $40), linking up with Dr Wagner's excellent boat tours (see p.17). No credit cards.

Gray Line ✆569-1401 or 1-800/535-7786. Bus tours of the city (2hr; $19); plantations (7hr 30min; $40); and nearby swamps (3hr 15min; $38). A one-day, hop-on-hop-off deal allows you to disembark at allocated stops along a loop route around the city as many times as you please ($19). They also offer a paddlewheeler-cruise and city-tour combination ($31).

New Orleans Tours ✆592-0560 or 1-800/543-6332. Similar to Gray Line, though fractionally cheaper, with a choice of van tours, walking tours and river cruises. They also do half-day and full-day trips to the plantations ($26/$40).

BUS TOURS

Roots of New Orleans ☏596-6889. African-American heritage tours ($30–55), including a "Roots 'n' the church" deal that includes a gospel mass and brunch. Times and days vary; call for schedules and to reserve.

"Haunted" tours

In recent years the choice of tours promising magic, voodoo, vampires and **ghosts** has become dizzying. There are, however, a few worth checking out among the high-camp, the overpriced and the plain silly.

Historic New Orleans Walking Tours ☏947-2120. Run by respected local historian Robert Florence. The "Cemetery & Voodoo" tour covers St Louis Cemetery No. 1, Congo Square, Marie Laveau's home, and a voodoo temple; meet at *Café Beignet*, 334 Royal St (Mon–Sat 10am & 1pm, Sun 10am; 2hr; $15). The "Garden District & Cemetery" tour emphasizes architecture and plant life; meet at the Garden District Bookshop, in The Rink at Washington and Prytania (daily 11am & 1.45pm; 2hr; $14). No reservations; arrive 15min before the tour is due to begin.

Magic Walking Tours ☏588-9693. "Serious" tours of the Quarter that mix informed historical detail with some tales quite as tall as those spun by other outfits – but without the costumes and to-go beers. They're run by the owner of the *Funky Butt* jazz club (see p.194); guides will happily lead you there afterward. Meet at *Lafitte's Blacksmith Shop* (daily 8pm; 2hr; $13; no reservations). They also do a tour of St Louis Cemetery No. 1 from *Pirate's Alley Café* next to St Louis Cathedral (daily 10.30am & 1.15pm; 2hr; $13).

New Orleans Ghost Tour ☏944-7424. If you're out less for authenticity than to whoop it up, consider the tours – featuring magic tricks and "psychic demonstrations" – led by Englishman Thomas Duran. Ghost tours leave from Washington Artillery Park, across Decatur from Jackson

Square (Mon & Wed–Sun 8pm; around 2hr; $15); your guide is the questionable-looking one in a top hat, twirling his cane and swirling his mustache. For the cemeteries tour, meet at *CC's Coffee House* on Royal and St Philip in the Quarter (Fri & Sat noon, Sun 10.30am; around 2hr; $15). No reservations.

New Orleans Historic Voodoo Museum Tours ℗523-7685. Cemetery, voodoo, and "undead" tours of the Quarter ($12–18), plus authentic voodoo ceremonies ($15) and van trips to swamps and "haunted plantations" ($45–59); prices include reduced or free museum admission (see p.50). Call for schedules.

Swamp tours

The popular fantasy of the misty, mysterious **Louisiana swamp** as an eerily quiet place, swathed in ghostly gray Spanish moss, is not so very far from the truth. New Orleans' local swamps – many of them only thirty minutes' drive from downtown – are otherworldly enclaves, brought to life by informed guides eager to share their knowledge of local flora and fauna. Most operators can arrange pick up from downtown, which adds to the total cost.

What you see on the swamp will be very different depending upon the time of year, how hungry the local animals are and sheer luck. In the chilly winters, with the water moving fast, you're less likely to see an **alligator** than during the summer, when they sleepily bask in the sun. Whatever time of year you come, bring a hat, sunscreen and, most importantly, bug repellent.

Dr Wagner's Honey Island Swamp Tours ℗641-1769. Based around ten miles outside suburban Slidell, north of Lake Pontchartrain, ecologist Dr Paul Wagner offers the best, most informative swamp tours available. Twelve-seater boats venture out onto the delta of the lower Pearl River, a

SWAMP TOURS

wilderness inhabited by racoons, nutrias, bobcats, wild pigs, black bears, and alligators; birdlife includes ibis, great blue herons and snowy egrets (daily; 1hr 45min–2hr; $20, $10 for under-12s; with transport from New Orleans $40/$20). Tour times change daily, so call to reserve. No credit cards.

Mockingbird Swamp Tours ☏386-7902. Boat tours of the Manchac swamp, around an hour's drive northwest of the city (daily 10am, noon & 2pm; $17, $8 for under-12s). No credit cards.

Turgeon Tours and Charters ☏689-2911. Lafitte-based firm offering daily swamp tours on six-person boats. "Early bird" (6am; 2hr) and "sunset" options (summer 6pm; winter 3pm; 2hr) ply local marshes and swamps, while the standard tour (9am; 4hr) zips down the bayou to the gulf, taking in a brown pelican nesting site on the way.

The French Quarter

T he heartbreakingly beautiful **French Quarter** – or Vieux Carré ("old square") – is where New Orleans started in 1718. Today, battered and bohemian, decaying and vibrant, it's the spiritual core of the city, its fanciful cast-iron balconies, hidden courtyards and time-stained stucco buildings exerting a haunting fascination that has long caught the imagination of artists and writers. Though most of the buildings of the French city burned in two devastating fires in 1788 and 1794, the culture of the Vieux Carré remained predominantly French-Creole right up to the Civil War, and today, though it has more of the feel of a seductive Caribbean port than a European city, it makes much of its Gallic heritage, from the French street names and real-estate signs stamped "fait accompli" ("sold"), to the beignets and café au lait served at the *Café du Monde*.

....

**The area covered by this chapter
is shown in detail on color map 4.**

....

The Quarter covers a compact **grid** – unchanged since it was laid out by military engineer Adrien de Pauger in 1721 – bounded by the Mississippi, Rampart Street, Canal Street and Esplanade Avenue. Its hub is Europeanate

Jackson Square, facing the river. Upriver, the **Upper Quarter** sees most of the **commercial activity**, concentrated in the blocks between brash Decatur Street and Bourbon Street. Here, as in the days of the Creole city, the gorgeous old buildings hold offices, shops, galleries, restaurants and bars on the lower floors, with apartments on the upper stories. In the streets beyond Bourbon, up toward Rampart Street, and in those of the **Lower Quarter**, downriver from Jackson Square, things become more peaceful – here you'll find quiet, predominantly **residential** neighborhoods that are home to much of the Quarter's **gay** community.

While there's no shortage of formal **attractions** – house tours, the superb Cabildo and Historic New Orleans Collection museums, and the eclectic decorative arts collection of the Presbytère, to name but a few – you could just as easily spend an entire week simply wandering the streets, absorbing the melange of sounds, sights and smells. Early morning, in the pearly light from the river, is a good time to explore, as sleepy locals wake themselves up with strong coffee in neighborhood patisseries, stores crank open their shutters, and busking brass bands set up to blast the roofs off Jackson Square.

....

Walking tours of the Quarter are reviewed on pp.14–15.

....

Some history

Despite inauspicious beginnings as a miserable colonial outpost built on an unprepossessing swamp, the French – then Spanish – city thrived thanks to its location on the river. Even after the Louisiana Purchase, when the new, Anglo-American Faubourg St Mary mushroomed around it, the Vieux Carré held its own, becoming the **first municipality** of the divided city (see p.266). Though New Orleans' **ante-bellum** "golden era" marked the ascendancy of the American sector, planters, bankers and lawyers continued to build homes in the old Creole quarter, entertaining in its famed theaters and ballrooms. During this period a third of the French Quarter was owned by **free people of color**, wealthy Francophones – many of them slave-owners – a significant number of whom sent their children to Paris to be educated.

For more on the history of New Orleans, see p.259.

After the **Civil War**, the district took a downturn, its old buildings used as tenements to house poor Italian and black families, or torn down to make room for new developments along the river and behind Canal Street. Things improved in the 1920s, however, when a colony of **artists**, including writers Sherwood Anderson and William Faulkner, flocked to the Quarter; their fascination with its architecture and rich cultural history led in the 1930s to the formation of the **Vieux Carré Commission** – whose remit was to preserve the district's "quaint and distinctive character" – and a WPA restoration program. Since then, the Quarter has become something of a battleground for preservationists, the hardest fight yet being against a 1946 proposal to build a highway right through it, which was only definitively won in the 1970s. However, as the mounting number of themed restaurants and fast-food outlets reveals, the Commission's remit extends neither to vetting what buildings are used for, nor what is done to their interiors.

In 1997, the overnight transformation of Bourbon Street's landmark *Old Absinthe House* into a lurid daiquiri bar was met with city-wide dismay and a growing concern that this historically evolving, vibrant neighborhood could transmogrify into a lifeless theme park. For now, however, the Quarter battles on. Its lopsided buildings, many of them buckling and rotting in the perpetual damp, still emanate a ghostly beauty, accentuated by the tiny aesthetic details – a string of Christmas-tree lights, a little cast-iron chair, voluptuous green ferns – added by residents.

French Quarter accommodation is reviewed on p.133, restaurants on p.150, bars on p.183 and music venues on pp.194 & 198.

JACKSON SQUARE

Map 4, F5–G5.
Ever since its earliest incarnation as the Place d'Armes, a dusty parade ground used for public meetings and executions, **Jackson Square** has been at the heart of the French Quarter. Its spruce appearance today owes much to the **Baroness Pontalba** (see opposite), who in 1851 revamped the drill ground into a landscaped park and renamed it for Andrew Jackson, hero of the Battle of New Orleans (see p.96), who went on to become seventh US president.

The square, with its iron benches, neat lawns and blaze of flowerbeds, somehow manages to stay tranquil despite the streams of photo-snapping tourists, overexcited school groups, waiters on their breaks, and the odd crashed-out casualty. Presiding over them all, an **equestrian statue** – the first in the nation, constructed by Clark Mills in 1856 – shows Jackson in uncharacteristically jaunty mode, waving his hat. It's a sculptural masterpiece, with the mighty horse, rearing on its hind legs, perfectly balanced on the plinth. The hectoring inscription, "The Union Must and Shall be Preserved" was pointedly added by General "Beast" Butler (see p.70) during the Civil War occupation.

The Baroness

Jackson Square, and the smart red buildings that flank it, are the result of a melodrama of murder and money starring the willful **Baroness Pontalba**, known in New Orleans simply as "the Baroness". Born Micaëla Almonester in 1795, the daughter of Don Andrés Almonester – who came to New Orleans in 1769 as a clerk and went on to become one of the city's richest and most influential philanthropists – at the age of 16 she was married in St Louis Cathedral to Célestin Pontalba, a distant cousin. The couple moved to Paris, where Micaëla, whose considerable inheritance included all the real estate fringing the Place d'Armes, became convinced that her father-in-law, the Baron Pontalba, had engineered the wedding in order to get at her wealth. After a decade of bitter wrangling over money, Micaëla eventually left Célestin, taking their three children, upon which her father-in-law promptly disinherited them. In 1834, during a violent row, the baron shot her four times in the chest, and proceeded to kill himself. Micaëla miraculously survived, though she lost two fingers defending herself. Four years later, by then a baroness, she divorced Célestin, and in 1849 – with Europe in revolutionary turmoil – returned to New Orleans.

Back in the city, the baroness set about recreating the elegance she had so admired in the French capital. By all accounts she was a harsh taskmistress, supervising construction to the last detail and refusing to pay for the many changes she demanded. In 1851 the Pontalba Buildings were completed, at a cost of $300,000, and renovations began on the square; the baroness, however, returned to Paris for a reconciliation with Célestin. Seriously ill, he handed over his affairs to Micaëla, who, in an ironic twist, succeeded in adding all his property to her own.

St Peter, Chartres and St Ann streets are pedestrianized where they border the square. In this enclave you'll find some of the city's major sights: the chic **Pontalba Buildings**, their street-level rooms taken up by shops and restaurants; **St Louis Cathedral**; and, flanking the cathedral like stout bodyguards, the **Cabildo** and **Presbytère** museums. During the day, everyone passes by at some time or another, weaving their way through the tangle of artists, Lucky Dog vendors, rainbow-clad palmists, magicians, shambolic brass bands and blues buskers. At night it's more peaceful, with just a few waifs and strays lingering in the shadows cast by the stately, floodlit buildings.

....

**Pick up free maps, leaflets and self-guided
walking tours at the Welcome Center (see p.8),
529 St Ann St in the lower Pontalba Building.**

....

St Louis Cathedral

Map 4, F5. Tours daily 7am–6.30pm, except during services; free.

A postcard-perfect backdrop for the Andrew Jackson statue, **St Louis Cathedral**, commanding the square across Chartres Street, is the oldest continuously active cathedral in the United States, and the third church on this spot. Its construction in 1794 – the second church had been destroyed by the fire of 1788 – was funded, along with the Cabildo and the overhaul of the Presbytère, by the philanthropist Don Almonester; in 1850, while Almonester's daughter was busy sprucing up Jackson Square (see p.23), it was enlarged and remodeled by eminent architect J.N.B. de Pouilly. Dominated by three tall slate steeples, the facade, which marries a Greek Revival symmetry with copious French arches, is oddly one-dimensional – an elaborate movie prop for the street theater below.

Though the cathedral has always been central to the life of this very Catholic city – Andrew Jackson laid his sword on the altar in thanks for victory at the Battle of New Orleans; voodoo queen Marie Laveau (see p.51) was baptized and married here – the modest interior, an unextraordinary assemblage of murals, sculpture and stained glass, is little to shout about. Tour guides point out the highlights, including Don Almonester's marble tomb, inscribed with a list of his many bequests, and an overblown tabernacle brimming with cherubs.

There's a great view of the cathedral from Washington Artillery Park (see p.91), across Decatur by the river.

Flanking the cathedral, two narrow flagstoned lanes link Jackson Square to Royal Street. Downriver, **Père Antoine Alley** is named for the beloved Capuchin priest Antonio de Sedella, who came to New Orleans in 1779. He was promptly banished by the Spanish authorities – they'd discovered that he had been sent to enforce the Inquisition – only to return a few years later to become rector of the cathedral. Adored by his parishioners, he is still regarded as one of the greatest heroes of a city that boasts many. On the other side of the cathedral, photogenic **Pirate's Alley**, supposedly where Jean Lafitte met Andrew Jackson to plan the Battle of New Orleans in 1815 (highly unlikely, since the alley wasn't built until the 1830s), is lined with vibrantly colored town houses. At no. 624, the sunshine-yellow Faulkner House Books (see p.221) occupies the ground-floor room where the verbose one wrote his first novel, *Soldier's Pay*, in 1927.

Behind the cathedral, on a patch of land that was the scene of numerous duels in the 1800s, the small, iron-fenced **St Anthony's Garden** is sandwiched between the

ST LOUIS CATHEDRAL

25

two alleys. In the centre, in front of the huge marble statue of the Sacred Heart of Jesus, an obelisk commemorates the crew of a French ship who in 1857 died of yellow fever in the Gulf of Mexico.

The Cabildo

Map 4, F5. Tues–Sun 9am–5pm; $5 (20 percent discount with admission to any other museum in the State Museum group; see opposite).

On the upriver side of the cathedral, the Hispanic **Cabildo** was built as the Casa Capitular, seat of the Spanish colonial government (the "Very Illustrious Cabildo"). Today, it is home to one of the best history museums you'll find anywhere. The building – which cuts an impressive dash with its columned arcade, fan windows and fine wrought-iron balconies – is another legacy of the philanthropist Don Almonester, who, after the original building burned down in the fire of 1788, offered funds to remodel it in the grand style of the home country. Historically, the Cabildo is hugely significant – not least for being where, in 1803, the Spanish colony was transferred back to France, and three weeks later, under the terms of the **Louisiana Purchase**, was sold on to the United States (see p.264).

Today the outstanding **museum** ably picks its way through the complex melange of cultures, classes and races that throng Louisiana's history. Bursting with well-captioned artifacts, it starts with the Native Americans and winds up with the demise of Reconstruction – rather than attempting to see the whole place, it's best to concentrate on a few sections that particularly interest you. It certainly pulls no punches – in keeping with the city's uncommon fascination with matters morbid, there's a gloomy room devoted to disease, death and mourning, while another displays the post-Civil War cartoons put out by the White League-dominated

Mardi Gras krewes, revealing the racist venom with which the New Orleans elite resisted Reconstruction. Black history is well-represented, with as much emphasis on the free people of color as on the city's role as the major slave-trading center of the South. Bills of sale show Alabama slaves going for $3850 each in 1856, while a worn-smooth auction block stands in front of a mural depicting the markets held in the old St Louis Hotel (see p.42).

The Cabildo – along with the Presbytère (below), 1850 House (p.32), the Old US Mint (p.34) and Madame John's Legacy (p.45) – is part of the Louisiana State Museum. Each site is open Tuesday to Sunday from 9am to 5pm; buying a ticket to two or more gives a total discount of 20 percent.

On the second floor you can see the bronze **death mask of Napoleon**, made and brought to New Orleans by the exiled emperor's doctor, Francesco Antommarchi, who displayed it in his office on Royal Street for thirteen years before donating it to the city in 1834. Also upstairs is the reconstructed **Sala Capitular**, where the Louisiana Purchase was signed in 1803, and where in 1892, the *Plessy vs Ferguson* case (see p.269), which legalized segregation throughout the South, was first argued.

The Presbytère

Map 4, G5. Tues–Sun 9am–5pm; $5 (20 percent discount with admission to any other museum in the State Museum group; see above).

Forming a matching pair with the Cabildo, the **Presbytère**, on the downriver side of the cathedral, was designed in 1791 as a rectory. It was never used as such, however; after the death of Don Almonester, its chief benefactor, put construction on hold, it was not completed until 1813, and went on to serve as a courthouse. Today it's a very good decorative arts museum, full of odd treasures. Alongside **oil paintings** of nineteenth-century Creole nobility, captions tell tales of the artists, many of whom, including numerous free men of color, were French-born and trained. The subjects are equally interesting – among the planters, manufacturers, generals and statesmen, look out for the life-size portrait of local hero Père Antoine, painted in 1822, seven years before his death, and likenesses of Don Almonester and his daughter, Baroness Pontalba, who is concealing her mutilated fingers (see p.23).

You can also see the **furniture** that marked out the wealthy Creoles as people of distinction and taste, including wooden armoires and chests carved by Prudent Mallard, the prominent local cabinet-maker, and silver fashioned by German smiths who had fled the homeland in the 1840s. **Folk art** includes a clutch of gnarled voodoo dolls and naive works by Clementine Hunter, a Louisiana plantation slave. One particularly fascinating room is devoted to a history of **cartography**, including Native American, Aztec and Japanese representational maps. Deliberately fictionalized eighteenth-century maps of North America show the Mississippi to be near New Mexico, fabled land of gold, in order to encourage speculation in the Mississippi Bubble (see p.260).

The bizarre, pod-shaped vessel that stands rusting outside the Presbytère is something of a mystery. The long-held theory that it was an early Confederate **submarine** has since been disproved, but no one has yet been able to come up with the true origins of the thing.

The Pontalba Buildings

Map 4, F5 & G5.

The elegant, three-story **Pontalba Buildings**, which line

St Peter and St Ann streets where they border Jackson Square, were commissioned in 1850 by the formidable Baroness Pontalba (see p.23). Having returned from France in 1849 to find her real estate palling in comparison to the American sector across Canal Street, her first project was to replace the shabby buildings around the Place d'Armes with elegant colonnaded structures resembling those she'd seen in Paris. The original **architect**, James Gallier Sr – whom the baroness eventually sacked because of their endless squabbling – was responsible for many of the buildings' Greek Revival elements, but the large courtyards at the back, and the arrangement of commercial units on the ground floor and living spaces above, are typically Creole. These were not, as is commonly claimed, the first apartment buildings in the US, but they were innovative in their use of mass-produced materials and, in particular, of **cast iron** – the iron was cast in New York, the red brick pressed in Baltimore, and the plate glass and slate roof tiles came from England. The stunning visual effect of the wide galleries and balconies, their decorative curlicues centering on cartouches inscribed with the initials A&P – Almonester and Pontalba – sparked off a city-wide fad for lacy cast iron, which came to replace the plainer, hand-wrought iron fashioned locally by African slaves.

As the Quarter declined after the Civil War, the apartments lost their exclusivity, and by the end of the nineteenth century they had become tenements. During one of the city's many yellow fever epidemics, health officials reported finding a cow living in one of the rooms. In the 1930s, however, restored by the WPA, they regained their former prestige and are today some of the city's most desirable places to live, with stores and restaurants, along with the **Welcome Center** (see p.8), on the ground floors.

THE PONTALBA BUILDINGS

29

French Quarter architecture

While the French Quarter streets are as straight as a die, its **architecture** is a fabulous jumble of different shapes and sizes, colors, styles and states of repair. Little exists from before the two great **fires** of 1788 and 1794, after which Spanish Governor Carondelet ordained that all buildings should be made of brick, plaster and stucco, with tiled roofs. That said, the streetscape is far from purely Spanish. Most structures marry French and Spanish colonial elements, and many reveal Caribbean influences. Others, dating from the antebellum era, meld Anglo-American and Creole styles.

Many of the vernacular buildings are **Creole cottages**, built about a foot off the ground, above a closed ventilated area known as a "crawl space", and with a high gabled roof. The interiors were designed without a hall, with four rooms in a checkerboard square; front doors, indistinguishable from the shuttered ceiling-to-floor windows, open straight from the street into the living quarters. Outside areas held slave quarters, kitchens and **garconnières**, where the sons of the house would take up residence after reaching adolescence. Planters from the **West Indies** brought the notion of building houses on pillars, protecting them from waterlogging, and added porches – known as galleries – to shield against the sun and rain. The ground floor was used for storage, with living space above and, during good weather, out on the gallery. Hot air inside the house could rise and escape through tall dormer windows, set in steep pitched roofs.

Under the Spanish, louvered shutters replaced heavier battened ones, and fine iron balconies were wrought by African craftsmen. Though they rarely stood higher than two stories, the public buildings especially became heavier-looking and more obviously Mediterranean in style. **Courtyards** were designed now as extra living areas, where residents cultivated lush tropical plants, along with potent flowers, spices and herbs to mask the odors from the street.

As the nineteenth century drew on, the **Anglo-Americans** tended to settle on the other side of Canal Street in today's CBD, but their influence was still felt in the Quarter, where a number of buildings were designed in simply elegant Federal or Greek Revival styles. With a concern for privacy alien to the Creoles, the Americans preferred their homes to have enclosed hallways and indoor toilets.

The ornate **cast iron** so associated with the Quarter didn't come in till the 1840s, when improved communications and technologies meant that it could be bought in bulk from the industrializing north. Inspired by Baroness Pontalba's apartment buildings (see p.29), a fad developed for filigree balconies and fences, curly brackets and fluted columns, which were added to old buildings and incorporated into new ones. At the same time, large two- or three-story **galleries** were tacked onto the front of buildings, held up by pillars. Extending over the sidewalk, these provided shade for pedestrians and more living space for residents. In the late 1800s, **shotgun houses** emerged in force: composed of a single row of rooms opening onto each other, they're supposedly named for the fact that you could, in theory, shoot a bullet from the front door to the back without it hitting anything. Long, narrow clapboard structures, the shotguns are most notable for the decorative wooden details that early owners ordered from catalogs and stuck to the fronts.

While exploring The Quarter, watch out for the bands of young boys taking advantage of the crowds out to have a good time, spend cash, and get drunk. They'll bet that they can tell where you got your shoes, or some such challenge – the answer, of course, is that you got your shoes on your feet . . .

FRENCH QUARTER ARCHITECTURE

1850 House

Map 4, G5. Tues–Sun 9am–5pm; $3 (20 percent discount with admission to any other museum in the State Museum group; see p.27).

In 1850, when New Orleans was one of the largest cities in the nation, riding on the wealth of its booming port, the Pontalba Buildings were the height of fashion among the prosperous middle class. The cordoned-off rooms of the **1850 House**, in the lower Pontalba Buildings at 523 St Ann St, recreate the tastes of a well-to-do Creole family from that era. Drawing attention to every piece of rococo revival furniture, Vieux Paris china and fine crystal, but leaving you with little sense of how the family might have lived, it is, in fact, the least interesting of the state museums. Part of the problem is that tours are self-guided; for enlivening historical detail, leaf through the folder of docents' notes by the entrance.

> **For a good view of the Mississippi,**
> **cross Decatur Street to the Moonwalk,**
> **a wooden promenade where sidewalk musicians**
> **serenade you as freighters and ferries negotiate the**
> **river's perilous current.**
> **For more on the river, see p.87.**

DECATUR STREET

Map 4, A6–N6.

When the French Quarter was laid out in 1721, **Decatur Street** (pronounced "deKAYder"), then known as Levee Street, abutted the Mississippi. Today, the land that separates it from the water – four whole blocks of it at Canal Street – has all been dumped by the dramatically shifting river. A broad thoroughfare, noisy with traffic and lined with cheap-and-cheerful tourist shops, bars and restaurants, Decatur becomes more countercultural as you head down-river, where, beyond the touristy **French Market**, a string of dive bars and thrift stores leads you toward the funky **Faubourg Marigny**.

The French Market and Farmers Market

Spanning the three riverside blocks downriver from Jackson Square, the low, red **French Market** buildings (Map 4, G6–I6) are said to stand on the site of a Native American trading area. There has certainly been an active market here, in one form or another, since the 1720s; nineteenth-century visitors marveled at the exotic, chaotic jumble of Native Americans, Africans, farmers and fisher-men, fast-talking in every language imaginable, trading fragrant herbs, mysterious wild birds and even alligators. Naturalist John James Audubon, shopping in 1821 for fowl to use as studies for his *Birds of America*, called it "the dirtiest place in all the cities of the United States". Today, the colonnaded arcades – much reworked and restored since the first was built in 1813 – are more sanitized, their specialty stores teeming with tourists snapping up the T-shirts, cookbooks and pralines, while musicians play jazz outside the overpriced cafés. The 24-hour **Café du Monde**, traditionally *the* place to snack on beignets and café au lait (see p.174), is the one place you won't want to miss. Come very early, or very late, and you can almost imagine yourself back at the old French Market coffee stands, where dockers, farmers, businessmen and society ladies would gather at the marble-topped tables to drink steaming, strong coffee before hurrying on with their affairs.

For market stalls, you'll need to head for the **Farmers**

Market (Map 4, J6–K6), just off Decatur on N Peters Street, where fresh produce, spices, hot sauce and the like are sold around the clock; the weekend **flea market**, next to it, is full of oddities, as are the quirky thrift and rummage stores opposite on Decatur.

For more on shopping in the French Market
and along Decatur Street, see p.210.

French Market Place, the innocuous alley that runs alongside the Farmers Market, was known in the second half of the nineteenth century as **Gallatin Street**, the dingiest, deadliest block in New Orleans. Blind-drunk sailors and swaggering young blades would enter this cesspit of brothels, barrel houses and dark gambling dens at their peril, many of them never to be seen again. Even policemen refused to set foot near the place, fearing encounters with garroters, murderous prostitutes and knife-wielding pimps, and, worst of all, the Live Oak Boys – who would crack your head open with an oak bludgeon as soon as look at you. There's little to show for all this derring-do today; just the market stalls on one side and the shabby back end of Decatur on the other.

Old US Mint

Map 4, L6. Tues–Sun 9am–5pm; $5 (20 percent discount with admission to any other museum in the State Museum group; see p.27).

From 1838 to 1909 – with a break during the Civil War and Reconstruction – the **Old US Mint** churned out $300 million worth of currency, including, for a year or so, Confederate gold coins. In 1862, at the outset of the city's occupation by Union troops, Confederate patriot William Mumford tore down the star-spangled banner from the flagpole here and dragged it through the streets – a crime for which Union General "Beast" Butler (see p.70) hanged him from the peristyle.

On the ground floor, an **architectural exhibit** tells how the building, a rust-colored Greek Revival hulk dating from 1835, was saved in the 1850s from sinking into the soggy earth by General Pierre Beauregard's engineering flair. Most people, however, are here for the **Jazz Museum**, on the floor above, which traces the history of the music that New Orleans calls its own through photographs, old letters – among them a pencil-written fan letter to pianist Amand Hug from a ten-year-old Harry Connick Jr – and advertising images. With its murmuring jazz soundtrack, it's a surprisingly understated place, its melancholy air exemplified by a letter from jazz great Willie "Bunk" Johnson. Poverty-stricken and forgotten in his fading years, Johnson was reduced to writing to his old employer on the plantation, asking him for a bicycle for his birthday so he could get into town to shop. Downstairs, a small branch of the excellent **record store** the Louisiana Music Factory (see p.232) sells jazz on vinyl and CD.

For more on the history of jazz in New Orleans, see p.285; for more on Mardi Gras, see p.271.

The Mint also features a **Mardi Gras exhibit**, displaying vintage carnival invitations, with their arcane wording and bizarre imagery, and a parade float built for Proteus, one of the old-line krewes. Among the flamboyant carnival costumes you'll see an extraordinary Mardi Gras Indian suit and oddly disturbing Cajun Mardi Gras get-ups, with their tall conical hats, Spanish-moss wigs and impassive full-face masks.

OLD US MINT

Esplanade Avenue and the Faubourg

The downriver boundary of the Quarter, **Esplanade Avenue** (Map 4, L7–L1) is a ravishing, if somewhat down-at-heel boulevard, lined with huge Live Oaks and decaying Italianate mansions. At the end of the nineteenth century this was the grandest residential street in the declining Creole city; today its faded glamour is part of its charm. Crossing Esplanade from the Quarter brings you to **Faubourg Marigny** (Map 4), a hip, low-rent area of Creole cottages populated by artists, musicians, and sundry bohemians. The Faubourg, as it's known, is named for the Creole Bernard de Marigny, a millionaire roué, expert duelist and hopeless gambler who in 1808, aged 18 and in in drastic debt, divided his vast plantation into lots and sold them off. Many were bought by the planters, among them numerous free people of color, who flooded the city in 1809 after the slave rebellions in Saint-Domingue (today's Haiti). By the 1820s, much of Esplanade and the Faubourg was populated by the free women of color, who, under the semi-institutionalized system of **plaçage** (see p.50), lived with their children in houses bought for them by their white "husbands".

Though the Faubourg is gentrifying, and its bars, coffee shops and restaurants are expanding further and further beyond the Quarter, it's best **not to wander** too far beyond the blocks around Decatur and Frenchmen, the district's main drag. Even Elysian Fields – where Stanley and Stella lived in Tennessee Williams' *A Streetcar Named Desire* – is probably best avoided, despite its heavenly name.

....
**The Faubourg's accommodation is reviewed on p.138,
its restaurants on p.162, bars on p.185,
and music venues on p.197.**
....

CHARTRES STREET

Map 4, A5–N5.

Cut in half by Jackson Square, **Chartres Street** (pronounced "Charders") is quieter and more characterful than Decatur, its appealing mix of bars, patisseries and offbeat shops geared as much to locals as to tourists. It was here, in the building on the riverside corner opposite *Keuffer's Bar* (see p.184), that the **great fire** of Good Friday 1788 broke out, after a candle in a small household shrine set light to a curtain. The family, along with most of the population, was at church, leaving the conflagration to rage unabated and 856 buildings, including the cathedral, to be destroyed in its wake.

The Napoleon House

Map 4, D5.

Now a hugely atmospheric bar and restaurant (see p.185), the **Napoleon House**, 500 Chartres St, is in fact made up of two houses. The original, 1797 building is a small, two-story structure on St Louis; the elegant three-story building on Chartres was added in 1814. With its weatherbeaten stucco walls, heavy wooden shutters and cupola, it's one of the loveliest buildings in the Quarter, and even more so inside – make sure to spend an hour or so in its historic, shadowy bar or lush courtyard, sipping a Pimm's Cup and snacking on some of the best muffulettas in the city (see p.147).

The main house was built for Mayor Nicholas Girod, who, so the story goes, volunteered to host the exiled French emperor in the New World. Sometimes the story goes even further, claiming that, with the help of pirates Jean Lafitte and Dominique You, Girod sent a boat, the *Seraphin*, to rescue Napoleon from the island of St Helena – unaware that he had died three days before it set sail.

CHARTRES STREET, THE NAPOLEON HOUSE

Historical Pharmacy Museum

Map 4, E5. Tues–Sun 10am–5pm; $2 (free with a Le Monde Creole walking tour; see p.15).

The quirky **Historical Pharmacy Museum**, 514 Chartres St, gives fascinating insights into the history of medicine from the eighteenth century onward. Lining the walls of the 1820s apothecary – in a Creole-American town house designed by J.N.B. de Pouilly – hand-carved rosewood cabinets hold dusty glass jars crammed with herbs, roots and leeches for blood-letting (to combat irritability), and froufrou china containers containing deodorizing powders and Creole tonics for "all the various forms of female weakness". Though the tatty, photocopied captions don't exactly scream for attention, they're packed with juicy snippets about medical setbacks. Finding a cure for the cholera that ravaged the city throughout the nineteenth century was certainly no easy task – doctors had tried blood-letting, opium, and alcohol to no avail, but must have felt particularly disheartened after experimenting with calomel, whose side effects included the rotting away of the skin and jaw.

The fragrance in the courtyard of the Pharmacy Museum comes from its sweet olive tree, cultivated in many New Orleans gardens; you can buy it in perfume form at Hové Parfumeur (see p.232).

The museum's **voodoo** cabinet is very enlightening about this often misrepresented religion (see p.51), unmasking many *gris-gris* – charms, or spells – as nothing more mysterious than the equivalent of today's essential oils. Look out, too, for the 1850s **trephination drill**, a gruesome saw-toothed corkscrew that was bored into the skull to cure headaches – and the pharmacist's financial **ledger**, which lists a loaf of bread at 7¢, a basket of coal at 6¢, and "blood-letting of wife" at 25¢.

The Beauregard-Keyes House

Map 4, J5. Tours on the hour Mon–Sat 10am–3pm; $4.

The **Beauregard-Keyes House**, a raised 1826 Creole cottage at 1113 Chartres St, owes the first part of its name to Confederate **General Pierre Beauregard**, who ordered the first shot of the Civil War at Fort Sumter and remained a hero in the South long after the war was lost. He rented a room in the house for a couple of years during Reconstruction. In the 1940s the house was bought by popular novelist **Frances Parkinson Keyes**, who wrote many of her New Orleans–based titles here.

You'll need to be a fan of the **decorative arts** to get the most out of this house, which showcases a wide range of fine old furniture from Beauregard's rosewood armoires to Keyes' New England-made pieces. Oil paintings include a likeness of the general's daughter Laurie, wearing a bracelet of brass buttons that he sent her from battle. The back rooms look much as they did in Keyes' day, when she set up a study in the old slave quarters and, in keeping with American custom, moved the bathroom and kitchen into the main building. While traveling around the world as editor of *Good Housekeeping* magazine, Keyes accumulated an extensive **doll collection**, some of which is on display in the carriage house, along with decorative porcelain *veilleuses* (nightlights) from Europe.

By no coincidence, tours draw to a close in the **gift shop**, which stocks secondhand copies of Keyes' titles (now out of print), including *Dinner at Antoine's*, which sold more than two million copies, and *Madame Castel's Lodger*, a romance about the house's Beauregard period; you can get them more cheaply, however, in local used bookstores (see pp.219–22). Before you leave, make sure to stop by the tranquil walled **garden**.

The Old Ursuline Convent

Map 4, J5. Tours Tues–Fri 10am, 11am, 1pm, 2pm & 3pm, Sat & Sun 11.15am, 1pm & 2pm; $5.

Built between 1745 and 1750, the tranquil **Old Ursuline Convent**, 1114 Chartres St, is the only intact French colonial structure in the city, and quite possibly the oldest building in the Mississippi valley. The Ursuline nuns arrived in town from France in 1727, invited by Bienville to establish a hospital for his soldiers. Their importance to the early settlement was incalculable: in 1729 they established an orphanage for the children of colonists killed in the Indian rebellion at Fort Rosalie (now Natchez, Mississippi); they also taught classes for young Creole, African and Native American girls. Since 1824, when the nuns moved to a new site, the imposing, dove-gray building – typically French-Canadian, with its tall casement windows and steeply pitched roof – has served variously as a school, the seat of the state legislature, and the archbishopric. It's said to be haunted by specters of the French **casket girls**, respectable white virgins shipped over in the early days of the colony, who were kept here by the nuns before being sold off as wives – an attempt by Bienville to impede his French soldiers from coupling with Indian or African women.

Inside, the mishmash of religious paraphernalia includes brightly colored bishops' slippers (red for martyrdom, green for hope) and a gold-embroidered red velvet canopy. Look out for the heavy wooden "Doorway to Heaven", a table on which bishops lay in state in St Louis Cathedral. In the 1846 **St Mary's chapel** next door, a Baroque marble altar displays an overwrought scene of the Revelation and the Virgin Mary, who pops up again on the stained-glass windows; to the right of the altar, she's shown above a foggy view of the Battle of New Orleans.

ROYAL STREET

Map 4, A4–N4.

Elegant **Royal Street** was the main commercial thoroughfare of the Creole city, inhabited by the wealthiest sugar planters and lined with the finest shops. Today, despite being one of the most touristed routes through the Quarter, it's still a dignified old place, lined with landmark buildings, antique stores and small, chic art galleries. Its fabulous cast-iron **balconies**, the cream of the Quarter's crop, create a stunning streetscape familiar from countless movies, coffee-table books and postcards.

Exchange Alley

Map 4, A4–C4.

Exchange Alley, today an uneventful pedestrianized lane running parallel to Royal Street between Canal and Conti, was originally intended to lead all the way to the Cabildo. It never got further than the St Louis Hotel, however – making a convenient conduit from the American sector straight into the hotel's slave exchange (see p.42).

In the 1830s the alley was known as the "street of the **fencing masters**", who would train young men in the art of dueling. Duels, or *affaires d'honneur*, had long been part of the fabric of the French and Spanish colony, fought with rapiers by proud young Creoles and settled at "first blood"; in the nineteenth century, however, as the city Americanized and rifles became the weapons of choice, they became a contest to the death. Many of the fencing masters were then able to hire themselves out as assassins, provoking their prey into unwinnable duels.

ROYAL STREET, EXCHANGE ALLEY

The Courthouse

Map 4, D4.

In 1910, when the Quarter was at its most run-down and the Vieux Carré Commission was barely dreamed of, an entire block, bounded by Royal, St Louis, Chartres and Conti, was demolished to make way for a colossal new **Courthouse**. A Beaux Arts behemoth of marble and terracotta, in the 1950s the building was abandoned in favor of more modern premises in the CBD, and eventually fell into disuse. Having been fenced off for years, it's currently being restored to house the Louisiana Supreme Court.

Omni Royal Orleans Hotel

Map 4, D4.

At the corner of Royal and St Louis, the swanky **Omni Royal Orleans Hotel** stands on the site of the famed **St Louis Hotel**, designed in 1838 by J.N.B. de Pouilly. With its copper dome, colossal spiral staircase and opulent frescoes, the St Louis was at the heart of Creole high society, hosting the grandest balls and, in its columned, marble rotunda, holding the city's largest **slave exchange**. To encourage traders to stay the full three hours between noon and 3pm, when auctioneering took place, management offered them a free lunch at the bar – a canny promotion that spread like wildfire through taverns around the nation until the onset of Prohibition.

The hotel's **demise** began with the Civil War. During the city's shambolic Reconstruction period it housed the State Capitol, but was abandoned in 1898 and left to decay for years. Visitors could pay a small fee to tour the ruins – in 1912, British author John Galsworthy was struck by his encounter with a wounded horse, stumbling alone through the broken marble. A hurricane blasted off the roof in

1915, and the wrecked building was finally demolished a year later to be replaced in 1960 with the *Omni Royal*. At the back of the hotel, on Chartres Street, you can still make out the shadow of the word "exchange", painted on an arcade taken from the original building.

Historic New Orleans Collection

Map 4, E4. Tues–Sat 10am–4.45pm; tours 10am, 11am, 2pm & 3pm; $4.

The bulk of the superb **Historic New Orleans Collection** is displayed in the **Merieult House**, 533 Royal St. In 1938, General and Mrs Leila Kemper Williams, wealthy plantation owners who struck oil on their property, bought and restored the building – one of the few survivors of the 1794 fire – along with a neighboring structure around the corner on Toulouse Street. Entry to the **temporary exhibitions** in the street-front room of the Merieult House is free, but to see the best of the collection, you'll need to take a **guided tour**, which might cover the galleries upstairs, or the **Williams House** on Toulouse, depending on the whim of the guide and the interests of the group.

> The Historic New Orleans Collection gift shop sells books, old prints and maps, and a good range of unusual postcards.

The extensive **main collection**, spread across the top floor of the Merieult House, is a fascinating treasure trove of old maps, drawings, architectural plans, documents relating to the Louisiana Purchase, furniture and paintings. Galleries, organized chronologically, span the years from French settlement to the end of the nineteenth century, with themed rooms covering the plantations and the river.

Though there is far more to see than can be taken in on one 45-minute tour, **highlights** include the only known portrait of Bienville painted from life and two revealing portraits of Andrew Jackson – furrow-browed and quizzical in 1819, and far more world weary 21 years later, after his stint as the seventh US president. Look out, too, for the 1720 engraving that portrays the colony as a land of milk and honey peopled with beaming natives – an early publicity poster to attract settlers from Europe. In contrast, an 1803 engraving showing the view from Bernard de Marigny's plantation (today's Faubourg Marigny; see p.36) reveals a vast swathe of open lots and unpromising swamp. Among artifacts from the antebellum era you can see decorative broadsides from the Creole Salle d'Orleans and the St Charles Theater, its equivalent in the American sector; a brace of dueling pistols; and designs for elaborate Mardi Gras floats.

For anyone interested in design and decorative arts, the 1889 **Williams House**, 718 Toulouse St (reached via the main building), is a must, revealing how rich, arty types lived in the revitalizing Quarter of the 1930s. The Williamses were prominent citizens – as a young deb during Mardi Gras 1936 she reigned as Comus' Queen, while he was Comus in 1953 – and a cultured pair, who filled their house with unusual, exotic objects. Treasures include a stool fashioned out of a column from a demolished plantation, lamps made from samovars and antique Chinese burial art, and a host of antique maps.

La Branche House

Map 4, F4.

The **La Branche House**, 706 Royal St, encapsulates all that people imagine the French Quarter to be. Its gorgeous cast-iron balconies and galleries, added a decade after the house was built, form a fanciful, filigree cage around the relatively plain, Greek Revival structure – the apotheosis of the style that the city went mad for in the 1850s. Today the building houses the *Royal Café* (see p.161), which dishes up good Creole food.

**The La Branche family originally came from Germany;
in New Orleans their name, Zweig,
meaning "twig", was Gallicized, a common fate
for many non-French surnames.**

Madame John's Legacy

Map 4, H4. Tues–Sun 9am–5pm; $3 (20 percent discount with admission to any other museum in the State Museum group; see p.27).

A rare example of the French Quarter's early, West Indies-style architecture (see p.30), **Madame John's Legacy**, just off Royal at 628 Dumaine St, was rebuilt after the fire of 1788 as an exact replica of the 1730 house that had previously stood on the site. It was constructed using the *briquete entre poteaux* technique, in which soft red brick is set between steadying, hand-hewn cypress beams, and raised off the ground on stucco-covered brick pillars. The deep wraparound gallery provided extra living space, cooler and airier than the indoor rooms.

Today it stands flush with the street; in the days of the French colony it would have been surrounded by far more land. Gates at the side open onto the wide carriageway that leads around the back, past the kitchen and *garconnière*. Inside, a **museum** displays Southern folk art, and an interpretative exhibition details the house's various inhabitants and changes in fortune.

There never was a real Madame John – the name was given to the house by nineteenth-century author George

MADAME JOHN'S LEGACY

Washington Cable (see p.278) in his tragic short story *'Tite Poulette*, and simply stuck.

Look out for the cast-iron fence fronting the
Cornstalk Hotel, 915 Royal St (see p.134).
Bought from a catalog in the 1850s, at the peak of the
city's craze for cast iron, the elaborate tangle of
brightly painted cornstalks entwined with morning
glories has a twin in the Garden District (see p.83).

Gallier House

Map 4, J4. Mon–Sat 10am–3.30pm, tours on the half-hour;
$5, $8 with Hermann-Grima House (see p.49).

The handsome 1857 **Gallier House**, 1132 Royal St – reputedly Anne Rice's inspiration for Louis and Lestat's dwelling in her novel *Interview with the Vampire* – was built by James Gallier Jr, a leading architect like his father before him, for himself and his family. Though it's in many ways a typical Creole structure, with a large carriageway leading to a courtyard, Gallier also incorporated a number of American elements, such as the enclosed hall and indoor bathroom. Innovations included a cooling system and a flushing toilet, while the filigree cast-iron galleries would have been the last word in chic.

Tours of the house, focusing on social history, are some of the liveliest in the Quarter. The place is set up to recreate the cluttered style of the antebellum era, when the city-wide fashion for fancy decoration had to be balanced with the practicalities of living in a swampy climate: fine oil paintings and hand-carved closets stand tilted away from the walls, to avoid being blighted by mildew. In summer – when wealthy Quarterites would have fled the unbearably hot, disease-ridden city for their plantations, or Europe –

the house adopts "summer dress": the furniture is swathed in gauze, and the carpets replaced with straw matting.

Though city slaves – valets, repairmen, cooks and nannies – were regarded as being better off than field laborers, who did the back-breaking work of the plantations, life was by no means easy; the **slave quarters**, conspicuous by their absence from other house tours, are minimally furnished with out-of-fashion or broken furniture from the main house.

....
Architects' Row, opposite the Gallier House, is one of the loveliest stretches in the Quarter: a parade of antebellum town houses fronted by spectacular cast-iron galleries.
....

The LaLaurie Home

Map 4, J4. Not open to the public.

The most famous **haunted house** in New Orleans, the French Empire **LaLaurie Home**, lurks at 1140 Royal St on the corner with Gov Nicholls. In the nineteenth century it belonged to the LaLauries, a doctor and his socialite wife Delphine, who, although seen wielding a whip as she chased a slave girl through the house to the roof, was merely fined when the child fell to her death. Whispers about the couple's cruelty were horribly verified when neighbors rushed in after a fire in 1834 – started intentionally by the shackled cook – to find seven emaciated slaves locked in the attic. There they saw men, women and children choked by neck braces, some with broken limbs; one had a worm-filled hole gouged out of his cheek. The doctor's protestation that this torture chamber was, in fact, an "experiment" met with vitriol; the next day the pair escaped the baying mob outside their home and fled to France. Since then,

THE LALAURIE HOME

many claim to have heard ghostly moans from the building at night; some say they have seen a girl stumble across the balcony.

During Reconstruction the building housed a desegregated girls' school, a hopeful venture that ended in December 1874 when the **White League** militia (see p.60) stormed in and evicted by force any of the pupils they believed to have African blood.

BOURBON STREET

Map 4, A3–N3.

Though you'd never guess it from the hype, there are two sides to world-renowned **Bourbon Street**. The tawdry, touristy, booze-swilled stretch spans the seven blocks from Canal to St Ann: a frat-pack cacophony of daiquiri stalls, novelty shops, and tired girlie bars offering "French style" entertainment. This self-contained enclave is best experienced after dark, when a couple – though by no means all – of its **bars** (see p.180) and **clubs** (pp.194 & 198) are worth a look, and the sheer mayhem takes on a life of its own. When the attraction of fighting your way through the crowds of weekending drunks starts to pall, however, it's easy to dip out again into the quieter parallel streets to regain some sort of sanity. If you manage to make it as far as St Ann, you come to a kind of crossroads, marked by the rambunctious gay dance clubs *Oz* and *Parade* (see p.236). Beyond here, Bourbon transforms into an appealing, predominantly gay, residential area, scattered with neighborhood bars, corner laundromats, and local restaurants.

Incidentally, the **name** has nothing to do with booze. One of the first streets laid out by Pauger in 1721, it was named for the royal family of France, and only took on its current character during World War II, when a rash of strip clubs and bars opened to cater to soldiers passing through the port.

Hermann-Grima House

Map 4, D3. Mon–Sat 10am–3.30pm, tours on the half-hour;
$5, $8 with the Gallier House (see p.46).

Half a block above Bourbon Street at 820 St Louis, the
1832 **Hermann-Grima House** illustrates the lifestyle of
two middle-class Creole families in the city's antebellum
golden era. Though in many ways a typically elegant,
Federal mansion, with a number of characteristic American
features – including the central hall – the house's loggia and
outside kitchen whisper of a lingering Creole sensibility. It
was built for Samuel Hermann, a wealthy German-Jewish
cotton and slave trader, who sold it in 1844 to Judge Felix
Grima. The Grimas lived here until the 1920s, after which
it became a women's hostel.

> **Creole cookery demonstrations are held in the
> Hermann-Grima House kitchen every Thursday
> from October to May.**

Though **tours** skimp on contextual detail to dwell rev-
erentially on replica antiques, they do at least give you
time to wander around the rooms rather than trooping
you past a succession of cordoned-off set pieces. Much of
the furniture was made by prominent local craftsman
Prudent Mallard; note especially the huge, ornate bed
with its characteristic egg motif, a visual pun on his sur-
name.

Bourbon-Orleans Hotel

Map 4, G3.

The **Bourbon-Orleans Hotel**, on the corner of those two
streets, stands on the site of the old **Salle d'Orleans** ball-

room, which in the antebellum era was the grandest venue for the much mythologized **quadroon balls**. Usually romanticized as glittering occasions where dashing white men had their hearts stolen by beautiful, dusky quadroon girls (one-quarter black, usually born to a white father and mulatto mother), the reality of the balls was less glamorous: put simply, these were dances where wealthy white planters and merchants were able to consort with poorer, mixed-race girls chaperoned by their mothers. Little would usually come of the encounters, but occasionally, under a formalized system known as **plaçage**, arrangements would be made whereby the girls would be taken as mistresses, supported by their white men. A lucky few were set up in homes of their own, raising the children of their paramour, who would usually also be supporting a "respectable" white family. The Salle d'Orleans closed at the onset of the Civil War, was reborn as a convent, and became a hotel (see p.133) in the 1960s.

The Historic Voodoo Museum

Map 4, H4. Daily 10am–8pm; $6.50.

A mesmerizing, if muffled, soundtrack of drumming and chanting heralds the **Historic Voodoo Museum**, between Bourbon and Royal at 724 Dumaine St. A rag-bag collection of ceremonial objects, paintings and *gris-gris*, the museum aims to debunk the myths that surround this misunderstood syncretic religion – an intention undermined somewhat by the self-consciously spooky atmosphere, not to mention its resident 12ft python, crumbling rat heads and desiccated bats. The gift shop sells *gris-gris* and voodoo dolls, while the gallery features more expensive folk art. Ask about their readings, rituals and city tours (see p.17).

Voodoo

Voodoo, today practiced by around fifteen percent of the
city's population, was brought to New Orleans by African
slaves from the Caribbean, where tribal beliefs had been
mixed up with Catholicism, the official religion of the French
colonies, to create a new cult based on spirit-worship. French
and, later, Spanish authorities tried to suppress the religion
(voodoo-worshippers had played an active role in the organization of the slave revolts in Haiti), but it continued to flourish
among the city's black population. Under American rule, the
weekly slave gatherings at **Congo Square** (see p.54), which
included ritual ceremonies, turned into a tourist attraction for
whites, fueled by sensationalized reports of hypnotized white
women dancing naked to the throbbing drum music.

Unlike in the Caribbean, where the religion was dominated
by priests, New Orleans had many voodoo priestesses. The
most famous was **Marie Laveau**, a hairdresser of African,
white and Native American blood. Using shrewd marketing
sense and inside knowledge of the lives of her clients, she
prepared **gris-gris** – spells or potions – for wealthy Creoles
and Americans, as well as Africans. Laveau died in 1881,
when another Marie, believed to be her daughter, continued
to practice under her name. The legend of both Maries lives
on, and their crumbling **tombs** are popular tourist attractions
(see pp.110 & 112).

Nowadays voodoo is big business in New Orleans, with
countless gift shops selling ersatz *gris-gris*. If you've got a
serious interest in the religion, head instead for the **Voodoo
Spiritual Temple**, 828 N Rampart St (daily 10am–8pm;
℗522-9627; Map 4, G1), which holds an open service on
Thursday evenings and offers various tours and consulta-
tions.

VOODOO

51

Lafitte's Blacksmith Shop

Map 4, I3.

The alarmingly tumbledown *Lafitte's Blacksmith Shop*, 941 Bourbon St at St Philip – now a great little bar (see p.184) – is one of the oldest buildings in the Quarter. Built around 1781, it's a typical early cottage, with a steeply pitched roof (the dormers are a later addition). On the outside walls, blotches of stucco have crumbled off to reveal its *briquete entre poteaux* construction (see p.45).

According to legend, the shop was used as a cover for pirate brothers Jean and Pierre **Lafitte**, leaders of the "Baratarians", a thousand-strong band of smugglers who hid out in the Barataria swamps at the mouth of the Mississippi. Though the importation of slaves was outlawed in 1804, there was such a high demand for labor in the thriving colony that illegal slave smuggling was a lucrative racket, and it was in murky little cottages like these that plans were hatched and raids were plotted.

BEYOND BOURBON STREET

Beyond Bourbon Street, the French Quarter becomes markedly more peaceful and residential, the tourists outnumbered by locals dog-walking, jogging, picking up provisions in a corner grocery, or chatting on stoops. These quiet streets are fringed by some of the Quarter's finest **vernacular architecture**, narrow shotguns and Creole cottages, the hues of hand-tinted antique photos, standing flush with the sidewalk. Small courtyards are tended lovingly, with myrtle and magnolia blossoms tangling over cast-iron fences and fountains tinkling at the heart of hidden patios.

The streets above Bourbon can be eerily **isolated** after dark; if you feel at all nervous, restrict your explorations to the daylight hours.

LAFITTE'S BLACKSMITH SHOP, BEYOND BOURBON STREET

Musée Conti Wax Museum

Map 4, D2. Mon–Sat 10am–5.30pm, Sun noon–5pm; $6.50.

The **Musée Conti Wax Museum**, 917 Conti St, tells the story of New Orleans through a series of lurid tableaux that includes the Battle of New Orleans, the arrival of the casket girls – portrayed here by a gaggle of department store mannequins with groovy 1960s make up – Napoleon proclaiming in his bathtub, wild-eyed voodoo dancers, and a hard-faced, whip-wielding Madame LaLaurie (see p.47). The grand finale, apropos of nothing, comes in the Haunted Dungeon, where encounters with Dracula, Frankenstein, and sundry ghouls are backed by recorded shrieking and wailing.

Rampart Street

Map 4, A1–N1.

Rampart Street, the run-down strip separating the Quarter from the black neighborhood of Tremé, is a boundary rarely crossed by tourists. Though it's home to a couple of the most popular clubs in the city (*Donna's* and *Funky Butt*; see p.194), both of which are just a short walk from the heart of the Quarter, it can feel unsafe at night, and only slightly less so during the day.

Our Lady of Guadalupe

Our Lady of Guadalupe, 411 N Rampart St (Map 4, D1), was built in 1826 as a mortuary chapel for the neighboring St Louis No. 1 cemetery; in those days both were outside the city limits, protecting the population from what were believed to be the poisonous miasmas that emanated from the mountains of corpses. The church's statue of "St Expedite", mysteriously delivered here, so the legend goes, in a crate simply stamped *expedite*, is said to be worshipped by the city's voodooists.

St Louis No. 1 Cemetery is covered on p.110,
in the chapter devoted to
New Orleans' Cities of the Dead.

Louis Armstrong Park and Congo Square

The entrance to **Louis Armstrong Park** (Map 4, F1–H1), a huge twinkling arch clearly visible the length of St Ann St, promises far more than the park itself delivers. Unprepossessing and windblown, with concrete bridges spanning a stagnant lagoon, it's a desolate space, little improved by the lumpen Mahalia Jackson Theater of the Performing Arts or the Municipal Auditorium. At its upriver edge, the small paved area ringed by benches is **Congo Square**. In colonial times this was the Place des Nègres, where every Sunday African slaves would meet to trade, make music and dance the **bamboula**, named after the large drums that beat the rhythm. In the American era, the gatherings quickly became tourist attractions, thronging with vendors and sideshows, from which white visitors would return with shocked tales of weird voodooist rituals and depravity. The slave gatherings were banned between 1834 and 1845, and in 1851, when the transformation of the Place d'Armes into Jackson Square left the soldiers without a parade ground, this open area was chosen as a replacement.

The CBD and Warehouse District

Neither as visually stunning nor as immediately appealing as the neighboring French Quarter, New Orleans' Central Business District, or **CBD**, is of more interest to visitors for its hotels and restaurants than for its sightseeing potential. Historically, however, its significance can't be overstressed: this was where American New Orleans started, created by vigorous Anglo newcomers who, after the Louisiana Purchase in 1803, built a new city of exchanges, insurance companies, banks and shops – along with grand theaters and hotels – as they set about making themselves rich. Rivaling their equivalents in the Creole city, the new developments marked the onset of New Orleans' **Americanization**, an era of phenomenal change and economic growth that lasted until the Civil War.

....

The area covered by this chapter is shown in detail on color map 3.

....

Upriver from the Quarter, across Canal Street, the CBD's sweep of offices, old bank buildings and fancy hotels stretches as far as the Pontchartrain Expressway, bounded riverside by the Mississippi and, lakeside, by I-10 (Claiborne Avenue). Apart from the gargantuan **Superdome**, which lies at the lakeside edge of the CBD, most of what there is to see is in the **Warehouse District**, a revitalizing area of low-rent studios and pricey loft apartments, loosely bounded by Poydras, the Expressway, Convention Center Blvd and St Charles Avenue. In the last decade, a number of the neglected warehouses and old factory buildings have been given over to galleries, restaurants and bars, with a spirited arts community thriving on and around **Julia Street**. There's still some way to go, however: assurances that the run-down, abandoned-looking buildings are, in fact, hives of creativity doesn't necessarily make the Warehouse District a great place to walk around at night.

Some history

In the eighteenth century, much of the area now covered by the CBD was a vast sugar plantation belonging to **Bertrand Gravier**. Following the devastating fire of 1788, which destroyed most of the French Quarter, Gravier sold off parcels of his land to allow settlement along the river. The emergent suburb, **Faubourg Ste Marie**, named after his wife, remained sparsely populated until the Louisiana Purchase in 1803. Within fifteen years or so of annexation, however, the faubourg – its name now Americanized to St Mary – expanded rapidly, populated by the factors, brokers, bankers and planters that flooded into New Orleans eager to exploit its booming port. The city's center of commerce swiftly shifted away from the French Quarter to the "**American sector**", as St Mary was referred to, and eventually, in 1836 New Orleans was carved into **municipalities**, each with its own council – a state of affairs which lasted until 1852.

Canal Street was the dividing line between the first (Creole) and second (American) municipalities, and gradually took over from Royal Street in the French Quarter as the city's chief commercial thoroughfare. The Americans also built fine East-coast style town houses for themselves, on and around **Julia Street**, while huge warehouses backed the bustling wharves.

After Reconstruction, as the French Quarter fell into decline, the CBD struggled on, keeping its head above water on the back of continuing cotton wealth; the warehouses, meanwhile, were turned over to wholesalers and meat packers. During the 1970s **oil boom**, many of the old banks and exchanges were torn down to make way for corporate towers (though building anything too high has always been a problem on this soggy soil – today the tallest building reaches just 51 stories, a tiddler in big-city terms), parking lots, business hotels, and the landmark hulk of the Superdome.

Hotels in the CBD are reviewed on p.139; restaurants on p.164.

In the 1980s, when the boom **bust** as suddenly as it had hit, the CBD experienced a mass exodus and turned to tourism for its salvation. While the towers, their rents drastically lowered, stand half-empty, many of the older buildings, capitalizing on their proximity to the French Quarter, have been converted into boutique hotels and ritzy restaurants. The Warehouse District, meanwhile, which had disintegrated into a forgotten wasteland, was reawoken by the 1984 **World's Fair**, held in restored buildings along the wharves. Since then it has gone from strength to strength, not least in the development of its **art galleries**.

CANAL STREET

Map 3, N6–N1.

The widest main street (170ft) in America, and on the parade route for all the super krewes at Mardi Gras (see p.276), the once glorious **Canal Street**, which runs from the river to Lake Pontchartrain, is looking a bit down at heel today. It is still the backbone of the city, however, literally dividing downtown (downriver) from uptown (upriver).

There never was a **canal** here, though one was planned in the early 1800s, and you'll see a phantom waterway marked on many early maps. The street started its days as a rough ditch cut along the ramparts of the city, separating it from the plantations – and later the American suburb – beyond. It was eventually filled to become the town commons, and as the Faubourg St Mary grew, settlers built homes along its muddy expanse. When New Orleans was divided into municipalities, this was the **"neutral ground"** in the middle, and many traders set up here in order to get business from both sides of the city. By the 1850s, all the homes had been replaced by department stores and opulent theaters.

> For a superb view of New Orleans,
> including the astonishing bend in the Mississippi,
> head for the World Trade Center,
> a woefully drab 1960s tower at the foot of Canal.
> There's a viewing platform on the 31st floor
> (daily 9am–5pm; $2) and a revolving cocktail bar
> two floors above (see p.187).

Though the grand old **department stores** that gave Canal Street so much of its character are disappearing one by one, the gorgeous **storefronts**, decorated in Beaux Arts,

Italianate and Art Deco styles, for the most part remain, safe from the demolition that richer cities would have inflicted upon them. Today the lovely old buildings are filled with tacky T-shirt and souvenir stores, fast-food outlets, and none-too-reputable electrical shops (stick to the national chains).

The casino

Map 3, M5.

Splayed out at the foot of Canal Street, the behemoth of the **casino** stands as a mute reproach to a decade-long saga of double-dealing and ineptitude. In the early 1990s, in the face of resistance from groups who felt it would drain resources, and character, from the rest of the city, and despite the state's gambling laws (which held that casinos had to be restricted to riverboats), Governor Edwin Edwards – a wheeler-dealer politician in the grand old Louisiana tradition – fixed it so that a land-based casino could be built in the city. In 1995, the Harrah's chain set up a temporary site in Louis Armstrong Park and started work on the Canal Street building, which was all set to become one of the largest casinos in the world. Less than a year after it opened, however, the temporary casino closed, blighted by low attendances. Harrah's promptly filed for bankruptcy, and the half-built Canal Street colossus stood eerily empty, windowless and fenced off for two years. In fall 1998, however, the project was resurrected, the developers promising to have the whole thing up and running by 2000. Whether it will succeed this time is anyone's guess – nobody but the politicians and Harrah's seems very enthusiastic – and whether its planned "reconstructed" French Quarter, complete with cast-iron balconies and beignet stands, will draw visitors away from the real thing, remains to be seen.

The Battle of Liberty Place

The riverside end of Canal Street, opposite the Custom House, was the site of one of the most significant battles in the city's bitter **Reconstruction** era (see p.268). On September 13, 1874, the Metropolitan police force, which included many freed slaves, seized a boat-load of arms destined for the **White League** – a militia formed by ex-Confederates committed to bringing down the radical Republican government and stamping out what they called the "Africanization" of their city. Claiming that the action of the police was an infringement of their constitutional right to bear arms, the League placed an advertisement in the *Times-Picayune*, calling for a mass demonstration in protest.

On September 14, some five thousand whites met at the Henry Clay statue, which stood at the heart of the city, on Canal Street where it crossed St Charles and Royal. After a morning of rabble-rousing, during which the call was made to depose the hated Republican Governor Kellogg, the White Leaguers armed themselves and marched down Canal Street to the river where they met a defensive line made up of the Metropolitan police and the black militia. A twenty-minute conflict ensued, which resulted in the police being chased back to Jackson Square in the French Quarter, where Kellogg was overthrown – just five days later President Grant sent in troops to reinstate him. Nonetheless, the **Battle of Liberty Place**, which left eleven policemen – six of them white – and sixteen rioters dead, was seen by the White League as a victory for freedom, a blow against the Reconstruction government and – despite lame public assurances that their motives weren't racist – an assertion of white supremacy. The League was formally disbanded two years later, when, Reconstruction over, Louisiana returned to home rule.

The ramifications of the battle did not end there, however. In 1891, the **Liberty Monument**, inscribed with a list of the White League members who had died fighting, was erected on the median at the foot of Canal Street. Well into the 1930s, Confederate supporters gathered at the granite obelisk every September 14 – their insistence that to do so was a celebration of political liberty was undermined somewhat by the plaque added to the monument in 1932, rejoicing at the demise of Reconstruction and the victory of "white supremacy".

In 1981, "Dutch" Morial, the city's first black mayor and the father of current mayor Marc Morial, ordered that the monument should be surrounded by tall bushes, effectively hiding it from view. Under increasing pressure from civil rights groups, who demanded that, as a racist symbol, it should be torn down, and white reactionaries, who insisted it was part of the city's history, the city council vacillated for years, until eventually, in 1989, the monument was removed and put into storage. Spearheaded by David Duke, a former Grand Wizard of the Ku Klux Klan and candidate for Louisiana governor in 1991, a lawsuit was filed to return the monument to the street, and in 1993, amid violent demonstrations, the Liberty Monument was rededicated in an inconspicuous spot next to a parking lot behind the aquarium. Though its supremacist plaque was replaced by a list of the Metropolitan police members killed in the battle, the monument remains an ugly, graffitied testament to a century of vexed race relations.

The Custom House

Map 3, N4. Mon–Fri 8am–4.30pm; free.

During the Civil War, the (then incomplete) gray granite **Custom House**, 423 Canal St, was headquarters to Union General "Beast" Butler (see p.70) and a prison for

Confederate soldiers. There's a surprise inside, behind the foreboding classical exterior: a huge **marble hall**, illuminated by a 55ft skylight, with fourteen columns of Italian marble supporting the dazzling white and gilt ceiling. Plans are afoot to turn the place into an insectarium, though the mind boggles at just how many bugs it would take to fill this block-spanning monster.

TOWARD THE WAREHOUSE DISTRICT

Turning off Canal at Baronne Street – look for the wonderful old neon Walgreen's sign – brings you to the oddly Moorish **Church of the Immaculate Conception**, or Jesuit Church (Map 3, M3), worth a look for its flamboyant arches, cast-iron spiral columns and pews. Designed by local architect James Freret, the gilt bronze altar, with its trio of onion domes, won first prize at the Paris Exposition of 1867. The original church, built in 1857, threatened to collapse into the city's soggy soil under its own weight; the structure you see today – a perfect replica – dates from the 1930s.

As you move upriver from the church and head down Common Street toward Carondelet, you come to the heart of the old CBD. Though it doesn't look like much today, the eleven-story **Latter and Blum** building, 203 Carondelet (Map 3, M3), was New Orleans' first "skyscraper", designed in 1895 by eminent local architect Thomas Sully who, though he is most famous for his St Charles Avenue mansions (see p.85), was inspired in this case by the Chicago School. Nearby, the 23-story **Hibernia National Bank**, 313 Carondelet (Map 3, M3), is another landmark. Built in 1921, it was the city's tallest building until 1962, and today its circular belvedere can be seen from anywhere in the CBD. It's especially striking when floodlit at night, and positively ethereal during Mardi Gras, when bathed in the carnival colors of purple, green and gold.

Another block toward the river, at 201 St Charles Ave, the **First NBC building** (Map 3, M4) is built on the site of the old **St Charles Hotel**, designed in 1835 by **James Gallier Sr** – one of New Orleans' premier architects, propelled to fame by his work on the hotel – and Charles Dakin. The equivalent of the St Louis Hotel in the French Quarter, this was the American sector's grandest building, a columned Greek Revival showpiece that was originally topped with a huge dome (the dome was destroyed in a fire in 1851, after which the hotel was rebuilt without it). Featuring a major slave exchange, the St Charles was at the commercial heart of antebellum, Anglo-American New Orleans, and *the* place to stay – among the famous names who slept here was "Beast" Butler (see p.70), who, during the Civil War occupation, took over the entire place after he was refused the VIP suite. Following another fire in 1894, Thomas Sully redesigned the building in Beaux Arts style, and it remained one of the city's top hotels until it was demolished in the 1970s.

Lafayette Square

Map 3, L4.
Laid out in 1788, **Lafayette Square** was the political hub of the American sector. Today, surrounded by dreary court buildings and offices, it centers on a bronze **statue** of early nineteenth-century statesman **Henry Clay**. When the statue was dedicated in 1860, it stood at the heart of the city, on Canal Street where Royal met St Charles, and provided a focal point for countless public meetings – including the rally that led to the Battle of Liberty Place (see p.60). In 1901 it was moved to this less conspicuous spot to make room for increasing traffic along Canal.

On the lakeside of the square, another bronze statue portrays **John McDonogh**, an outspoken abolitionist and leading light in the American Colonization Society, which advocated the return of slaves to Africa. McDonogh was regarded as a miser during his lifetime, but, when he died in 1850, he left his considerable riches to be divided between New Orleans and his native Baltimore for the establishment of racially mixed public schools. Today, many of New Orleans' public schools are the result of that legacy; the statue, designed in 1898 at a cost of $7000, was funded by nickel donations from the city's schoolchildren.

Gallier Hall

The magnificent **Gallier Hall** (Map 3, L4), across from Lafayette Square on St Charles Avenue, is the grandest example of Greek Revival architecture in New Orleans. Fronted by an ornate 90ft facade with ten fluted white Ionic columns and a pediment featuring Justice, Liberty and Commerce, it was designed by James Gallier Sr as the City Hall for the second municipality (the first municipality had its own, the Cabildo, on the Place d'Armes (see p.26). By the time it was dedicated in 1853, however, New Orleans had reunited; thus the building served as seat of government for the whole city right up to the 1950s, when the new City Hall was built on Poydras near the Superdome.

Today, Gallier Hall hosts civic events and receptions. Traditionally, too, it's the site of one of the premier **Mardi Gras** parade-viewing platforms, packed with assorted bigwigs, including the mayor. The enormous floats stop for quite a while here, and experienced bead-beggars know to stake out the spot across the street.

St Patrick's Church

Map 3, L5.

James Gallier Sr, though best known for his accomplished Greek Revival buildings, also had a hand in the neo-Gothic

St Patrick's Church, near Lafayette Square at 710 Camp St. In 1838 Irish architects Charles and James Dakin set to work on rebuilding the small wooden church that had stood on this site since 1833 – the second municipality was thriving, and needed a Catholic place of worship to equal St Louis Cathedral, where sermons were held only in French. Work was completed by Gallier, who designed the interior with its fine stained glass, elaborate altar, sweeping vaulting and neo-Gothic tracery.

THE WAREHOUSE DISTRICT

Map 3, J6–M5.

During the antebellum era, the **Warehouse District** was a bustling area of factories and warehouses storing sugar, cotton, grain and tobacco ready to be loaded onto ocean-going ships, and manufactured goods from overseas waiting to be transported upriver by steamboat. After Reconstruction, however, as the port went into decline, the district deteriorated into a dangerous no-go zone, only reviving after it was chosen as the site of the 1984 **World's Fair**. Today, tourist literature pushes the district as a thriving **arts community**, buzzing with workshops, galleries and designer stores. However, though it is certainly a desirable place to live – the spacious lofts, river views and easy parking making it an agreeable alternative to the bohemian funkiness of the congested Quarter – for the visitor, the attractions are not always immediate. It's also important to bear in mind that the Warehouse District is not interchangeable with the **Arts District**, the outcrop of cutting-edge galleries concentrated around Julia and Camp streets and the **Contemporary Arts Center**.

There's a lively farmers' market every Saturday morning at the corner of Camp and Girod streets.

Though many buildings were demolished in the 1970s, much of the area's original **architecture** – churches, factories and tall brick town houses, as well as warehouses – remains, offering a counterpoint to the Creole flavor of the Quarter. Here, Federal, Neoclassical and Greek Revival styles dominate, reflecting the very American nature of the antebellum Faubourg St Mary.

Julia Street and the galleries

Map 3, K5.

Though the low-rent buildings all over the Warehouse District are filling with studios and workshops, when people talk about the **Arts District** they're mainly referring to the stretch of **Julia Street** from Commerce Street up to St Charles Avenue. On the first Saturday of every month from October to May the hip **galleries** along here hold receptions (6–9pm) open to all: these pull a mixed crowd of uptowners, art students and conventioneers, all nibbling cheese, sipping Chablis and checking out each other as much as the art.

Many of the Arts District galleries close for summer, and some shut up shop during the day on reception days; call to check, or consult the listings papers *Lagniappe* or *Gambit* (see p.8) before setting off.

The biggest shindig of all, *the* place for the local art world to see and be seen, is **Art for Arts Sake**, the day-

The Julia Street galleries

The following are some of the most consistently interesting galleries on Julia Street. However, exhibitions rotate regularly, and it's a matter of taste as to which ones will appeal – for a full rundown check the listings papers. You can also pick up leaflets in the Welcome Center (see p.8), the Preservation Resource Center (see opposite) and *True Brew* (p.177).

LeMieux Galleries, no. 332 (Tues–Sat 10am–5.30pm; ℡522-5988). Contemporary art, folk art and crafts from Louisiana and the Gulf Coast. Retrospectives have included the bold "Caribbean-Cubist" images of New Orleans by Paul Niñas, who painted the mural in the swanky *Sazerac Bar* (see p.187).

Arthur Roger Gallery, no. 432 (Mon–Sat 10am–5pm; ℡522-1999). Large, swish space for an eclectic and always fascinating range of cutting-edge art, sculpture and video. If you only see one Arts District gallery, make it this one.

George Schmidt, no. 608 (Mon–Sat 12.30–4.30pm; ℡524-8137). Thought-provoking work, including Schmidt's own, which features quirky historical and religious tableaux and smudgy dreamlike drawings of decadent Mardi Gras aristocrats.

Sylvia Schmidt, no. 400a (Tues–Sat 10am–4pm; ℡524-8137). Arresting contemporary fine art and abstracts, photographs, prints, sculpture and drawings from local and international artists.

Galerie Simonne Stern, no. 518 (Mon noon–5pm, Tues–Fri 10am–6pm, Sat 10am–5pm; ℡529-1118). One of the first galleries to set up in the area, with strong shows of contemporary painting, photography and sculpture.

JULIA STREET AND THE GALLERIES

long festival held on the first Saturday in October. From 6pm to 9pm the streets around Julia and Camp are closed off, and a shuttle bus runs between here and the galleries on Magazine Street. There's a street-party ambience, with stalls selling wine and beer, and nervous artists milling around; after 9pm the revels shift to the Contemporary Arts Center (see p.72). The **Julia Street Jump**, on the first Saturday in May, is a similar, though smaller-scale event.

In addition to the galleries, Julia is a good place to check out the **architecture** that characterized the American sector. At no. 545 you'll see three of the district's earliest warehouses, simple, shuttered structures built in 1833; compare these with the larger, utilitarian building at no. 329, New Orleans' first reinforced concrete construction. In the block between St Charles and Camp stands a parade of beautifully renovated row houses known as the **Thirteen Sisters**. When they were built in 1833 these red-brick residences were the most desirable in the American sector, reminiscent of the Federal style favored in the northeastern states; just sixty years later they had declined into slums. Today no. 604 houses the **Preservation Resource Center** (see p.66), at the vanguard of local restoration efforts.

Louisiana Children's Museum

Map 3, L5. Sept–May Tues–Sat 9.30am–4.30pm, Sun noon–4.30pm; June–Aug Mon–Sat 9.30am–4.30pm, Sun noon–4.30pm; $5.

In a characteristic 1861 warehouse topped by an elaborate cornice, the **Louisiana Children's Museum**, 420 Julia St, is only worth a trip if you've got very bored kids in tow. Many of the exhibits don't work, and some are wearyingly earnest, geared toward school groups rather than out-for-fun visitors. However, there are enough things to wind up, push, pull and plunge to keep the younger ones diverted for an hour or so, and though the scope for role play is mostly

somewhat dreary, few people – kids or adults – will be able
to resist pretending to be a news anchor in the KidWatch
studio.

Confederate Museum

Map 3, J5. Mon–Sat 10am–4pm; $5.

A gloomy Romanesque Revival hulk, purpose-designed by
Thomas Sully in 1891 as a place for Confederate veterans to
display their mementos, the **Confederate Museum**, 929
Camp St at Lee Circle, is a relic from a bygone age.
Jefferson Davis, who died in New Orleans' Garden District
in 1889 (see p.81), lay in state here for a while, and there
remains a funereal air about the place, with its bittersweet
remembrances of long-lost generals and their forgotten
families. It's easy to forget that freewheeling New Orleans
has its roots entrenched in the Deep South, but this memo-
rial hall – the "Battle Abbey of the South" – is no better
reminder. Its aim, more than a century after the event,
remains to tell "the story of insult and oppression . . . pil-
lage and ruin . . . want and suffering and humiliation and
insult and punishment".

> **The Confederate Museum is a stone's throw from
> Lee Circle, which centers on a bronze statue of the
> Confederate general atop a 60ft marble column,
> built in 1884. The statue faces north, of course.**

Inside the church-like hall, glass cases are filled with flags,
swords, mess-kits, uniforms and helmets. There are wordy
accounts of battles and of generals, but very little background detail – when the museum was built the "lost
cause" would have been fresh in visitors' minds – and certainly no attempt at hindsight or analysis.

CONFEDERATE MUSEUM |

"Beast" Butler

Though he was in New Orleans for just nine months, **Major Benjamin Butler**, who commanded the military rule of the city after it fell to Union troops in 1862, is one of its most demonized figures. Dubbed **"Beast" Butler** by die-hard Rebels, for what they saw as his cruelty and injustice – in June 1862 he hanged a man who had torn down a Union flag *before* the city was occupied – he was also known as **"Spoons"**, due to a rumored kleptomaniac habit of pilfering cutlery. The truth, however, is that during occupation families who refused to swear allegiance to the Union may have had property – including silver – confiscated. "Spoons" did not pocket the cutlery himself, though he may have personally profited from its sale.

So unpopular was the Beast that local belles – who, it is said, had his likeness painted in their chamber pots – would retch loudly as Union soldiers walked by. After a month or so of this, in a fit of pique at the behavior of what he called "these she-adders", Butler announced the **General Order 28**, claiming "When any female shall by word, gesture, or movement, insult or show contempt for any officer of the United States, she shall be regarded and held liable to be treated as a woman of the town plying her vocation". The order, denounced by Jefferson Davis (who announced that the general deserved to be hanged) and the British parliament (who saw it as terribly ungentlemanly), was recalled, as was Butler himself in December 1862.

That said, the place has an undeniable pull. Along with affecting sepia photos – of the wealthy, muddy antebellum city, and wide-eyed youths dandied up in uniform – oddities include a crown of thorns hand-woven by Pope Pius IX and sent to Jefferson as an encouraging gift. There's also an account of the **Confederate Native Guards**, free men of color who signed up but weren't allowed to fight by the other Confederate states because of the color of their skin.

For more on the Civil War in New Orleans, see p.267;
for Reconstruction see p.268.

The curators obviously feel that the exhibit on notorious Union **General "Beast" Butler** (see opposite) needs no introduction, and concentrate instead on the now legendary tales of his corruption and cruelty. The throwaway line at the end, "justice requires that it be stated that he did feed the poor, clean up the streets and prevent disease", strikes an odd note, as does the startling assertion that after the war he befriended the widow of William Mumford – the man he hanged for tearing down the Union flag – and secured her "a government position".

Reconstruction, too, is covered in the bitterest terms, charging that the US government deliberately kept the southern states from recovery. Accounts of white supremacist groups, such as the **White League** (see p.60), are puffed up with patriotic outrage, couched in terms of individuals seeking political liberty in order to protect themselves from the "police state". That the Metropolitan police was composed of many Union sympathizers and freed slaves is seen as an affirmation of White League beliefs rather than a challenge to them.

The Ogden Museum of Southern Art, on Lee Circle,
and the state-of-the-art D-Day Museum,
a few blocks away, both slated for completion in 2000,
are set to draw even more visitors to
the Warehouse District.

CONFEDERATE MUSEUM

The Contemporary Arts Center

Map 3, K5. Mon–Sat 10am–5pm, Sun 11am–5pm; closed July;
ground floor galleries, cybercafé and giftshop free; changing
exhibitions $5.

Housed in a restored nineteenth-century warehouse and
ice-cream factory, the **Contemporary Arts Center**
(**CAC**), 900 Camp St, is the city's premier modern art
gallery. A kind of anchor for the Arts District, it's a beautifully designed space, and there's always something interesting going on, from the temporary shows on the ground
floor to major exhibitions upstairs. It also hosts a number of
lively fundraisers, climaxing in October's **Art for Art's
Sake** bash (see p.66), when you can wander the galleries
with a beer and a gumbo, dance to live bands, or watch a
fashion show.

Check the listings papers for the CAC's **schedule** of cutting-edge performances, classic and art-house movies, lec-
tures and workshops.

THE SUPERDOME

Map 3, K1–2. Tours daily, except during special events, on the hour
10am–4pm; $6.

The lakeside edge of the CBD, a tangle of busy gray high-
ways, would be pretty grim without the colossal home of
the beleaguered New Orleans Saints football team, the
Superdome. At 52 acres, 27 stories high and spanning a
diameter of 680ft, this is one of the largest buildings in the
world, completed in 1975 at a cost of nearly $200 million.
The investment paid off: more **Superbowl** games have
been held here than in any other US city, bringing in huge
amounts of revenue. You can't really appreciate the sheer
enormity of the place until you venture inside, either by
seating yourself with 76,999 others to see a **Saints game**

(Aug–Dec; $25–50) or, second-best, by joining one of the superlatives- and statistics-heavy guided tours.

....

The wildly popular intercollegiate football championship, the Sugarbowl, is held at the Superdome every New Year's Day.

....

The dome is also used for major gigs and special events – guides proudly quote that it hosted not only the largest ever rock concert audience (for The Rolling Stones in 1981), but also the largest movie audience (the world premiere of Disney's *The Hunchback of Notre Dame* in 1996). It was also designed as a hurricane shelter, much needed in this storm-battered city – a function first put to the test in September 1998 in the run-up to Hurricane Georges, when it sheltered 14,000 people for two days before the hurricane veered sharply east at the last minute and bypassed the city altogether.

Tours lead you around the stalls and behind the scenes to the visitors' locker room (the Saints' is out of bounds for security reasons) and the press box. Disappointingly, you can't walk, let alone kick a ball, on the astroturf (called, wearisomely, "Mardi Grass") – a source of frustration to restive Georges evacuees, some of whom whiled away the hours by sneaking into the Saints' luxury suites, raiding the minibars, and pilfering anything that wasn't stuck down.

THE SUPERDOME

The Garden District and uptown

The grand, residential **Garden District**, around two miles upriver from the French Quarter, was created in the 1840s by the energetic breed of Anglo-Americans who, having outgrown the Faubourg St Mary (today's CBD, see p.56), announced their ever-accumulating wealth by building sumptuous mansions in huge, lush gardens. Shaded by jungles of subtropical foliage, the glorious houses – some of them spick-and-span showpieces, others in ruins – evoke a nostalgic vision of the Deep South in a profusion of galleries, columns and balconies. It's a ravishing spectacle, if somewhat Gothic – perfect for horror author **Anne Rice**, who was born nearby and has since bought and restored a number of local properties, as well as featuring several of them in her fiction.

The Garden District began its days in 1834 as the city of **Lafayette**, which remained separate from New Orleans until 1852. Development sped up with the arrival, in 1835, of the **New Orleans and Carrollton Railroad** – forerunner of today's streetcar – which ran along St

Charles Avenue, the broad street bordering the suburb on its lakeside edge. Lafayette's construction frenzy was brought to a rude halt by the Civil War, when occupying troops made themselves comfortable in the capacious homes; the turn of the century, however, saw another spate of mansion-building, this time along **St Charles Avenue** and the crucial streetcar line, extending further and further upriver with each passing year. The august residences of the Garden District, meanwhile, remained in the hands of the monied elite, as they continue to do today.

The area covered by this chapter is shown in detail on color maps 2 & 3.

The Garden District heralds the onset of **uptown** New Orleans, the big chunk of the city that extends from Jackson Avenue to Audubon Park. The **St Charles Avenue streetcar**, which follows the same route as the early railroad, is still by far the best way to explore the area, affording front-row views of "the avenue", as St Charles is locally known. Clanging its way from Canal Street, it courses through the low-rent **Lower Garden District** before arriving at the Garden District proper, beyond which it continues past increasingly opulent turn-of-the-century mansions. It eventually reaches peaceful **Audubon Park** and its excellent **zoo**; a little farther, the track turns inland to the studenty **Riverbend** area, which has some great bars and restaurants.

Running parallel to St Charles, and forming the riverside boundary of the Garden District, **Magazine Street**, its shotgun houses filled with thrift stores, antique shops and designer studios, is the other main channel between Canal Street and uptown.

The St Charles streetcar

There can be few more romantic ways of passing an hour or so in New Orleans than planting yourself on a mahogany bench on the **St Charles streetcar**, catching the breeze from the open window, and watching as one of America's loveliest avenues unfolds in front of you.

The streetcar, now a National Historic Monument, began in 1835 as the **New Orleans and Carrollton Railroad**, a steam-powered train that took a whole day to cover the six-and-a-half miles from Canal Street, via Lafayette and a string of small faubourgs, to the resort town of Carrollton. After the Civil War, the inefficient steam engines were replaced with mules – a cleaner, quieter form of transport – until overhead electricity was introduced in 1893.

The streetcar network spread quickly, with cars traveling three abreast along tracks crisscrossing Canal Street and the French Quarter. Though Tennessee Williams was said to be inspired by the clanging of the trolley bell beneath his French Quarter apartment to pen his 1947 play *A Streetcar Named Desire*, the service was already dwindling by then, faced with competition from motorbuses, and by 1964 only the St Charles line remained.

In the 1980s, a new streetcar line, geared primarily toward tourists, was developed along a two-mile stretch of the river-front (see p.12). Plans are now afoot to resurrect the Canal Street route and link all three tracks. For more on the **practicalities** of streetcar travel, see pp.11–12.

Hotels in the Garden District and uptown are reviewed on p.141, restaurants on p.166, bars on p.188 and clubs on p.202.

THE ST CHARLES STREETCAR

THE LOWER GARDEN DISTRICT

Map 3, G6–I6.

The **Lower Garden District** – designated the hippest neighborhood in the US by funkier-than-thou lifestyle paper *Utne Reader* in December 1997 – is a loose term for the area between the Warehouse District and the Garden District proper. Sprawling down through a cluster of unpronounceable streets named after the Greek muses, via **Coliseum Park** to the river, it's a racially mixed neighborhood, the once decorative, now decaying, nineteenth-century buildings housing a motley population of artists and poor families. While it's no great shakes for sightseeing, it does have a number of good budget **hotels**. On top of that, lower **Magazine Street** – more countercultural here than along its uptown stretch – holds various alternative galleries and thrift stores. This end of the street is studded with desolate, run-down blocks, however, so keep your wits about you if you decide to walk it. The #11 bus runs the length of the road, but services are sporadic.

THE GARDEN DISTRICT

Map 3, B5–F5.

Pride of uptown New Orleans, the **Garden District** drapes itself seductively across an area just thirteen blocks wide and five deep, bounded by Magazine Street and St Charles, Jackson and Louisiana avenues. Here some of the swankiest homes in the city – during Carnival season, many fly the official Mardi Gras banner, announcing that a resident has been honored as King or Queen of Rex – stand in the shadow of hauntingly derelict piles.

The mansions of Lafayette were built in a variety of **architectural styles**, each according to the whim of its owner. The earliest homes stood one to a block, situated on the corners and fronted by brick flagstones that came over as ballast on ships returning from Europe. As fortunes were made, tastes became more and more flamboyant, each nouveau-riche planter and merchant trying to outdo his neighbor. Today you'll see ordered, columned Greek Revival structures; romantic, Italianate villas; Moorish follies; Second Empire piles and fanciful Queen Anne mansions, plus a number of buildings that defy categorization, with motifs mixed up together to form transitional, or hybrid, styles.

It's no coincidence that so many gallery ceilings in the Garden District are painted sky-blue – it's a well-known ploy to deter dimwitted insects, who thrive in the copious foliage, from nesting there.

Though most people are here to gaze upon the houses, the neighborhood also lives up to its name with its fabulous **greenery**. Unlike the Creoles of the French Quarter, who were constrained by lack of space, the planters and traders who built in Lafayette reveled in its expansiveness, setting their mansions back from the street by surrounding them with lush gardens. Today, everywhere you turn, foliage threatens to overtake the place: huge, mossy Live Oaks form a canopy over the streets, while broad oleander trees and banana plants fight for space with vividly flowering azaleas, camellias and crepe myrtles. The air is scented by jasmine, sweet olive and waxy magnolia blossoms – originally planted, it is said, to mask the odors from the tanneries and slaughterhouses of the **Irish Channel**, the working-class district that spread out beneath Lafayette toward the river.

....

**The Garden District's cemetery, Lafayette No. 1,
is covered on p.109, in the chapter devoted to
New Orleans' Cities of the Dead.**

....

The Garden District mansions are only open to the public during New Orleans' Spring Fiesta (see p.249). The neighborhood is best explored on an official **walking tour** (see p.14) or one of the self-guided tours available from the Welcome Center (see p.8). Other than a handful of fellow tourists, you'll see little human activity on these rarefied streets, where the uncanny hush is interrupted only by birdsong and the buzzing of distant lawnmowers – worlds away from the crash and clatter of the Quarter.

Toby's Corner and McGehee School

Map 3, E5.
The Greek Revival mansion known as **Toby's Corner**, 2340 Prytania at First, is the oldest surviving house in the Garden District. It was built in 1838, in unadorned plantation-style, with a raised floor to prevent waterlogging. Thomas Toby himself, a native of Philadelphia, had made a fortune by inventing a revolutionary cotton hauler, then promptly lost most of it backing the doomed Texan revolution of 1835.

Covering the entire block opposite Toby's Corner, fronted by mighty Corinthian columns, the private **McGehee School for Girls**, 2434 Prytania at First, was the envy of every sugar planter in town. Built during Reconstruction for Union sympathizer Bradish Johnson, the showy Second Empire trophy boasted not only an exquisite domed marble staircase, but also a newfangled elevator, a sure sign of wealth and distinction.

Joseph Morris House and the White House

Map 3, E6.
The **Joseph Morris House**, the lovely rose-pink villa on the corner of First Street and Coliseum, is a quintessential example of the dreamy Italianate style that swept through the Garden District in the 1860s. Its romantic aspect, enhanced by a web of cast-iron galleries, is set off perfectly by the orderly, straight-down-the-line Greek Revival **White House**, opposite at 1312 First St.

Anne Rice's house

Map 3, E6.
A gorgeous Italianate-Greek Revival hybrid on the corner of Chestnut and First, **Anne Rice's residence** is also the fictional home of her Mayfair witches. Built in 1856, it was the first house on the block, and today its elaborate floriate iron fence encloses other, newer houses. Notice the Egyptian "keyhole" front door, flaring out at the base, and the sky-blue gallery ceilings so common in the Garden District (see p.78). Peering out from the first-story balcony, the bizarre fiberglass German Shepherd – representing the mastiff that befriends the vampire Lestat – is said to have been a gift to Rice from her vet. You'll usually see at least one of the author's stretch limos parked outside the house; she has three, with the registration plates Seraphim, Cherubim and Ophanim.

....

**Anne Rice leaves long voicemail messages, which
include her views on topical events, her favorite TV
programs and books, and updates on her current state
of mind, on ⓒ522-8634.**

....

In recent years, Rice has sporadically offered free tours of her home, usually for just a couple of hours a week. Anyone interested should contact her Web site (see p.9) to check the latest situation.

Payne-Strachan House

Map 3, E6.

One block south of Anne Rice's house, the relatively unostentatious, columned **Payne-Strachan House**, 1134 First St at Camp, is a prime specimen of antebellum Greek Revival styling. Built in 1849 for the pro-Union planter Jacob Payne, the house is most notable for being where Jefferson Davis, president of the Confederacy, died in 1889, while visiting Payne's son-in-law. A granite slab outside commemorates the event.

Musson House and Showboat House

Map 3, E5.

Back up on Coliseum Sreet and Third, the Italianate **Musson House**, a fanciful pink clapboard structure fronted with fabulous cast-iron balconies, was built in 1850 for Michel Musson, the Creole uncle of the French Impressionist painter **Edgar Degas**. After the Civil War, having lost much of his wealth, Musson abandoned the Anglo-dominated Garden District in favor of Esplanade Avenue, the Creole equivalent of St Charles Avenue. He went on to join the supremacist White League, and was a voluble presence at the rally that led to the Battle of Liberty Place (see p.60).

....

Michel Musson can be seen testing a cotton sample in the foreground of Degas' *A Cotton Office in New Orleans* (see p.101).

....

Opposite the Musson House, the gallery-swathed **Showboat House**, 1415 Third St, is one of the Garden District's most palatial mansions. A transitional Italianate-Greek Revival structure built in 1860 by eminent architect Henry Howard, it is best known, prosaically, for its early form of indoor plumbing, whereby the roof acted as a large vessel to collect rainwater that was then channeled down into the house.

Lonsdale-Rice House and Briggs House

Map 3, E5.

The enormous Italianate **Lonsdale-Rice House**, 2521 Prytania St at Third, was built by Henry Howard in 1856 for coffee magnate Henry Lonsdale, who lost his fortune in the Civil War. It was later turned over to a religious order, who added a chapel, and, in 1996, Anne Rice – who had attended services here as a child – bought it outright.

On the other side of the road, the Garden District's only neo-Gothic mansion, the stern-looking **Briggs House**, 2605 Prytania at Third, was designed by James Gallier Sr in 1847. Though there are a couple of significant neo-Gothic buildings – also the work of Gallier – in the CBD, as a rule Southerners weren't that keen on the narrow windows and arches that characterized the style. This building, whose pared-down aspect does look a little out of place, was built for an English insurance broker.

Colonel Short's Villa

Map 3, D5.

Yet another Henry Howard structure, the Italianate **Colonel Short's Villa**, 1448 Fourth St at Prytania, was built for $25,000 in 1859 – a relatively paltry sum, even then. Just a few years later, it was commandeered by

Yankee forces, who enjoyed its facilities for the duration of the Civil War. While the building itself, with its columns and galleries, is undeniably striking, it's the cast-iron **cornstalk fence** that grabs your attention. A rural tangle of corn cobs and morning glories, it was picked, during the city's cast-iron craze, from the same catalog as its twin in the French Quarter (see p.46). You'll spot crumbly patches, where the fence is rusting away: cast iron, despite its decorative qualities, tends to be less durable than the simpler, hand-wrought iron favored in the early nineteenth century.

The turquoise Queen Anne building at 1403 Washington Ave is *Commander's Palace*, one of the finest Creole restaurants in the city (see p.167).

ST CHARLES AVENUE

A stately, Live Oak-lined swathe sweeping its way from Canal Street upriver to Audubon Park, **St Charles Avenue** is uptown's showpiece boulevard. Most of its ostentatious homes were built in the late nineteenth and early twentieth centuries – after 1893, when the streetcar line was electrified, merchants flourishing in the post-Civil War South found that to live on "the avenue", as it is still called, was an ideal way to display their new wealth.

The **streetcar** is still by far the best way to see the avenue, which gets more magnificent the further uptown you go. **Lower St Charles** is a scrappy ragbag of empty lots and architectural nonentities; beyond the Garden District, however, the private mansions cut as impressive a dash as they did a century ago, their cut-glass doors sparkling like priceless crystal.

ST CHARLES AVENUE

The *Columns Hotel*, 3811 St Charles
(on the lakeside of the avenue), is a fabulous place to
stop off for a drink, either in the faded bar
or on the avenue-side verandah,
fronted by its stout Doric columns (see p.188).

St Elizabeth's Orphanage

Map 2, I6. Tues–Sun 11am–3pm; $7 donation.

A couple of blocks south of St Charles, the red-brick
Second Empire **St Elizabeth's Orphanage**, 1314
Napoleon Ave at Prytania, is the most visited of Anne
Rice's properties. Rice has converted the massive structure,
which covers the entire block, into a glorious, opulent
palace, filling it with her personal effects, including ranks
of overwrought Roman Catholic art and husband Stan's
bright paintings. **Dolls** from her prodigous collection pop
up all over the place, casting a vaguely surreal spell. Rice
hosts frequent charity events in the ballroom, while newly-
weds can hold receptions in the huge white chapel, illuminated by vivid stained glass and bursting with religious
icons.

For details of Anne Rice's spectacular Memnoch Ball,
a tickets-only costume party held in
the orphanage every Halloween,
call the Lestat fan club ©529-0560.

Houses on the avenue

St Charles Avenue's showy **mansions** display a variety of
styles, from Italianate through Romanesque to Queen

Anne. Many of them – including his own little Queen Anne gingerbread home at 4010 St Charles (riverside; Map 2, J6) – are the work of eminent architect **Thomas Sully**, also responsible for some of the most important buildings in the CBD.

You can hardly miss the **Brown House**, a limestone Romanesque behemoth at no. 4717; it's the largest mansion on the avenue (lakeside; Map 2, H6). Further along, at no. 5705, look out for the gleaming white 1941 replica of **Tara**, the plantation home in *Gone with the Wind* (lakeside; Map 2, F5); close on its heels at no. 5809, the aptly nick-named **Wedding Cake House** (lakeside; Map 2, E5) is an ostentatious Greek Revival building, frosted with a layer of balconies, balustrades, cornices and columns. Beyond, the handsome **university campuses** of Loyola and Tulane (lakeside; Map 2, D4 & E3) stand side by side facing Audubon Park.

AUDUBON PARK

Map 2, B8–D4.

Built on plantation lands once belonging to Etienne de Boré – who in 1795 perfected the sugar granulation process, and went on to become the city's first mayor – Upper City Park was laid out in 1871. After hosting the 1884 Cotton Exposition, which, though it proved to be a financial flop, marked the onset of a nascent tourist indus-try in New Orleans, the park was redeveloped and renamed for Haitian artist and naturalist John James Audubon, who stayed in the city for a few months in 1821 while compiling *Birds of America*. Today the 350-acre **Audubon Park** is a lovely, much-used space, dotted with lagoons and picnic areas, shaded by Spanish moss-swathed trees, and looped by an extensive cycling and jogging path.

Audubon Zoo

Map 2, C7. Daily 9.30am–5.30pm; summer Mon–Fri 9.30am–
5.30pm, Sat & Sun 9.30am–6pm; $8.75, children $5; zoo and
aquarium (see p.94) $15.50, children $7.50.

New Orleanians are justifiably proud of the superb
Audubon Zoo – a fifteen-minute walk or short shuttle
ride from the park's St Charles entrance – where a number
of carefully recreated habitats feature a couple of very rare
snow white tigers, komodo dragons and, star attraction, the
mysterious blue-eyed **white alligator**, which became an
overnight celebrity after being discovered in a nearby
swamp in 1987. In 1994, another group of white baby
gators was found in the same place, but no one has yet been
able to track down the mother.

**Each October, Audubon Zoo hosts the excellent
Swampfest, featuring the best in Cajun and zydeco
music, food and crafts.**

Don't miss the **Louisiana swamp**, complete with Cajun
houseboat, wallowing alligators and knobbly cypress knees
poking out of the stagnant water. It's populated by raccoons,
bears, cougars, and snapping turtles, who entice hapless fish by
wiggling a worm-like growth on the end of their tongues. You
can also wander through an **African savannah** – where most
visitors, underwhelmed by the small hillock proudly labeled as
the highest point in the city, prefer instead to watch the hippos
and giraffes – and "**Jaguar Jungle**", where jaguars, sloths and
monkeys prowl, doze and swing among mock Maya ruins.

One appealing way to get to or from the zoo – perhaps
combining it with a streetcar ride in the opposite direction
– is to take a narrated cruise on the **John James Audubon
riverboat**, which plies the Mississippi between Audubon
Park and the aquarium (see p.94). For details, see p.89.

The Mississippi River

A resonant, romantic, and extraordinary physical presence, the **Mississippi River** is New Orleans' lifeblood and its *raison d'etre*. Nearly half a mile wide, it writhes through the city like an out-of-control snake, swelling against the constraining, man-made levees as it courses toward the Gulf. Nineteenth-century visitors marveled at this mighty highway into a still unexplored interior, writing long, lyrical accounts of its power and its hazards; as the city's port boomed, however, river traffic increased, New Orleans gradually cut itself off from the water altogether, hemming it in behind a string of warehouses and freight railroads.

More recently, as the importance of the port has diminished, a couple of downtown **parks**, plazas and riverside walks, accessible from the French Quarter and the CBD, have focused attention back onto the waterfront, capitalizing on its magnetic appeal. Most tourists combine a river walk with a **shopping** trip at the historic French Market, Jackson Brewery or Riverwalk malls (for more details on these, see Shopping, which starts on p.211) or a visit to the superb **Aquarium of the Americas**. The main draw, however, is the river itself, best seen from the **Moonwalk** or **Woldenberg Park**, or, even better, on a **cruise** aboard a restored steamboat or paddlewheeler. Some of these, which share river space with tugs and towboats, barges, naval tankers and darting water-taxis, take you as far as **Chalmette**, riverfront site of the 1815 Battle of New Orleans.

You can also get out onto the water on the free ferry from Canal Street, which struggles against the current to deliver you within minutes to the old shipbuilding community of **Algiers** on the west bank. Though taking the ferry is an adventure in itself, it's worth disembarking at the other end and strolling the Spanish moss-draped streets to the quirky **Mardi Gras museum**.

Some history

It took considerable persistence for the French-Canadian explorer Jean Baptiste le Moyne, **Sieur de Bienville**, to impose a city on the banks of as powerful a force of nature as the Mississippi River. His dream, however, of a mighty metropolis built on the back of lucrative river trade – a vision not shared by his critics, who saw only a soggy handful of cypress huts doomed by endless flooding – was eventually realized. By the nineteenth century, New Orleans' position, on a portage between the river and Lake Pontchartrain, which opened into the Gulf of Mexico, made it an ideal **entrepôt** – the meeting point for the riverboats carrying cotton, sugar, tobacco and lumber down from the interior, ocean-going ships hauling the goods out to the rest of the world, and foreign vessels bringing manufactured and luxury commodities from overseas. In 1803, as the United States began its inexorable sweep westward, the Americans snapped the city up, under the terms of the

River cruises

Quite apart from the sheer delight of churning along one of the world's greatest rivers on a big old sternwheeler, a short **cruise** on the Mississippi offers a fascinating glimpse into the workings of the nation's most important waterway. If you're after a cruise plain and simple, the three-deck **Natchez steamboat** – heralded by its hauntingly off-key calliope tunes, which float through the French Quarter about thirty minutes before the boat sets off – is by far the best choice. It leaves twice a day from the Toulouse Street wharf behind Jackson Brewery and heads downriver, turning back near the Chalmette battlefield. You can sit on deck or lunch inside on fried chicken and red beans, with a live Dixieland jazz accompaniment (daily 11.30am & 2.30pm; 2hr; $14.75, $20.70 with lunch; ©586-8777).

Though less atmospheric than the historic *Natchez,* the **John James Audubon riverboat** is a great option if you want to combine a cruise with a trip to the aquarium (see p.94) or Audubon Zoo (p.86), or both. Cruises leave daily from the aquarium at 10am, noon, 2pm and 4pm, and from the zoo an hour later ($10.50 one-way, $13.50 round-trip; $21.50 with aquarium; $19.50 with zoo; $26.50 with both; children half-price; ©586-8777).

The only boat that stops at Chalmette, site of the Battle of New Orleans, is the **Creole Queen paddlewheeler** (10.30am & 2pm; 2hr 30min; $14, $20 with lunch; ©524-0814), which leaves from the Plaza d'España.

Tickets for all cruises are sold at riverside booths behind Jackson Brewery.

Louisiana Purchase, which ensured them control of the entire river. Within a year, tonnage using New Orleans' port had increased by fifty percent, and, for the next quarter century, flat boats and keelboats docking at the end of

Tchoupitoulas Street averaged around a thousand per year. The flatboats, unable to negotiate the current and return upstream, were sold for lumber or transformed into floating brothels and gambling dens, while the boatmen – a lawless, brawling breed known derisively by the Creoles as "**Kaintocks**" (many came from Kentucky) – would kick up hell in the city for a while before making their way back into the interior by land. **Pirates** plied the Mississippi, too, ready to hijack the cumbersome vessels; most notorious among them were Jean and Pierre Lafitte and their **Baratarians** – named for their swampy hideout, around twenty miles downriver – who hatched countless dastardly plots in the coffee houses and bars of New Orleans.

In 1811 the **steamboat** exploded – sometimes literally – onto the scene. Though these "floating palaces", with their puffing chimneys, fancy galleries, and enormous paddlewheels, have become icons of the great days of river travel, the earliest packets, with their propensity to overheat and burst into flames, were seen as novelties only, far too dangerous to carry passengers. By the 1840s, however, hundreds of them churned along the river, bringing goods, news, travelers and sharp-suited card sharks to the city, while their cousins, the flamboyant **showboats** – a common sight on the Mississippi well into the 1930s – staged vaudeville, circus, melodrama and Shakespeare for plantation owners, rough boatmen and straggling river communities.

Today, though New Orleans' antebellum golden era as the world's biggest export **port** – when scores of steamboats, ocean-going ships, keelboats and barges lined the waterfront for miles on end – is a distant memory, in terms of tonnage New Orleans is still one of the busiest ports in the world. The river, meanwhile, continues to bide its time behind the levee, as unpredictable and intractible as ever.

The Riverfront streetcar (see p.12), which makes
ten stops between Esplanade Avenue and the
Convention Center, can be useful if you're footsore;
views, however, are blocked by
floodwalls and parking lots.

WASHINGTON ARTILLERY PARK AND THE MOONWALK

Map 4, F6–H6.

Directly across Decatur Street from Jackson Square (see
p.22), **Washington Artillery Park** is a rather grand name
for a small, elevated strip of concrete, reached by steps, that
gives superb views of the square and St Louis Cathedral,
and, on the other side, of the Mississippi. Street performers
use the space below, on Decatur, as a stage, playing to spectators sitting on the stairs.

Descending the steps on the river side, and walking
through the concrete flood walls, over the Riverfront streetcar tracks, and up another flight of steps, brings you to the
Moonwalk, a riverfront boardwalk named for "Moon"
Landrieu, mayor of the city from 1970 to 1978. It's a great
spot, its wooden benches usually full with tourists gazing at
the panorama upriver to the Mississippi River Bridge and,
downriver, to the wharves that begin at Governor Nicholls
Street. Gulls dip and dive in front of you, in the vain hope
of plucking catfish out of the whirling eddies, while ships
battle against the current at **Algiers Point**, the sharpest
bend in the entire river, churned by a savage centrifugal
force. Safe enough during the day – though you'll have to
contend with buskers, panhandlers and **hustlers** – the
Moonwalk is best avoided at night.

WASHINGTON ARTILLERY PARK AND THE MOONWALK

The Big Muddy

North America's principal waterway, the **Mississippi** – the name comes from the Algonquin words for "big" and "river" – starts just ninety miles south of the Canadian border in Minnesota and writhes its way 2348 miles to the Gulf of Mexico, 217 river miles (65 miles as the crow flies) from New Orleans. On its way it takes in more than one hundred tributaries and drains 41 percent of continental America, an area of more than a million square miles.

The **Big Muddy** – so nicknamed because it carries 2lb of dirt for every 1000lb of water – is one of the busiest commercial rivers in the world and one of the least conventional. Instead of widening toward its mouth, like most rivers, the Mississippi grows narrower and deeper. Its "**delta**", near Memphis, Tennessee, over three hundred miles upstream from the river's mouth, is not a delta at all but a fertile alluvial flood plain. On the other hand, its estuary deposits, which extend the land six miles out to sea every century, are comparatively paltry; Gulf currents disperse the sediment before it has time to settle. The Mississippi is also, in the words of Mark Twain, who spent four years as a riverboat pilot, "the **crookedest** river in the world". As it weaves and curls its way extravagantly along its channel, it continually cuts through narrow necks of land to create oxbow lakes, meander scars, cutoffs and marshy backwaters. Some engineers predict that eventually the mighty river will desert its present channel altogether and find a shorter route to the sea, bypassing New Orleans entirely.

Another manifestation of the Mississippi's power is its huge propensity to **flood** – a particularly serious threat to New Orleans, which at its highest point reaches just 15ft above sea level. Although the city was settled on a natural levee, formed by sediment dumped by the river, this was little safeguard against further flooding and wasn't enough to prevent the swollen river from sporadically wiping out valuable sugar crops and entire cotton plantations. As the city developed, it became increasingly crucial to find effective ways to tame this destructive force, and in 1792 Governor Carondelet ordained that landowners had to build and maintain artificial **levees**, imposing steep fines for non-compliance. The plan backfired somewhat, however, as landowners would send men out at night, under the guise of checking their own levees for *crevasses* (tiny cracks that could be caused by something as small as a crawfish), but in reality to force holes into the levees of their neighbors.

Since disastrous flooding along the Mississippi valley in the late 1920s, the federal government has been responsible for a wide range of flood-protection measures all along the river; in New Orleans, the levee is backed by a series of flood walls. Recently these have been rendered less necessary with the building of the **Spillway**, which, when the river gets to dangerous levels, automatically drains into Lake Pontchartrain – to the dismay of conservationists, who claim that it pours polluted water into the lake.

WOLDENBERG PARK TO THE RIVERWALK MALL

Map 4, E7–A9.

Long, thin **Woldenberg Park** curves upriver from the end of Toulouse Street in the French Quarter to the **Aquarium of the Americas**. Though in itself the park is nothing to get excited about, its riverside location makes it a good place to sprawl on the grass with a picnic, watching the traffic on the Mississippi and the stream of tourists flowing to and from the aquarium or one of the river-cruise terminals. Beyond the aquarium, you have to cut through the ugly concrete **Canal Street wharf**, terminal for the free ferry to **Algiers**, to reach the **Plaza d'España** and the **Riverwalk** shopping mall.

....

On Lundi Gras, the day before Mardi Gras, Zulu hosts a superb day-long party in Woldenberg Park; see p.244.

....

Aquarium of the Americas

Map 4, B8. Daily from 9am; closing hours vary; $11.25, children $5; IMAX $7.75, children $5; aquarium and IMAX $15.50, children $9; aquarium and Audubon Zoo (see p.86) $15.50, children $7.50; ✆1-800/774-7394 or 581-4629.

As you enter New Orleans' superb **aquarium**, through a clear **tunnel** where angel fish, flapping rays and hawksbill turtles whirl above and around you, you know you're in for something good. It's a vast place, where different environments are recreated in lively detail – the misty **Amazonian rainforest**, for example, demonstrates how monstrous fish, grown fat on the river's bounty, develop sensitive whiskers and an acute sense of hearing in order to make their way through the silty, muddy water. Tropical birds fly above a tree-top pathway, while thumbnail-sized poisoned-dart frogs and bird-eating spiders lurk menacingly in glass enclosures. The **Mississippi delta**, meanwhile, complete with its own mossy cypress trees, features one of New Orleans' white alligators (see p.86), ancient paddlefish, and the unnerving giant flathead catfish, who feed on geese, ducks and dogs.

There are so many other things to see – including a recreated Gulf oil platform, a penguin enclosure and hands-on exhibits – that it can be a challenge to get around it all. Do, however, make time for the **sharks**, which range from weird-looking Australian wobbegongs to leathery nurse sharks – which you're encouraged to stroke – and the **jelly-fish**, the most agreeable of which are the infinitesimal specks that sparkle like tiny Christmas-tree lights. The five-story **IMAX** theater shows the usual overblown epics of mountaineering, space exploration and other derring-do.

For details of the narrated John James Audubon **river-boat cruise**, a great way of getting from the aquarium to uptown's Audubon Zoo, see p.89.

....

To enjoy an unmatched bird's-eye view of the river,
head for the 1960s World Trade Center (see p.58), at
the foot of Canal near the aquarium.

....

Plaza d'España and the Riverwalk Mall

Nudged in between the river and the World Trade Center, the sunken **Plaza d'España** (Map 4, A9), ringed with Spanish coats of arms and centering on a fountain, is most lively on Lundi Gras, when a free, touristy party, following the Zulu bash in Woldenberg Park (see p.244), celebrates the mayor handing over the city to Rex, King of Carnival.

From the plaza you can enter the half-mile-long **Riverwalk mall** (Map 3, M6–M7) – even if you're not shopping, it's worth strolling along the mall's outdoor promenade, raised above the river and dotted with illuminating historical plaques. It does, however, cut off at a number of points in order to channel people into the stores. Inside, parts of the mall are still undergoing repairs since a Chinese freighter, losing control against the current at Algiers Point, ploughed into it in 1996. For more on **shopping** in the Riverwalk mall, see p.212.

CHALMETTE BATTLEFIELD

Daily 8am–5pm; free.

About six miles downriver from the city, off Hwy-46, the **Chalmette Battlefield National Historical Park** was the site of the **Battle of New Orleans**, final skirmish of the War of 1812. In 1814, having captured Washington DC, the British turned their sights to the Gulf, inviting the notorious Lafitte pirates to join them in the campaign against General Andrew Jackson. The double-crossing Lafittes, however, aligned themselves with Jackson and, though neither of them actually fought, furnished him with arms and troops, in exchange for which they were pardoned of all piracy charges.

On December 23, 1814, British General Edward Pakenham and his nine thousand Redcoats arrived five miles downriver of the city, to be met by Jackson's five-thousand-strong volunteer force of Creoles, Anglo-American adventurers, free men of color, Baratarian pirates and Native Americans. Though at first the British troops succeeded in pushing back the ragbag American army, on **January 8, 1815**, after a battle of minutes, Jackson's men routed their opponents. The death toll came to seven hundred Redcoats, including Pakenham, and just a dozen or so Americans. Ironically, the battle, from which Jackson went on to become a national hero – and eventually US president – was unnecessary. Soon after it was fought, the news reached the city that the Treaty of Ghent had already ended the war in December 1814.

Today the Battle of New Orleans is commemorated by a 110ft **obelisk** and an **interpretative exhibit** – a source of delight to war buffs but probably too much of a good thing for casual visitors. Though you can look around the plantation house, there's very little else to see. For details of getting to Chalmette on a **river cruise**, see p.89.

ALGIERS

Map 1, G7.

A free **ferry ride** from the bottom of Canal Street brings you within ten minutes or so to the west bank and the quiet neighborhood of **Algiers**. Seen from the lofty heights of the World Trade Center (see p.58), the **ferry** looks tiny, swirling alarmingly with the river's flow – the Mississippi is at its deepest (nearly 200ft) here, and the current fierce, furiously churning around the drastic bend in the river. Even if you don't disembark, the splendid views of both banks – especially at sunset – and the chance to see the river traffic up close make it well worth a trip in itself.

**During rush hours ferries run every 15min each way;
at other times they leave Canal on the hour and half hour,
and Algiers at quarter past and quarter to the hour.
Always check the schedule, however. Pedestrians ride free;
it's $1 each way for bikes and cars.**

Settled a couple of years after New Orleans was established on the east bank, Algiers, a swathe of plantations originally belonging to Bienville, was entirely separate from the early city. The origins of its **name** are obscure, though one theory holds that, as a major eighteenth-century disembarkation point for the slave boats, it may have been named for the slave port in Africa. In 1819 the first **shipyard** opened on the point, and settlement increased rapidly as a rash of dry docks, boat-builders and related industries spread along the riverfront. The coming of the **railways** and the development of the **shipbuilding industry** during the Civil War led to further growth, and in 1870 the city was incorporated into New Orleans. Here, as across the river, the saloons – haunts of gamblers, dockers, seamen and prostitutes – spawned some of the earliest **jazz** music, often

ALGIERS

created by freed slaves who had played in brass bands on the local plantations. Practically the whole town had to be rebuilt after a devastating **fire** in 1895; most of the buildings you see today date from just after that time. Algiers fell into decline after the 1920s, and was touched little by the oil boom and subsequent modernizations that were inflicted on the east bank.

....

Though you're safe enough walking around Algiers during the day, it's best not to wander too far off the beaten track, especially if you're alone.

....

Visitors to the **Mardi Gras museum**, the district's one real "sight", are shuttled to and from the ferry landing; to pass the time before catching the ferry back you could take a stroll through quiet streets lined with a host of **architectural styles** and lovely subtropical gardens. Take time, too, to climb up onto the **levee**: the downtown skyline is at its most photogenic from here.

Blaine Kern's Mardi Gras World

Map I. G7. Daily 9.30am–4.30pm; $8.50.

Free buses from the Algiers ferry whisk you off to the cavernous "dens" of **Blaine Kern's Mardi Gras World**, 223 Newton St at Brooklyn, where year-round (except during the fortnight or so before Mardi Gras itself) you can see artists preparing, constructing and painting the overblown papier mâché floats used in the carnival parades. Kern's team makes floats for around forty or so of the krewes, including super krewe Bacchus, whose trademark Mr and Mrs King Kong hibernate here for most of the year. It's a surreal experience wandering these paint-splattered warehouses, past piles of dusty, grimacing has-beens from parades gone by. Many of the figures – from limbless cartoon characters to giant caved-in crawfish, and from superstars to presidents – are recycled and adapted for future parades, so little is ever thrown away. In keeping with the carnival spirit, there are plenty of opportunities to dress up, fool about and take photos – before the tour, you're free to try on colossal Marilyn and Nixon papier mâché heads, velvet cloaks and towering plumed headdresses.

Exploring Algiers

A block or so from the ferry landing, the turreted **Algiers Courthouse**, 225 Morgan Ave (Mon–Fri 8.30am–7pm), has piles of free self-guided walking tours of Algiers, concentrating either on architecture or the area's jazz history. Turning onto the 100 block of **Bermuda**, trimmed with gingerbread homes and cast-iron fences, then again onto the 300 block of **Delaronde** – more gingerbread, lovingly restored – brings you to a rare survivor of the 1895 fire, the **Seger-Rees-Donner House**, at no. 405: an austere Greek Revival home with Gothic-style iron railings, built in 1850. If you continue along Delaronde, you'll come to **Olivier Street**, the first few blocks of which feature some of Algiers' best-preserved architecture, a jumble of Creole cottages, Greek Revival, Italianate, Queen Anne and Edwardian styles. Turn right again onto Alix; a block away at Verret, the towering neo-Gothic **Holy Name of Mary Church**, built in 1929, retains its Carrara marble altars and stained-glass windows from a nineteenth-century church that stood on the same site.

Conveniently situated opposite the church, an ideal place to hang out before walking the few blocks back to the ferry landing, **News 'n' Brews**, 347 Verret St at Alix, is a laid-back hangout serving good **espresso**, bagels, muffins and cookies (Mon–Thurs 7am–8pm, Fri 7am–10pm, Sat 7.30am–10pm, Sun 7.30am–8pm).

Mid-City and City Park

Predominantly residential **Mid-City**, the large swathe of land that fans up from Tremé toward Lake Pontchartrain, is of most interest to visitors for **City Park** and the eclectic **New Orleans Museum of Art**. Snaking down the eastern side of the park and a mile or so beyond, **Bayou St John**, once an important waterway, today flows placidly through a desirable residential area; nearby, the **Fair Grounds** racetrack hosts New Orleans' annual **JazzFest** (see p.246), when it bursts at the seams with tens of thousands of music fans from around the world.

You may well also venture into Mid-City for its **restaurants** (see p.171). There's an especially good cluster along **Esplanade Ridge** – the "high" ground (about 4ft above sea level) that hugs either side of Esplanade Avenue. Beyond the ridge, however, it's not a good idea to wander around the poverty-scarred outskirts of **Tremé**; bus #48, which runs from the corner of Rampart in the French Quarter, along Esplanade all the way to City Park, is a safe way to travel during the day, but you should call a **taxi** (see p.12) after dark.

ESPLANADE AVENUE

Map 1, F6–D4.

In the antebellum era, wealthy Creoles turned their sights toward **Esplanade Avenue**, the broad, Live Oak-lined street that sweeps up from the Mississippi to City Park. Escaping the congested French Quarter, they lined the grand boulevard with large, fashionable homes, fronting them with voluminous cast-iron galleries. Today, many of the houses, though still hauntingly lovely, are decidedly run-down, and stretches of the road lie blighted and desolate. Restoration, monitored by an active preservation group, is gradually improving matters, and a handful of the homes have been converted into luxurious **B&Bs** (see p.138).

Degas House

Map 1, F5. Mon–Fri 9am–5pm, Sat & Sun 10am–2pm; $6.

Art fans shouldn't get too excited about the Italianate **Degas House**, 2306 Esplanade Ave at Tonti. Built in 1854, it was rented in the 1870s by the Mussons – Creole relatives of the French Impressionist painter Edgar Degas – who were forced to sell their Garden District mansion following a downturn in their fortunes after the Civil War (see p.81). Degas lived here for a while in 1872, and though he returned to Paris the next year, frustrated by the degenerative eye problem that prevented him from painting outdoors, he did produce at least one important work during his stay: *A Cotton Office in New Orleans*, a complex commercial scene that works just as well as a family portrait, showing Michel Musson, Degas' uncle, at work in his cotton exchange, along with sundry nephews and sons-in-law. The artist also made numerous portraits of his blind cousin Estelle, who was married to his brother René until he ran off with a neighbor. Today the house – which is, in fact,

ESPLANADE AVENUE, DEGAS HOUSE

just half of the original building (the other half stands next door on the left) – is used as a B&B. Tours, though anecdotal, have little to divulge about the building itself, which, lined with reproductions of the artist's work, rather overdoes the tenuous Degas connection.

BAYOU ST JOHN

Map 1, E2–D5.

Were it not for **Bayou St John**, New Orleans might never have existed. Local Indians had long used the site of today's city as a portage: the bayou, an inlet of Lake Pontchartrain, provided a handy short-cut between the Mississippi and the Gulf of Mexico via the lake, bypassing the river's perilous lower reaches. As the city grew, the countryside around the bayou was carved into plantations worked by African slaves, and in the early 1800s, it evolved into a popular gathering place for local **voodooists** (see p.51). Though it remained a key waterway until the 1920s, today Bayou St John is little more than a sluggish stream, flowing through the heart of a well-heeled residential neighborhood.

St Louis No. 3 Cemetery, near Bayou St John on Esplanade Avenue, is covered in the chapter devoted to New Orleans' Cities of the Dead; see p.113.

Pitot House

Map 1, D5. Wed–Sat 10am–3pm; $5.

The **Pitot House**, 1440 Moss St, near the upper end of Esplanade on the banks of the bayou, is the only remaining West Indies-style plantation home in the city. Built in the 1790s, it's named for its second owner, James Pitot, a French merchant who came to the US fleeing the 1792 slave rebellions in Haiti. Pitot built one of the city's first cotton presses, and succeeded Etienne de Boré as mayor in 1805. With its stucco-covered *briquete entre poteaux* (bricks between posts) walls, ground-floor basement, airy galleries and double-pitched roof, it's a typical Caribbean-New Orleans structure (see p.30), more interesting architecturally than for the antique furniture that fills the place.

CITY PARK

Map 1, D3–4.

City Park covers some 1500 acres between Bayou St John and Lake Pontchartrain. Crisscrossed with roads, and by no means as peaceful as Audubon Park uptown (see p.85), it's nonetheless an impressively landscaped space, streaked with lagoons and shaded by centuries-old **Live Oaks** swathed with ragged streamers of Spanish moss. Built in the 1860s, the park expanded in the 1920s, when the Beaux Arts Delgado Museum, now the **New Orleans Museum of Art**, established itself as the city's most important gallery.

Today the art museum remains the chief attraction, though visitors who've overdone it pounding the streets of the French Quarter might take solace in the atmospheric Art Deco **Botanical Garden** (Tues–Sun 10am–4.30pm; $3), filled with thousands of native plants, including blooming azaleas, magnolias and camellias. And anyone with young children in tow can head for the **Storyland** playground (Wed–Fri 10am–12.30pm, Sat & Sun 10am–4pm; $2), which, designed in the 1950s, is as dated as you'd expect, though not unpleasantly so. Kids also like the neighboring **carousel gardens**, where an antique merry-go-round is joined by a miniature railroad, bumper cars and a ferris wheel (Wed–Fri 10am–2.30pm, Sat & Sun 10am–4.30pm; $1 per ride, $8 unlimited rides).

To the left of the museum, the venerable **Dueling Oak**,

CITY PARK

with a diameter of more than 15ft, was a favorite spot for volatile young adversaries to settle the *affaires d'honneur* that felled so much of the male population of antebellum New Orleans.

New Orleans Museum of Art

Map 1, D4. Tues–Sun 10am–5pm; $6.

Near the Esplanade entrance to City Park, the **New Orleans Museum of Art** (**NOMA**) holds an impressive, wide-ranging collection and hosts major touring exhibitions, film shows and lecture series. Some works suffer from poor or non-existent captioning – **Art of the Americas**, for example, where Maya stelae, delicate Costa Rican jade and gold, Navajo kachinas, and fabulous Plains Indians beadwork are sporadically labeled. Not so the **Asian galleries**, however, where everything from tiny eighth-century Jain bronzes to Zen ink paintings is put into context. Similarly, the **African galleries** – a dizzying array of masks, beaded ceremonial costumes and fetishes – and the **Oceanic galleries** – which include wizened heads from Papua New Guinea and fierce eighteenth-century Hawaiian temple figures – plot admirably clear courses through their jaw-dropping treasures.

Of the **paintings**, watch out for the intensely symbolic portrait of Marie Antoinette by the young French court painter **Elizabeth Louise Vigée le Brun**, and **Edgar Degas**' 1872 painting of his New Orleans cousin, Estelle Musson (see p.101) – a poignant image of an unseeing woman reaching out to a blazing red gladiola. **Claude Monet**'s *Snow at Giverny* (1893), painted when the artist's eyesight was very poor, shrouds his beloved French home in a lavender-white blur. You'll also see one or two minor works each from names such as Braque, Modigliani, Miró, Picasso, Pollock, Dubuffet, Giacometti, Chagall and Warhol.

Finally, under no circumstances miss NOMA's outstanding collection of **Fabergé eggs**, exquisite pieces of end-of-Empire decadence. Russian jeweler Peter Carl Fabergé, commissioned in the mid-1880s by Tsar Nicholas II to make a precious egg for his precious daughter, went on to design sixty ever more elaborate creations for the autocratic Russian court. That first piece, an extravagant take on traditional Russian stacking dolls, is among those on show: a silver egg containing a hinged jeweled chicken, holding a gold crown hiding an emerald ring. Fabergé also created fabulous fairytale flowers, some of which are displayed here: humble dandelions and lilies magically transformed with platinum pods, gold stems, translucent nephrite leaves and seeds made from infinitesimal diamonds.

The cemeteries

T hough picking your way through a crumbling, overgrown graveyard may sound more like a nightmare
than a dream vacation, New Orleans' above-ground
cemeteries, scattered throughout the city, are fascinating
places. They're known as Cities of the Dead, and amid their
tangled pathways, lopsided marble-fronted tombs, and
decaying monuments to long-forgotten families, the city's
history and folklore, and its strange love affair with death,
seem somehow to come alive.

New Orleans' **first settlers** buried their dead – and there
were many of them, felled by epidemics, or killed in fires,
floods, duels or violent crime – underground. The set-up
wasn't ideal, however: so much of the city is at, or below,
sea level that during the frequent floods, great waves of
moldy coffins would float to the surface of the sodden
earth. Meanwhile, as the colony grew, so did the **death
rate**, reaching a peak in 1783 when a yellow fever epidemic
wiped out fifty percent of the population. With dismal sani-
tation, sailors bringing in infections from the Caribbean,
and fever-carrying mosquitoes proliferating in stagnant
swamps and cisterns, the hot, filthy city was an ideal breeding ground for disease.

Believing that germs were carried in miasmas emitted by
decaying bodies, New Orleanians began to build their

cemeteries outside the city limits, where, in traditional Spanish style, bodies were stored in **above-ground** brick and stucco vaults, or in smaller vaults packed into the walls. Not only did this protect the coffins from flooding, but also it meant families could reuse tombs – a situation that remains today, despite being a felony in other states.

By the **antebellum** period, New Orleans had the highest mortality rate in the country: in any given year, about one fifth of the population died, and in the summer of 1853 alone some 11,000 people – one tenth of the population – were killed by **yellow fever**. At the same time, the economy was booming, and a fad for French funerary design, as perfected in Père Lachaise cemetery in Paris, led to a desire for increasingly ornate resting places. The finest architects were commissioned to build tombs in various decorative styles, from Baroque and neo-Gothic to Italianate and Neoclassical. Many were set in little gardens surrounded by cast-iron railings, with benches where families could greet friends on All Saints' Day (see p.109). Wide avenues, to accommodate grand funeral processions, divided the cemeteries into blocks.

Family tombs stood two or more stories high. The first coffin, placed on the top level, would remain there until the death of another family member, when it would be shifted down to the next level, and so on, until all levels were filled. After a year and a day, with the heat and humidity having sped up decomposition, the first body could be removed from its coffin, and the desiccated remains and ashes poked down into the damp pit at the base of the tomb. Eventually, the remains of numerous family members would be mixed together in this *caveau*, as the long lists of names on the tombs attest.

Bodies could also be stored in rented **wall vaults**, which followed the same "year and a day" principle but held only one coffin at a time. Jewish families built tombs in **copings**

– elevated, walled frames containing soil, allowing the body to be buried in the earth, as the religion demands, and yet above ground, as geography insists. The largest, most ornate tombs, with dozens of vaults, belong to the city's many mutual **benevolent societies**.

Because the marble enclosure tablets needed to be kept clear for the long lists of names, epitaphs are rare – as if to compensate, there's an overload of **symbolism** throughout the cemeteries, with a profusion of broken columns (signifying a life cut short), winged hourglasses (the passage of time), roses with broken stems (death), rose buds (the death of a child, also represented by a lamb), and waterlilies (death while pregnant or in childbirth).

Visiting and safety

Today, though part of the thrill of venturing into the Cities of the Dead is the frisson fueled by the vampires-and-witches tales of local horror author Anne Rice, many of which refer to specific cemetery locations, the real **danger** comes from a different source – the threat of being mugged, or worse. Though statistically the probability that you'll be attacked is slim, you should *never* venture into the cemeteries alone, least of all after dark. Nearly all the city **tours** include a quick trip around at least one of them; if you're interested in more than an overview, contact Historic New Orleans Walking Tours (see p.16) or Save our Cemeteries (see p.15).

The most touristed cemeteries are **Lafayette No. 1**, in the Garden District opposite *Commander's Palace* (see p.167), and **St Louis No. 1**, on the lakeside edge of the French Quarter. The nearby **St Louis No. 2**, surrounded by a run-down housing project, and **St Louis No. 3**, out in Mid-City near City Park, are less popular. The only cemetery that is safe to tour independently – by car – is ostentatious **Metairie**, upriver from City Park on the Pontchartrain Expressway.

All Saints' Day

In New Orleans **All Saints' Day**, November 1, is traditionally when families come to whitewash and repaint their tombs, trim the grass and shrubbery, and add fresh flowers – especially the long-lasting and vibrant red coxcomb – to their plot. In the nineteenth century this was a lively social occasion, when old friends, settling down on the iron benches with picnics, would exchange news and gossip. Orphans and nuns sold pralines and fruit outside the gates, while stallholders hawked raisin-filled "funeral pies" and hard Italian cookies called *ossi de muerte*, or bones of the dead – you'll still find both in the city's bakeries at the end of October.

Today, as many of the old families have died off and younger members have moved away, the All Saints' tradition is waning. People still tend their tombs around this time, but not necessarily on the day itself, and while devout Catholics make sure to attend afternoon mass, said by priests who drive along the ceremonial alleys sprinkling holy water on the tombs, few make a day of it.

Though it is not recommended otherwise (see opposite), All Saints' Day, when the cemeteries are protected by police guard, is the only time when you can safely attempt to tour them without a guide.

LAFAYETTE NO. 1

Map 3, D5. Mon–Fri 7.30am–2.30pm, Sat 7.30am–noon; free.

Lafayette Cemetery, in the heart of the Garden District at 1400 Washington Ave, was built in 1833 for the wealthy, Anglo-American population of Lafayette City (see p.74). The place was filled to capacity by 1852; in that year alone 2000 yellow fever victims were buried here.

ALL SAINTS' DAY AND LAFAYETTE NO. 1

Today, Lafayette No. 1 is an extraordinarily atmospheric place, its wide intersecting avenues tangled with overgrown foliage. Many of the tombs are sinking into the gunge below, and as the soft red brick cracks and the marble tablets buckle, some of them are slowly opening, revealing the *caveau* within. It's no surprise that all this decaying grandeur should capture the imagination of **Anne Rice**, who has used the place in many of her books – in 1995, she even staged a mock jazz funeral here to launch publication of *Memnoch the Devil*; the "corpse" was herself, dressed in an antique wedding dress, in an open coffin carried by pall-bearers.

ST LOUIS NO. 1

Map 4, D1. Mon–Sat 9am–3pm, Sun 9am–noon; free.

St Louis No. 1, 400 Basin St between Conti and St Louis, is the oldest cemetery in the Mississippi valley. It was built in 1789, outside the city limits in an attempt to protect the population from the fatal fumes they believed emanated from corpses, and its tombs vary from early Spanish structures made of brick and plaster to later mausolea designed by eminent architects including Benjamin Latrobe and Jacques de Pouilly.

On the lakeside fringe of the French Quarter, the cemetery is a regular on the tour bus circuit. There is invariably a huddle of people by the simple tomb of "voodoo queen" **Marie Laveau** (see p.51), graffitied with countless brick-dust crosses. They're usually being told some nonsense about how, if you knock on the slab three times and mark a cross on her tomb, her spirit will grant you any favor. The family who own it have asked that this bogus, destructive tradition should stop, not least because people are taking chunks of brick from other tombs to make the crosses. Voodoo practitioners – responsible for the candles, plastic

Storyville

St Louis No. 1 and No. 2 are on the fringes of what was once New Orleans' notorious red-light district, **Storyville**, long since torn down to make room for housing projects. In 1897, in an attempt to control the prostitution that had been rampant in the city since its earliest days, an ordinance was passed that confined the brothels to a fixed area formed by Basin, Iberville, North Robertson and St Louis streets. The law, rather than legalizing prostitution within these boundaries, simply decreed it to be illegal *outside* them; nonetheless, the trade continued to exist throughout the city and Storyville – nicknamed for the alderman who passed the ordinance – simply became its most famous locale.

The district soon developed into a tourist attraction, with newspapers reporting the movements of its various **stars**, among them "Mayor" Tom Anderson, state legislator and oil company president, who owned many of the most famous saloons. Anderson also produced the famed **blue book**, which advertised the palaces of madams such as brawling Josie Arlington, who prided herself on her exotic continental girls; Emma Johnson, who staged exhibitionist circuses in her "House of All Nations", and, Queen of Storyville, the diamond-bedecked Lulu White – Mae West's inspiration in her 1934 movie *Belle of the Nineties*. Though **jazz** was not, as is often claimed, invented here, many of the palaces' "professors", who played rumbustious piano to entertain the clients, went on to become well-known musicians.

In 1917, the Secretary of the Navy decreed that red-light areas were bad for wartime morale, and Storyville was **closed** down. Its denizens, however, are immortalized in the extraordinary, humane portraits taken by **E.J. Bellocq**, the hydrocephalic photographer adopted by the madams as their official recorder.

STORYVILLE |

flowers, beads, and rum bottles surrounding the plot – deplore the practice, too, regarding it as a desecration that chases Laveau's spirit away. Nearby, the enormous white marble circular structure, topped by a cross and angel, is the 1857 **Italian Benevolent Society** mausoleum, where Peter Fonda and Dennis Hopper writhed and gibbered in an LSD-induced hell in the movie *Easy Rider*.

St. Louis's other famous dead include the city's first African-American mayor, **Ernest "Dutch" Morial** – father of the current mayor, Marc Morial – and **Homer Plessy**, whose refusal in 1892 to move from the whites-only section of a train led to the historic *Plessy vs Ferguson* case. His defeat gave rise to the Supreme Court's "separate but equal" ruling, which effectively established segregation in the South for more than fifty years.

At the back of the cemetery, in the non-consecrated **Protestant section**, a sinking tomb engraved with the words "For the virtuous there is a better world" was designed by Benjamin Latrobe for the wife and baby of **Governor Claiborne** – the city's first American governor – who both died of yellow fever. Claiborne's second wife is buried in the cemetery's Catholic section.

ST LOUIS NO. 2

Map 1, E6. Daily 10am–3pm; free.

St Louis No. 2, on N Claiborne Ave between Iberville and St Louis, is one of the most desolate of the Cities of the Dead, hemmed in between the Iberville housing project and the interstate. Built in 1823, it's a prime example of local cemetery design, with a dead-straight center aisle, and many grandiose Greek Revival mausolea, designed by de Pouilly. A second **Marie Laveau**, thought to be *the* Marie Laveau's daughter, has a tomb here – daubed with red-chalk crosses, like her mother's in St Louis No. 1 (see p.110) – as do Baratarian swashbuckler **Dominique You** and his friend **Mayor Nicholas Girod**, who plotted together to return Napoleon from exile (see p.37).

ST LOUIS NO. 3

Map 1, E4. Daily 10am–3pm; free.

Built in 1856 on the site of a leper colony, **St Louis No. 3**, in Mid-City at 3421 Esplanade Ave, is a peaceful burial ground used mostly by religious orders; all the **priests** of the diocese are buried here, and fragile angels balance on top of the tombs. It also holds the family tomb of **James Gallier Jr**, designed by the architect himself, and that of photographer **E.J. Bellocq**, whose remarkable images of the Storyville prostitutes (see p.111) have become icons of a lost era.

METAIRIE

Map 1, B4–C5. Daily 8.30am–4pm; free.

Metairie Cemetery, 5100 Pontchartrain Blvd, is quite different from the other Cities of the Dead, resembling a huge, formal park more than a haunted secret garden. Built after the Civil War on a racetrack, it covers 155 landscaped acres and is criss-crossed by wide, driveable streets. Though it may be less evocative than the older cemeteries, there's a certain fascination in the sheer hubris of these mighty granite tombs: every bombastic funerary style conceivable, from Egyptian and Moorish through Neoclassical to Gothic, is employed to honor mayors, governors, Confederate generals, and countless Rexes, kings of Carnival. Metairie is **safe** to tour alone, but you'll need a **car** to get to and around the place. The funeral home at the gate can lend you a free **audio tour**, for which you should allow an hour.

Highlights include the overblown **Brunswig mausoleum** – a pyramid fronted by a marble sphinx – and the tomb of **David Hennessy**, topped with a 26ft broken column covered by a pall, a police belt and baton. Police chief Hennessy was fatally shot in 1890 when New Orleans was in the grip of a wave of anti-Sicilian racism; his death provoked an international incident when eleven of the nineteen Sicilian immigrants charged with his murder were themselves killed by a thousands-strong lynch mob, and the Italian government demanded $25,000 compensation for the families of the victims. The cemetery's largest memorial, topped by a 60ft obelisk, was built in 1914 by wealthy Irishman **Daniel Moriarty** for his wife Mary, a woman twice his age, who had never been accepted in polite society.

Until recently, notorious Storyville madam **Josie Arlington** (see p.111) was also entombed in Metairie. Her cenotaph, fronted by a statue of a young woman reaching out to a closed door – symbolizing Arlington's boast that no virgins were allowed in her "palace" – became such a tourist attraction that eventually her descendants sold it and removed Arlington's remains to an unmarked tomb in a secret location.

Out of the city

By far the most popular side trip from New Orleans is the drive along the **River Road**, which hugs the banks of the Mississippi all the way to Baton Rouge, seventy miles upriver. A series of bridges and ferries allows you to crisscross the water, stopping off and touring several restored antebellum **plantation homes** along the way.

There's a color map of the River Road at the back of this book.

In the nineteenth century, these spectacular homes were the focal points of the vast estates from where wealthy planters – or rather, their slaves – loaded cotton, sugar or indigo onto steamboats berthed virtually at their front doors, ready to be transported to the markets in the city. Most of the plantations that you can visit today grew **sugar**, which from the earliest days of the colony was vital to the economy, protected by tariffs that blocked imports from the Caribbean. Though some sugar farms still exist, the golden era was over by the 1930s, when many of the houses, too expensive to maintain, were abandoned. At the same time, the construction of the levee – a response to drastic flooding in the 1920s – enabled ocean-going tankers to ply the river as far as Baton Rouge and heralded the era of the **petrochemical** companies.

If you prefer not to drive, Cukie's, Gray Line, New Orleans Tours and the Historic Voodoo Museum all offer bus tours along the River Road; see pp.15 & 17.

Today, the levee runs the length of the banks, blocking the river from view, and though you'd never guess it from the tourist brochures – which romanticize the area as a magnolia-scented idyll swathed in azaleas and dreamy Spanish moss – it's the hulking chemical plants that dominate the River Road **landscape**. Almost as soon as you've crossed the soupy swamp that surrounds New Orleans you're confronted with a vista of grim refineries, whose rusty pipes, according to local environmental groups, annually spew out millions of pounds of toxins into the Mississippi. There *are* rural stretches, where wide sugarcane fields are interrupted only by moss-covered, tumbledown shacks, but you'll more often find yourself driving through straggling communities of boarded-up lounges and laundromats, scarred by scrap piles and smokestacks.

In the last few decades, some – but by no means all – of the neglected old **plantation houses** have faced a reprieve, as wealthy individuals, hoping to combat the local dependence on chemical industries, or PR-savvy oil companies, looking to clean up their image, have set about restoring them as tourist attractions. Generally speaking – the superb **Laura** plantation is an exception – **tours**, more often than not led by ballgown-garbed guides, skimp on detail about the estates as a whole, which included huge mills and vast complexes of slave quarters, and concentrate instead on the big houses, presenting them as showcase museums filled with fine antiques. The cumulative effect of these endless evocations of a long-lost "gracious" era can be stultifying, to say the least, making it a bad idea to try to visit too many homes in one day. Pick out just one or two, and even better, reckon

Plantation practicalities

To **drive to the River Road** from New Orleans, take I-10 west to exit 220, turn onto I-310 and follow it to Hwy-44/48, on the east bank. On the west bank, the River Road is Hwy-18. Since signs for the plantations are few and far between, it's worth investing in the detailed *Louisiana River Road Plantation* **map** ($2.95), sold in bookstores around town and at all the houses (remember that the kinks in the river mean that distances are larger than they may appear). When timing your trip, it's best to get an early start, and certainly to avoid the last tours of the day; not only do they tend to be the most hurried, but also you'll be hitting rush hour on the River Road. **Tours** last between 45 minutes and an hour.

If you're going to make a day of it, you'd do best to bring your own picnic supplies, as **restaurants** in the plantations tend to serve overpriced, ordinary food, and there are few lunchtime alternatives nearby. If, on the other hand, you want to stay overnight, Oak Alley (p.122), Tezcuco (p.123), Madewood (p.125) and Nottoway (p.126) offer **accommodation**. Although each place has its own style, from the affordable cottages at Tezcuco to the full-board pampering at Madewood, all of them throw in a free house tour and a good breakfast.

on spending the night, maybe taking in another one on the drive back to the city. Many of the houses have peaceful, luxurious **B&B rooms**, which as well as being rather wonderful places to sleep, allow you to absorb more of the atmosphere of the plantations than is possible on the tours.

Few of the tours even mention the presence of slaves on the plantations; by far the best on the subject is Laura; see p.120.

DESTREHAN

Map 5, F6. Daily 9.30am–4pm; $7.

Destrehan, on the east bank, thirty minutes' drive from downtown New Orleans, is the oldest intact plantation house in the lower Mississippi valley, and a beautifully preserved example of Louisiana's early West Indies-style architecture (see p.30). Built in 1787, the house is named for Jean d'Estrehan, who, with his brother-in-law Etienne de Boré, invented the sugar granulation process that revolutionized New Orleans' nineteenth-century economy. D'Estrehan bought the house in 1792 and added two wings; it underwent further remodeling in the 1830s, when a number of Greek Revival features, including the eight thick Doric columns, were added.

....

**If you're staying the night at one of the plantations,
make sure to get out on the road after dark
– an extraordinary spectacle,
with the refineries twinkling like alien cities
in the post-apocalyptic gloom.**

....

In the 1970s the plantation was bought from oil giant Amoco by the non-profit River Road Historical Society, whose restoration emphasizes the architectural features of the **main house**. Built using the *bouisallage entre poteaux* technique (horse hair and Spanish moss, providing insulation, packed between steadying cypress pillars), it is raised a story off the soggy ground to prevent flooding, and surrounded by double galleries to catch the breezes.

It was at Destrehan, after the **slave rebellion** in January 1811 (see p.265), that a tribunal sentenced twenty slaves to death, ordering their heads to be exhibited on spikes strung out along the River Road.

SAN FRANCISCO

Map 5, D5. Daily: Nov–Feb 10am–4pm;
March–Oct 10am–4.30pm; $7.

Some twenty miles beyond Destrehan, **San Francisco**, near the village of Reserve on the east bank, was built in 1856 by Creole planter Edmond Marmillion. Its fantastic combination of Italianate, Gothic Revival and gingerbread style was dubbed "Steamboat Gothic" by novelist Frances Parkinson Keyes; painted in carousel shades of green, turquoise and peach, its rails, awnings, galleries and pillars recreate the ambience of a Mississippi showboat. San Francisco was a sugar estate until 1974, when the land was bought by a local oil company – their huge tanks now surround the place – which has funded its restoration.

Tours of San Francisco focus on the gorgeous **interior** of the main house. Designed in the old Creole style, which was already out of fashion when it was built, its rooms open directly onto each other, with no hallway. The main rooms were on the top story, decorated in bold colors and featuring cypress-paneled tongue-and-groove ceilings rather than plaster. Its exquisite ceilings, walls, blinds, moldings and doors, a riot of pastoral trompe l'oeils, floral motifs and Italian cherubs, were the result of a redecoration masterminded by Marmillion's Bavarian daughter-in-law.

The house used to stand in more than 1000 feet of **gardens**, over half of which were swallowed up when the levee was built in the 1930s.

The name San Francisco is a corruption of the Creole
"sans fruscin", or "without a penny"
– a moniker coined by Marmillion's son,
due to the colossal amount of money that
went into decorating the place in 1860.

LAURA

Map 5, D6. Daily 9.30am–5pm; $7.

A ferry at Lutcher, the tiny settlement a few miles beyond San Francisco on the east bank, crosses the river to Vacherie, where **Laura** is causing something of a stir on the River Road scene. Rather than dwelling lovingly on priceless antiques, **tours** here, which draw upon a wealth of recently discovered historical documents – from slave accounts and photographs to private diaries – sketch a vivid picture of day-to-day plantation life in multicultural Louisiana.

The earliest **inhabitants** of the Laura plantation were the local Colapissa tribe, who lived in huts behind the main house – built in 1805 by the Spanish Guillaume DuParc – until around 1815. In the antebellum era, a multiracial mix of some 500 people lived on the estate – 200 of them slaves, whose quarters were strung along a three-mile road out into the fields.

DuParc died before the first crop came in, and his wife Nanette ran the place for the next twenty years before handing it down to her daughter, Elizabeth. The plantation was managed by the women of the family until 1891, when the thoroughly modern **Laura Locoul** – DuParc's great-granddaughter, for whom the plantation is named – rejected the life carved out for her, sold the estate to the German Creole Waguespack family and moved to St Louis. It was bought in 1993 by a group of enthusiastic investors who embarked on an extensive restoration process that continues to this day.

The **house** looks as it did in the Waguespacks' era: the original building would have been simpler, without the front door and double steps. Built long before the construction of the levee, it stands high off the ground in order to safeguard it from flooding; its columns, rooted 8ft into the earth, fan out to create a firm foundation. Guides chart the evolution of the building, emphasizing the craftsmanship of the Senegalese slaves who built the place in just eleven days – after a full eleven months gathering the cypress and the bricks – and pointing out details such as the narrow doors to the men's quarters, designed to impede hoop-skirted women from entering. The facade, brightly colored in red, blue, green and yellow, gives the place a distinctly Caribbean feel and identifies it as a Creole structure: Anglo-American planters preferred their homes to be snowy white.

**The Locoul saga is continued in
Le Monde Creole's superb walking tours
of the French Quarter (see p.15),
where the family kept their city apartments.**

Brimming with human-interest stories, tours of Laura bring to light the hard-nosed realities of Creole **plantation management**. Traditionally, the business had to stay within the family – while the owner could hand it down to whichever child he or she wished, the recipient would have to bear children themselves in order to inherit. Brutally, any family member not involved in the business had no right to live in the big house – even the doughty Nanette, in the last years of her life, had to buy land from the estate in order to build her own home near her family, while in a climate of sibling squabbles and backbiting, the big house was subjected to a frenzy of wing-claiming and annex-building.

Incidentally, Laura also calls itself "the home of **Brer Rabbit**". Retold by the plantation's Senegalese slaves, the African folk tales of the wily Compair Lapin were transcribed by a local Frenchman, Alcée Fortier, friend of author Joel Chandler Harris.

LAURA

121

OAK ALLEY

Map 5, C6. Daily: March–Oct 9am–5.30pm; Nov–Feb 9am–5pm; $8.

The quintessential image of the antebellum plantation home, **Oak Alley**, some nine miles upriver from Laura on the west bank, dates from 1839, when, as the tourist brochure puts it, "Southern aristocracy ruled the land". The 28 monumental **Live Oaks** that form a magnificent canopy over the driveway from the front door to the river are 150 years older and are expected to live another three hundred years.

Built on the site of an early Creole plantation, the Greek Revival house, surrounded by fluted Doric columns – 28 of them, mirroring the number of Live Oaks – was originally called Beau Séjour. Abandoned in 1917, in the 1920s it was bought by the Stewarts, whose meticulous restoration set a trend for rescuing the old homes along the river. Today, 25 acres of the original estate are open to the public, while the remaining 1000 acres are leased out to sugar planters.

> You'll notice that Oak Alley's famous Live Oaks are bare of the Spanish moss that drapes the greenery elsewhere in the region: in the 1920s Mrs Stewart thought that the ghostly gray wraiths were creepy and had them all removed.

Supremely photogenic Oak Alley is one of the most touristed of the River Road plantations. The anecdotal **tours**, led by crinoline-garbed guides, are lively enough, though their version of events is somewhat sanitized; they're most interesting when pointing out domestic objects long since abandoned, such as the chaperone mirror, its huge convex eye guaranteed to catch any hanky-panky, and the "rolling pin" headboard, with a detachable wooden pole to smooth out the lumpy Spanish moss- and horsehair-filled mattress.

Oak Alley's **restaurant** (daily 8.30–10am & 11am–3pm) does decent, if scandalously overpriced, Creole standards, including gumbo, red beans and rice, and crawfish etouffé. You can also **stay** in pretty B&B cottages on the grounds (℃261-2151; ④).

....

**The accommodation price codes used in this book
are explained on p.132.**

....

TEZCUCO

Map 5, C5. Daily 9am–5pm; $7.

Some 25 miles from San Francisco, near the village of Burnside, on the east bank, **Tezcuco** – or "resting place", named after the lake in Mexico – is an antebellum raised cottage built in the Greek Revival style. **Tours**, led by guides dressed up as Southern belles, concentrate on the columned main house, which was constructed between 1855 and 1860 as a summer retreat. Though it appears to have three stories, the top floor, too hot for habitation, was used only for storage. To combat the debilitating heat, rooms were built with 15ft ceilings and hinged doors that could be removed in the stuffiest months. Although planters displayed their wealth in the big house – using enough excess material in the drapes, for example, to form a luxurious puddle on the floor – their families didn't live a life of leisure, and children as young as five were expected to contribute to the running of the estate. Little money was spent on childish pleasures such as toys, which were generally rough little things, home-made from scraps.

Beyond the main house, the grounds are dotted with buildings including a blacksmith, a chapel, and, unusually, a good **African-American Museum** (Wed–Sun 1–5pm).

Tezcuco's **restaurant** (daily 11am–3pm) serves reasonably priced, if unremarkable, salads, po-boys and hot lunches. The **accommodation** is far more distinctive, and very good value, with a wide range of options from cute one-bedroom cottages – most with porches, rocking chairs and fireplaces – to a gorgeous two-bedroom suite in the main house. Rates include a bottle of wine, a full Creole breakfast served in your room and a free house tour (©562-3929; ③–⑦).

HOUMAS HOUSE

Map 5, B5. Daily: Feb–Oct 10am–5pm; Nov–Jan 10am–4pm; $8.

Flanked by colossal chemical plants, **Houmas House**, a couple of miles beyond Tezcuco on Hwy-942, is, in fact, two houses: the first, an early **Spanish colonial** structure, stands in the shadow of a far grander **antebellum** pile. In 1774 business partners Alexandre Latil and Maurice Conway snapped up 10,000 acres of land for 4¢ an acre from the local Houmas Indians, and proceeded to make their fortunes chopping down the forest of cypress around them. The simple, four-room house that they built was neither large nor ostentatious enough for the planters who lived here in the 1840s, who stuck a white, columned Greek Revival edifice in front of it.

In 1858 the plantation was bought for $2 million by **John Burnside**, the so-called "Prince of Sugar". Under his ownership it grew to become Louisiana's biggest sugar estate, its four mills and thousand slaves producing the largest volume of sugar in the nation. Though Burnside left no heirs, the 20,000-acre plantation was eventually handed down to the son-in-law of one of his friends and continued to thrive until the Depression, when it fell into disuse. A decade later the house was bought by a doctor, who began a process of elegant restoration.

OUT OF THE CITY

Tours start in the colonial building, where the kitchen, centering on a giant cypress table, displays racks of rustic domestic implements including a herb-filled spoon and rudimentary fat-skimmer. A holy water cabinet on the wall attests to the Creoles' Catholic piety. The dining room is similarly plain, and very Spanish-looking, with its low, beamed ceilings and whitewashed walls. In contrast, the antebellum home, filled with a wealth of paintings and sculpture, reflects the golden era of the plantation. Unlike in the earlier house, where cypress predominates, here you'll see an abundance of marble, especially on the fireplaces and mantels. Even the richest families couldn't outwit the climate, however: the oppressive parlor, with its Victorian furniture overstuffed with Spanish moss, features a press to squeeze buckled and dampened books into shape.

Two unusual hexagonal *garconnières* (see p.30) stand in the pretty **grounds**, which are planted with fragrant rose bushes and azaleas. The gnarled Live Oaks that form a shaded alley from the river to the main house are at least 150 years old – there used to be sixteen more of them until the construction of the levee in the 1930s swallowed up six acres of land.

MADEWOOD

Map 5, B7. Daily 10am–5pm; $6.

Taking a detour off the River Road, turning off Hwy-18 onto Hwy-308, which hugs Bayou La Fourche, brings you to the glorious Greek Revival **Madewood**, designed by eminent architect Henry Howard. It took four years to gather enough cypress and brick to build the 21-room house; and another four years till construction was completed in 1850. The owner died two years later, leaving his wife to raise fourteen children and manage the estate until

MADEWOOD

her death in 1896. In the 1960s, the New Orleans-based Marshall family bought and restored the big house; they keep an apartment in the *garconnière* (see p.30) while a local family owns the land and maintains the sugar cane.

Everything about Madewood is imposing, without being oppressive: the walls, 18in to 24in thick, are made of solid brick covered with stucco and plaster, and the ceilings soar as high as 25ft. **Tours** are particularly good on architectural detail and the history of the restoration, but it's the **B&B** at Madewood that's the real treat (©1-800/375-7151 or 369-7151; ⑧ including dinner). There are five huge rooms in the main building – most of them with balconies and giant four-poster beds – and three suites in a relocated 1820s cottage originally owned by a riverboat captain. Sleeping in these peaceful surroundings, with the freedom to pad around pretty much at will, is a great way to get the feel of the place. Evenings start with a wine and cheese reception with your hosts and other guests; dinner is served in the old dining room. In the morning, you get coffee in bed, then it's back to the dining room for a superb full breakfast.

NOTTOWAY

Map 5, A5. Daily 9am–5pm; $8.

Back on the River Road, **Nottoway**, the largest surviving antebellum plantation home in the South, lies eighteen miles south of Baton Rouge on the west bank. Built in 1859 as the main house on a 7000-acre sugar estate, the 64-room white Italianate and Greek Revival edifice was designed by Henry Howard about a decade after his work on the nearby Madewood plantation. At the time it was built, its indoor plumbing, gas lighting and coal fireplaces were innovations, but today it's the unfeasible opulence of the place that is most striking – in particular in the stupendous columned ballroom, all white and gilt, with sparkling crystal chandeliers.

Nottoway has a **restaurant** (daily 11am–3pm & 6–9pm) and luxurious **B&B** rooms (℗545-2730; ⑦), where rates include a welcoming bottle of sherry, a wake-up call of coffee, muffins and juice, a full breakfast, and a house tour.

LISTINGS

Accommodation

New Orleans has some fantastic **places to stay**, from rambling old guesthouses and beautiful boutique hotels to the extraordinarily genteel *Windsor Court*, deemed best hotel in the world by *Condé Nast Traveler* in 1998. **Room rates**, never low (you'll be pushed to find anything half decent for less than $50), increase considerably for Mardi Gras, JazzFest and the Sugar Bowl, when prices can go up by as much as 200 percent. At other times, and especially during summer, when things slow down, it's worth asking about **special deals**. Guesthouse owners, especially, are often more willing to negotiate prices than to let rooms go empty.

New Orleans is not a city in which you want to be stranded overnight, and though it's possible to take a chance on last-minute deals, you should ideally make **reservations** well ahead of time. This is especially true during the big festivals and special events – when hotels get booked solid months in advance – and weekends throughout the year. However, if you do turn up on spec, head immediately for the **Welcome Center** (see p.8), which has a room-booking service and racks of **discount leaflets** offering savings on same-day bookings (weekdays only).

Accommodation price codes

Accommodation prices throughout this book have been coded using the following symbols. Prices are for the least expensive double rooms available between October and May – the city's high season – though during Mardi Gras and JazzFest, rates can be double those quoted here. Where places have rooms with shared or private bath, we have quoted the cheapest room with bath, and where there is a large disparity between the cheapest and the most expensive rooms, we have quoted codes for both. Rates do not include the room tax of 11 percent.

① $40 and under	② $40–60	③ $60–75
④ $75–90	⑤ $90–100	⑥ $100–120
⑦ $120–150	⑧ $150–200	⑨ above $200

Many places, especially in the Quarter, have minimum stays of two nights on weekends – longer during special events.

Most people choose to stay in the **French Quarter**, in the heart of things. Many accommodations here are in **guesthouses**, most of them in old Creole cottages or town houses, furnished with antiques. These are some of the most beautiful, and atmospheric, lodgings in the city, ranging from shabbily decadent places with iffy plumbing to romantic honeymooners' hideaways. The odd few can be dark and a little musty inside – in the Creole tradition, they're shaded from the heat, sun and rain by lush patios and cranky wooden shutters – but many also have courtyards, balconies, verandahs and pools. Most serve continental breakfast, and in the more expensive places you may also get complimentary evening drinks and hors d'oeuvres.

As for possibilities outside the Quarter, the **Lower Garden District** offers a number of budget options near the streetcar line, while the funky **Faubourg Marigny** specializes in atmospheric, good-value bed and breakfasts and the **Garden District** proper has a couple of gorgeous old hotels. The **CBD** and **Warehouse District** are the domain of the city's upmarket chain hotels, catering mostly to conventioneers – they're much the same here as in any other American city, and contactable on the national 1-800 numbers.

Also, many of the grand old **plantation homes** strung along the River Road offer B&B accommodation; they're reviewed in the Out of the City chapter, which begins on p.115.

Drivers should note that hardly any of the French Quarter hotels offer free on-site parking.

FRENCH QUARTER

Biscuit Palace

Map 4, H4. 730 Dumaine St at Royal ☏525-9949.
Well-run, friendly and spotless hotel, named for the old biscuit ad painted on its outside wall. It's housed in an 1820 mansion, complete with a pretty flagstoned courtyard, fish pond and tropical plants. The characterful rooms, many of them suites, with balconies and antique baths, are creatively decorated – if you hanker after an opium-den ambience, ask for room no. 3. The attic apartment sleeps six. Rates drop considerably in summer, but there's a three-day minimum stay over weekends. ③–⑦.

Bourbon-Orleans

Map 4, G3. 717 Orleans St at Bourbon ☏523-2222.
Colossal hotel that was once the site of the grandest Mardi Gras and quadroon balls (see p.50). It's right in the heart of

everything, with good-sized rooms and suites, all with mini-bars, plus a restaurant and pool. Service is excellent, and rates can be surprisingly low for this standard of accommodation. ⑥.

Chateau Hotel

Map 4, I5. 1001 Chartres St at St Philip ℂ524-9636.
Simple rooms in a prime position. Some are better than others, so if you feel yours is too small or a bit dark, check to see what else is available. There's an outdoor café and pool, and complimentary continental breakfast. ⑤.

Cornstalk Hotel

Map 4, H4. 915 Royal St at St Philip ℂ523-1515.
Friendly, elegant hotel in a turreted Queen Anne house surrounded by a landmark cast-iron fence (see p.46). The comfortable rooms are each individually furnished with antiques and feature plenty of period detail; all have showers, and four have baths. Continental breakfast can be taken in your room, on the balcony, or on the large front verandah. ⑦.

A Creole House

Map 4, G2. 1013 St Ann St at Burgundy ℂ524-8076 or 1-800/535-7858.
Unfussy, friendly guesthouse, bordering on shabby in places, with a variety of rooms ranging from cozy hideaways with shared bath to antique-filled suites. Be specific about your needs when making reservations and feel free to negotiate. Rates include continental breakfast and 24-hour coffee. ③–⑥.

Dauphine Orleans

Map 4, D2. 415 Dauphine St at Conti ℂ586-1800 or 1-800/521-7111.
Beautiful historic hotel – once a bordello – with exemplary attention to detail throughout. The best rooms, with jacuzzis,

are set in brick cottages around tranquil, lush courtyards. There's a pretty outdoor pool, a bar, and a library, and they serve superb complimentary breakfast, afternoon tea, hors d'oeuvres and cocktails. Highly recommended. ⑦.

Lafitte Guest House

Map 4, I3. 1003 Bourbon St at St Philip ℂ581-2678 or 1-800/331-7971.
The unpromising mushroom-colored exterior of this galleried antebellum house, on the quieter end of Bourbon Street, right by the historic *Lafitte's Blacksmith Shop* (see p.184), hides a romantic, welcoming, gay-friendly hotel, complete with resident ghost. The comfortable, antique-furnished rooms vary in size and style, though all feature original architectural details, and many have balconies. Ask about the tranquil sound machines and sleep masks. Wine and cheese is served in the living room every evening, and rates include in-room continental breakfast. ⑤–⑧.

Hotel Maison de Ville

Map 4, E4. 727 Toulouse St at Royal ℂ561-5858 or 1-800/634-1600.
Very classy small hotel, favored by Elizabeth Taylor and Tennessee Williams (who stayed in room 9) among others. Service is luxurious, with free evening sherry, overnight shoe shine, and breakfast brought to your room. Rooms in the main building, with its fabulous courtyard and fountain, are attractive, though small; a complex of secluded cottages, a block away on Dauphine Street, offers larger rooms, patios and a pool. Two-night minimum stay over weekends. ⑨.

Monteleone Hotel

Map 4, B4. 214 Royal St at Bienville ℂ523-3341 or 1-800/535-9595.
Opened in 1886, New Orleans' oldest existing hotel is also the tallest building in the Quarter, its sixteen stories making it

something of a giant towering above Royal Street's classy antique stores. It's been restored and modernized, and now has more than 600 rooms, but it manages to keep its distinctive character, with a handsome baroque facade and revolving *Carousel* bar (see p.183). There's a gym, heated rooftop pool and three restaurants. ⑦.

Olivier House

Map 4, E3. 828 Toulouse St at Bourbon ©525-8456.
Family-run place in a Creole town house with a warren of corridors, balconies and stairwells. Like many of the Quarter's buildings, it can feel a bit dark, but it's immensely atmospheric and good value. The 42 rooms (all with bath) vary considerably in size and quality, but most of them are appealingly old-fashioned, with antique furniture, chandeliers, plush sofas, and tall shuttered windows. It's worth negotiating about rates at quiet times; if money's no object, go for room 112, which has its own garden and fountain. There's a gorgeous tropical court-yard, and a small pool (though it's not always spotless), and coffee is served all day in the parlor. ④–⑨.

Hotel Provincial

Map 4, I5. 1024 Chartres St at Ursulines ©581-4995 or 1-800/535-7922.
Intimate and relaxed place in a quiet part of the Quarter, with very nice, antique-filled rooms opening onto peaceful, gaslit courtyards. They also have an outdoor pool, a popular, reasonably priced restaurant, and a bar. ⑦.

Le Richelieu

Map 4, K5. 1234 Chartres St at Barracks ©529-2492 or 1-800/535-9653.
Handsome historic hotel in a restored factory and neighboring town house. The old-world ambience of the lovely lobby is not continued in the rooms, which are nonetheless comfortable and

attractive, equipped with all mod cons. There's a small outdoor pool, overlooked by a café serving lunch and coffee, and free on-site parking – a rarity in the French Quarter. ⑤–⑨.

Rue Royal Inn

Map 4, I4. 1006 Royal St at St Philip ℅524-3900 or 1-800/776-3901.
Superb, exceptionally good value, gay-friendly hotel, whose owners and their big fluffy cats make everyone feel welcome. The enormous, brick-walled, high-ceilinged rooms, which easily sleep four, all have bath, fridge and minibar; the priciest have balconies and jacuzzis. Rates include complimentary coffee and continental breakfast, which you can eat in the pretty courtyard. Two-night minimum stay over weekends. ④.

St Peter Guest House

Map 4, F2. 1005 St Peter St at Burgundy ℅1-800/535-7815.
Darkish, comfortable rooms – some set around a courtyard, others with balconies – popular with a mixed gay and straight clientele. Though it's less characterful than some of the older Creole guesthouses, and can be noisy if you're staying at the front, it's clean, efficiently run and perfectly adequate. Rates include continental breakfast. ③–⑧.

Hotel St Pierre

Map 4, H2. 911 Burgundy St at Dumaine ℅524-4401 or 1-800/225-4401.
Quirky, gay-friendly hotel in a quiet street. Rooms, in two-story Creole cottages set around courtyards, come in all shapes, sizes and decor, and there are two small outdoor swimming pools. Rates include continental breakfast. ⑥.

Ursuline Guest House

Map 4, J4. 708 Ursulines St at Royal ℅525-8509 or 1-800/654-2351.
Peaceful and unfussy place, with a courtyard and jacuzzi, catering

ACCOMMODATION: FRENCH QUARTER

to a mixed gay and straight clientele. Rates include continental breakfast and evening drinks. ④–⑦.

Hotel Villa Convento

Map 4, J4. 616 Ursulines St at Chartres ©522-1793.
Friendly, family-run guesthouse with a bustling atmosphere. The no-frills rooms all have their own bath; some have balconies overlooking the street, while others lead on to the patio. Complimentary continental breakfast is served in the covered courtyard. ⑤–⑧.

FAUBOURG MARIGNY AND ESPLANADE RIDGE

The Frenchmen

Map 4, L6. 417 Frenchmen St at Esplanade ©948-2166 or 1-800/831-1781.
Excellent, gay-friendly B&B in a great Faubourg location across from the Old US Mint. Located in two quiet 1860 town houses overlooking a tropical patio, the rooms, which range from tiny to spacious, are all different, decorated with good-looking antiques. There's a small pool on site and a jacuzzi. ④–⑧.

Maison Esplanade

Map 1, F6. 1244 Esplanade Ave at Tremé ©523-8080 or 1-800/892-5529.
Good-value B&B in a lovely mint-green mansion, with huge, individually decorated rooms named after local musicians. It's friendly and lived-in, with good-looking antiques and stripped hardwood floors, but you're on the fringes of the Faubourg here, near Tremé; don't wander around the neighborhood at night. Rates include continental breakfast. ③.

Melrose Mansion

Map 4, L2. 937 Esplanade Ave at Burgundy ©944-2255.
Extremely luxurious B&B – a honeymooners' favorite – in a

Gothic mansion designed in 1884 by esteemed local architect
James Freret. All eight rooms are superbly furnished with
antiques; the suites have jacuzzis and complimentary brandy.
There's also a tropical patio, heated pool, gym and reading
room. Rates include a fabulous breakfast, open bar and stretch
limo airport pick-up. ⑨.

Rathbone Inn

Map 4, M1. 1227 Esplanade Ave at St Claude ℂ947-2100 or
1-800/947-2101.

Good-value guesthouse in an elegant 1850s mansion, with a
tropical patio and small jacuzzi. All rooms have private bath and
small kitchenettes; the sizeable suites sleep four. Rates include
continental breakfast. Reservations and deposit required; two-
day minimum stay over weekends. See *Maison Esplanade*, opposite, for a caution about the neighborhood. ⑤.

Royal Street Inn

Map 4, M4. 1431 Royal St at Kerlerec ℂ948-7499 or
1-800/449-5535.

Characterful accommodation above the funky *R-Bar* (see
p.186), and run by the same people. The five, good-looking
rooms (all with private bath) are individually decorated on
themes ranging from Art Deco to bordello; those for two
people are smallish, but the four-person suites are excellent
value. Favored by a young, hip crowd who spend evenings
hanging out in the bar. ④.

CBD AND WAREHOUSE DISTRICT

Depot House at Mme Julia's

Map 3, K4. 748 O'Keefe Ave at Julia ℂ529-2952.

Budget rooms in an old railroad boarding house at the lakeside
end of the CBD, a short walk from the Arts District and seven
blocks from the Quarter. The newest venture from the people

behind the *St Charles Guest House* (see p.143), it's very similar, with simple, small rooms, shared bath, no phones or TV, and continental breakfast served in the small garden. ②.

Pelham Hotel
Map 3, M4. 440 Common St at Magazine ©522-4444 or 1-800/659-5621.
Boutique hotel in a nineteenth-century building a couple of blocks from Canal Street, with comfortable, attractive rooms. Despite its upscale ambience, it's a no-hassle, no-attitude kind of place. Ask about special weekend deals or check the tourist office for brochures – and make sure to eat in the superb *Metro* restaurant downstairs (see p.165). ⑧.

La Salle Hotel
Map 4, A1. 1113 Canal St at Basin ©523-5831 or 1-800/521-9450.
Reliable, popular budget option near the Quarter. Few frills here, just plain rooms – some with private bath – free coffee and daily newspapers. The area, on the fringes of the run-down Tremé neighborhood, can feel unsafe at night. ②.

Windsor Court
Map 3, M5. 300 Gravier St at Tchoupitoulas ©523-6000 or 1-800/262-2662.
Extremely luxurious hotel, voted the best in the world by *Condé Nast Traveler* in 1998, dripping with Italian marble, Old Master paintings, colossal flower arrangements and priceless antiques. The rooms themselves are huge and very comfortable, while pampering perks include in-room massages. ⑨.

YMCA
Map 3, J5. 920 St Charles Ave at Lee Circle ©568-9622.
Budget option on the streetcar route, offering drab singles, doubles, triples and quads (with bunk beds) – all with TV and shared shower. There's a good veggie restaurant (see p.164),

and you can use the adjoining gym and pool. It gets booked up very fast, especially during Mardi Gras, when the rooms overlooking St Charles give great parade views. No curfew. ①.

LOWER GARDEN DISTRICT, GARDEN DISTRICT AND UPTOWN

Columns Hotel

Map 2, J6. 3811 St Charles Ave at General Taylor ©899-9308. Atmospheric Garden District hotel in an 1883 Italianate mansion designed by Thomas Sully. Standing in for a Storyville bordello in the 1977 movie *Pretty Baby*, the whole place seeps louche glamour, especially the superb bar (see p.188) and the columned verandah. The characterful rooms have hardwood floors and are decorated with antiques; some come with private bath and balcony, but there are no TVs. Complimentary continental breakfast is taken in a little tearoom. Rates increase by more than 200 percent at Mardi Gras, because of its excellent parade-viewing location on the streetcar line. ⑤–⑨.

HI-New Orleans Marquette House

Map 3, F5. 2253 Carondelet St at Jackson ©523-3014. Large multi-building hostel a block from the streetcar in the Garden District. Dorm beds cost $15–18, and there are a few functional budget rooms, including doubles and apartments, some with bath. Reservations recommended; for Mardi Gras and JazzFest you'll need to pay in full in advance. No curfew. ③.

Josephine Guest House

Map 3, F5. 1450 Josephine St at Prytania ©524-6361 or 1-800/779-6361.
Exquisite guesthouse in the gorgeous 1870s Italianate home of M and Mme Fuselier, set on the fringes of the Garden District. Rooms are artistically decorated with unusual

antiques and baroque flourishes; each has private bath and a balcony. Continental Creole breakfast comes with fresh orange juice, warm bread and café au lait, and drinks are served in the parlor. Excellent value. ⑤.

Longpré House

Map 3, H5. 1726 Prytania St at Euterpe ℭ581-4540.
Run-down Italianate house in the Lower Garden District, with cramped dorms ($12; $25 during special events) and nine private rooms, some of which sleep four or five. The cheaper rooms are not bad value at $30, but the place as a whole is only for die-hard hostelers. No curfew, and no smoking in rooms. ①.

McKendrick-Breaux House

Map 3, H6. 1474 Magazine St at Race ℭ586-1700.
Laid-back B&B housed in two nineteenth-century homes in the Lower Garden District. The rooms are large and all have private bath; some feature balconies overlooking the lush patio. Rates include continental breakfast, served by the knowledge-able, personable hosts. ⑤.

Park View Guest House

Map 2, C4. 7004 St Charles Ave at Walnut ℭ861-7564.
Built for the 1884 Cotton Exposition, this uptown hotel on the edge of Audubon Park has an appealing, lived-in feel, with mismatched antique furniture and a roomy verandah. Rooms, some with shared bath, are comfortable and good value; many have views of the park. Rates include continental breakfast. ④.

Pontchartrain Hotel

Map 3, G5. 2031 St Charles Ave at Josephine ℭ524-0581 or 1-800/777-6193.
Stylish Garden District hotel dating from 1927. It's on the streetcar line, with an uptown grandeur that attracts visiting dignitaries and privacy-seeking celebs – the atmospheric *Bayou*

Bar (see p.188), with its dark wood and romantic corners, is a
favorite of local author Anne Rice. ⑦.

Prytania Inns I, II & III
Map 3, I5. 1415 Prytania St at Thalia ℂ566-1515 (main office);
also at 2041 & 2127 Prytania St.
German-owned historic houses, each a block from the streetcar
in the Lower Garden District, with a total of around one hundred
rooms varying in size and style. The cheapest have shared bath,
and rates are often negotiable. There's a communal TV room in
no. 1415, where a gourmet breakfast is served for $5. ②.

Prytania Park Hotel
Map 3, H5. 1525 Prytania St at Terpsichore ℂ524-0427 or 1-
800/862-1984.
Spruce, peaceful small hotel in the Lower Garden District. The
varied selection of historic and modern rooms includes good-
value lofts that sleep four or five; all have fridges and
microwaves. Rates include continental breakfast, which you
can eat in the courtyard or in your room. ⑥.

St Charles Guest House
Map 3, H5. 1748 Prytania St at Polymina ℂ523-6556.
Bohemian guesthouse in the Lower Garden District with
rooms (all non-smoking) ranging from extremely basic cabins
to en-suite doubles, none with phone or TV. It's a favorite
with European backpackers who go for the 6ft by 8ft cabins for
$30, but for the pricier rooms you can get better value else-
where. It's friendly enough, though, with a pool and a small
café serving free breakfast. They give discounts for students,
but cash deposits are required with reservations. ①–④.

St Charles Inn
Map 3, C3. 3636 St Charles Ave at Foucher ℂ899-8888 or
1-800/489-9908.

Sizeable and good value, if unexciting, motel rooms in a prime
location just beyond the Garden District, right by the streetcar
stop. There's a communal lounge, and rates include continental
breakfast taken in your room. ③.

St Vincent's Guest House

Map 3, H6. 1507 Magazine St at Race ℂ523-3411.
Lower Garden District lodging, run by the same people as the
Prytania Inns (see p.143), with more than seventy simple,
economical rooms in a huge 1861 orphanage. The atmosphere
is cheery, if a little institutional, with its long echoing corridors; meals (starting at $10 for full buffet breakfast) are served
in the tearoom. There's a pool, too. ②.

Whitney Inn

Map 3, H5. 1509 St Charles Ave at Melpomene ℂ521-8000 or
1-800/379-5322.
Renovated nineteenth-century town houses on the streetcar
line in the Lower Garden District. The simply furnished rooms
range from motel-type singles to a penthouse suite; all have
private bath. Complimentary continental breakfast is served in
a small kitchen, and there's a little courtyard. No smoking. ⑤.

Eating

ew Orleans is a gourmand's dream. Many visitors come here for the restaurants alone, while locals will spend hours arguing about where to find the fattest po-boy, the briniest raw oysters or the tastiest gumbo. The comings, goings and latest creations of local celebrity chefs is daily gossip, food festivals litter the calendar and restaurant openings make regular headlines.

The **food** itself, commonly defined as **Creole**, is a spicy, substantial – and usually very fattening – blend of French, Spanish, African, Caribbean and Cajun cuisine, mixed up with a host of other influences including Native American, Italian and German. It tends to be rich, and fragrant, using heaps of herbs, peppers, garlic and onion. Some of the simpler dishes, like red beans and rice (traditionally served for Monday lunch), reveal a strong Caribbean influence, while others are more French, cooked with long-simmered sauces based on a **roux** (fat and flour heated together) and herby stocks. You'll often get surprising twinnings – oysters and tasso, say, or crabmeat and veal – and many dishes are served **étouffé**, literally "smothered" in a tasty Creole sauce (a roux with tomato, onion and spices), on a bed of rice.

Seafood is abundant and can be very cheap – hardly surprising when you consider the city is almost entirely surrounded by water. Along with shrimp and soft-shell

Some New Orleans food terms

Andouille (on-*doo*-we) Spicy pork sausage.

Bananas Foster Flamboyant dessert invented at *Brennan's* restaurant. Sliced bananas, doused in rum and banana liqueur, are added to a mountain of brown sugar and set alight at your table to create boozy comfort food.

Barbecue shrimp Not BBQ as we know it; the shrimp are baked in their shells and served in a buttery, garlicky sauce.

Beignets (*ben*-yay) Hot fried doughnuts without a hole, smothered in powdered sugar. Commonly thought to be French, in fact they derive from Spanish *sopapillas*, or fritters, and were renamed in the 1960s as a tourist gimmick. They're best eaten with café au lait at the *Café du Monde* (see p.174).

Biscuits Sourmilk scones, eaten at breakfast.

Boudin Spicy Cajun sausage, filled with pork, crawfish or dirty rice.

Bread pudding Gooey little raisin-filled dessert, made with French bread and often drenched in custard.

Chicken-fried Breaded and deep fried.

Debris Crispy meat leftovers, usually from roast beef, often served in a po-boy.

Dirty rice Rice cooked with chicken livers, giblets, onions, peppers and spices.

Grillades (*gree*-yards) Sliced veal or beef served in a rich gravy, usually with grits, often for breakfast.

Grits Southern breakfast staple of mushy ground corn boiled and served with a dollop of butter, maple syrup or gravy.

Gumbo Thick soup-cum-stew made with seafood, chicken, vegetables or sausage. The name may come from *kombo*, a Native American word for filé (sassafras, ground by the local Choctaw to thicken soups, and often added to gumbos today) or *gombo*, the Bantu word for okra, which is another thickening agent. Gumbo z'herbes is a vegetarian option, created by African slaves for Lent.

Hush puppies Fried corn balls.

Jambalaya Rice jumbled together with seafood, sausage, chicken, bell peppers, celery and onion. The name is thought to come from the Spanish or French words for ham (*jamon* and *jambon*), tacked onto the Spanish *paella*.

Mirliton Squash.

Muffuletta Italian sandwich; a big round bun stuffed full of aromatic meats and cheese, dripping with olive and garlic dressing.

Oysters Rockefeller Invented at *Antoines* at the turn of the century, and named for the oil magnate. Most come baked in a creamy spinach sauce with a splash of anise, but the original, secret recipe uses greens.

Pain perdu French toast.

Panéed Lightly breaded and fried in butter.

Po-boy French-bread sandwich crammed with oysters, shrimp, roast beef or almost anything else. They were created by two local bakers in 1929, who handed them out free to striking streetcar drivers ("poor" boys).

Praline (praw-leen) Tooth-rottingly sweet candy made from caramelized sugar, butter and pecans (pi-*cons*).

Ravigote Piquant mix of mayonnaise and capers, usually served with cold shellfish.

Remoulade Chilled spicy sauce made with peppers, spring onion, horseradish and lemon, and slathered over cold shrimp.

Tasso Lean, spicy smoked ham.

crabs, you'll get famously good **oysters**, shucked and slurped in their hundreds along marble-topped counters all around the city; they're in season from September to April. Once looked down on as "trash" food, but now a favorite delicacy, **crawfish** or mudbugs (which closely resemble

langoustines and are best between March and October), are
served in everything from omelettes to bisques, or simply
boiled in a spicy stock. To eat them, tug off the overlarge
head, pinch the tail and suck out the juicy, very delicious
flesh.

New Orleans' swankiest, **old-guard restaurants** –
including *Brennan's*, *Commander's Palace* and *Galatoire's* –
serve haute-Creole cuisine in elegant, jacket-and-tie surroundings; the atmosphere alone in these places makes it
worth splashing out for a special occasion. Many of them
are owned by members of the extended Brennan family, a
dynasty that has ruled the city's dining roost since the
1950s. There's no shortage of vibrant, **cutting-edge
restaurants**, either, where stellar chefs throw even more
influences – Southwestern, New American, Asian – into
the pot. Currently, the most famous is *Emeril's*, brainchild
of TV darling Emeril Lagasse, who stormed the restaurant
scene in 1990 after cutting his teeth at *Commander's*. (His
other two restaurants, *Nola* in the French Quarter and
Delmonico's on St Charles Avenue, are overrated and overpriced.) Other top restaurants to try include *Bayona*,
Peristyle and *Upperline* – and keep an eye on the papers for
news on the latest wunderkind chef stealing the show.

Although New Orleans does have a couple of good
restaurants calling themselves **Cajun**, few of the menu
items they serve have much in common with the country
food, cooked in a very dark roux, that is dished up on the
bayous. After all, despite the non-stop accordion music that
jangles from the tackiest tourist shops, New Orleans is not
actually in Cajun country, which lies well to the west and
southwest. What passes for Cajun food in the city is often a
modern hybrid, tasty but not authentic; "blackened" fish
and chicken, for example, slathered in butter and hot
spices, was made famous by chef Paul Prudhomme in the
1980s.

New Orleans also has some good **ethnic** restaurants for Japanese, Chinese, Indian, Thai and North African food. Along with the handful of **vegetarian** places, these are the best bets for non-meat eaters, who otherwise need to be careful; even dishes that sound innocent – red beans and rice, collard greens – will probably yield fat chunks of smoked sausage or ham hocks, or will at the very least have been stewed with some juicy lump of flesh.

Gratifyingly, **prices** are not that high compared to other US cities – even at the very best restaurants you can get away with $50 per head for a three-course feast with wine. And if you're on a really tight budget, don't despair: one of the great pleasures of New Orleans' dining scene is the scores of great little local joints serving colossal portions at low prices.

New Orleans' best coffee houses, most of which serve light lunches and snacks, are reviewed from p.174; if you're planning a picnic, turn to the reviews of delis and food stores, which start on p.177.

No neighborhood can rival the **French Quarter** for sheer volume and variety of eating options, its narrow old streets jam-packed with everything from down-home holes in the wall to old-guard dining rooms serving glorious haute cuisine. If you can drag yourself away from the Quarter, your best bet for a special occasion is one of the swanky restaurants in the **CBD**, **Garden District**, or uptown, while at the other end of the scale you'll find a clutch of good local places in the **Faubourg**, along Esplanade Avenue in **Mid-City**, in the **Lower Garden District** and throughout the studenty **Riverbend** area uptown.

EATING

149

RESTAURANTS

In the reviews below we've used broad **price categorizations**, estimating how much you might pay, on average, for an appetizer and entrée, or an entrée and dessert, not including service or taxes. In places classified as **inexpensive** you'll get away with spending less than $15 per head, while at a **moderate** restaurant you're looking at between $15 and $25 and at an **expensive** establishment, you could easily spend well over $25. All this depends, of course, upon what you order; most restaurants offer a wide range of options, varying in price. Eating lobster at a restaurant we've classed as inexpensive will obviously push costs up, while many of even the swankiest restaurants offer reasonable lunchtime deals.

Reservations are not accepted in many places (which generally means having to wait in line); we've stated below where this is the case and where you should call in advance. Also, we've noted the very few restaurants where a **dress code** applies.

THE FRENCH QUARTER

Acme Oyster House
Map 4, B4. 724 Iberville St at Bourbon ©522-5973.
Mon–Sat 11am–10pm, Sun noon–7pm. Inexpensive.
With its checked tablecloths, tangle of neon signs, marble-topped oyster bar and fast, smart-talking staff, this noisy, characterful place has been *the* French Quarter hangout for raw oysters and ice-cold beer since early this century. A dozen briny bivalves on the half shell costs just $6, or you can get them fried for around $10. If they're in season, don't miss the fresh, buttery mudbugs, boiled in a delicious stock. Or try the gut-busting medley of gumbo, spicy jambalaya and red beans and rice – a mere $7.

Bacco

Map 4, C5. 310 Chartres St at Bienville ℭ522-2426.
Mon–Sat 11.30am–2.30pm & 6–10pm, Sun 10am–2pm & 6–10pm.
Expensive.

Owned by Ralph and Cindy Brennan of the city's top
restaurant clan, this gorgeous-looking nouvelle Italian – all
Venetian chandeliers, elegant iron gates, and ivory-colored
booths scrawled with Italian love proclamations – is less
expensive than you might expect, especially at lunch. Dinner
can set you back a bit, however, especially if you order a foie
gras pizza, and the pasta, though tasty, is overpriced. Good
appetizers include roasted garlic and Tuscan bread soup, rich
with Romano cheese, while for an entrée (around $20) you
could try wood-oven roasted Gulf shrimp on mushroom
risotto cake. Of the decadent desserts, the chocolate custard,
sozzled with orange liqueur, is a must.

Look out for the absurd *Lucky Dogs*
giant hot-dog-shaped carts, which trundle
through the Quarter at all hours. Featured in
John Kennedy Toole's farce *A Confederacy of Dunces*
(see p.279), they're something of an institution –
though the "dogs" themselves are nothing
to write home about.

Bayona

Map 4, D3. 430 Dauphine St at Conti ℭ525-4455.
Mon–Thurs 11am–2pm & 6–10pm, Fri 11am–2pm & 6–11pm,
Sat 6–11pm. Expensive.

Splendid, romantic and attitude-free restaurant in a seventeenth-
century Creole cottage with a lovely tropical courtyard. Chef
Susan Spicer creates dazzling "New World Cuisine", giving
local ingredients and dishes an oriental, Southwestern or
Mediterranean twist – grilled shrimp with black-bean cake and

RESTAURANTS: THE FRENCH QUARTER

cilantro sauce, say, or seared scallops with Asian noodle salad and Szechuan dressing. It's creative without being fussy; the simply prepared garlic soup ($4) and saffron-infused bouillabaisse are outstanding ($14). To cut costs a little, go for lunch, when you can get three fantastic courses for around $25.

Brennan's

Map 4, D4. 417 Royal St at Conti ℂ525-9711.

Daily 8am–2.30pm & 6–10pm. Expensive.

Historic Creole restaurant, the first in the Brennan empire, with a dozen rooms and a tropical courtyard. It's famed for its long, luxurious breakfasts – choose from more than twenty poached egg dishes, hair-of-the-dog cocktails, grillades and grits and the like; though locals balk at spending $50 on eggs, tourists can't get enough of the place. Dinner proves better value, with fixed-price four-course meals: the long menu includes turtle and oyster soups, crawfish sardou (spicy fried crawfish tails in an artichoke, creamed spinach and hollandaise sauce), redfish with lump crabmeat in a rich mushroom and red wine sauce and the definitive Bananas Foster (see p.146). The wine list is outstanding. Dress up and reserve.

Clover Grill

Map 4, H3. 900 Bourbon St at Dumaine ℂ598-1010.

Daily 24hr. Inexpensive.

All-night diner with counter seating and a few booths, usually crowded with a gay Bourbon Street clientele filling up on fries, burgers, omelettes and shakes. It's always lively and can get rowdy: come for a post bar-crawl breakfast of waffles, pancakes or Froot Loops, then sit back and enjoy the show.

Country Flame

Map 4, B4. 620 Iberville St at Exchange Alley ℂ522-1138.

Mon–Thurs & Sun 11am–10pm, Fri & Sat 11am–11pm.

Inexpensive.

Tiny dive-like place, worth seeking out for hearty Spanish, Mexican and Cuban food at rock-bottom prices. It's all very meaty and lip-lickingly greasy – check out the Cuban sandwich with ham, cheese and roast pork, or *puerco frito*, pork marinated for days, fried and served with yucca. You can also get tamales, fajitas, burritos and juicy quesadillas, which come with thick dollops of guacamole and sour cream. Daily lunch specials – half a BBQ chicken, broiled catfish and so on – cost less than $5.

Croissant d'Or

Map 4, J5. 617 Ursulines St at Chartres ℂ524-4663.
Daily 7am–5pm. Inexpensive.
Peaceful, absurdly cheap little place serving the best French pastries and stuffed croissants this side of Paris, plus quiches, salads and steaming café au lait. There's a pretty courtyard, but inside, with its marble floor, tiled walls, stained-glass murals and iron chairs, is even more atmospheric, usually filled with locals reading, writing and chatting. No smoking indoors and no credit cards.

G&E Courtyard Grill

Map 4, J6. 1113 Decatur St at Ursulines ℂ528-9376.
Mon–Thurs 6–10pm, Fri & Sat 11.30am–2.30pm & 6–11pm, Sun 11.30am–2.30pm & 6–10pm. Expensive.
Though the New American food isn't at all bad, the best thing about the *G&E* is its brick-walled courtyard. Dotted with pottery fragments, plants and Christmas-tree lights, it focuses on the open hearth, where you can watch fat scallops and crispy duck roasting on the spit; the highlight, though, is the chicken, which might come with a mozzarella and tomato curry, or in a garlic sauce, for around $20. It's very New Orleans, but with a Californian edge, using organic produce and putting creative spins on tradition with dishes such as Oyster Rockefeller soup.

RESTAURANTS: THE FRENCH QUARTER

Galatoire's

Map 4, B3. 209 Bourbon St at Iberville ✆525-2021.

Tues–Sun 11.30am–9pm. Expensive.

Grand French-Creole restaurant, run by the same family since 1905. With its dark-wood, mirrored dining room, it's quintessential New Orleans and great fun, though newcomers may feel a little left out as regulars have favorite waiters who seat them at their preferred tables. It's best at lunchtime, on Friday or Sunday especially, when long, convivial hours can be spent gorging on turtle soup, shrimp remoulade, oysters en brochette (with crispy bacon and a meunière sauce), crabmeat Yvonne (sautéed with artichoke, mushrooms, peppers and parsley) and filet mignon. Reservations are only taken for parties of eight or more: smaller groups should go as early as possible and be prepared to wait. Jackets required after 5pm and all day Sun.

Girod's Bistro

Map 4, D5. 500 Chartres St at St Louis ✆522-4152.

Tues–Sat 6–10.30pm. Moderate.

Wonderful, romantic restaurant, linked to the *Napoleon House* (see p.185) and hidden away beside its courtyard. Like the bar itself, the bistro is all peeling walls, candlelight and old paintings – the perfect setting to linger over robust, creative Creole food with Mediterranean and Caribbean accents. Appetizers ($5–7) are a meal in themselves: try the baked oysters with tasso, or savory cheesecake with mushrooms and crispy prosciutto. Of the entrées ($15–18), most of which come with unusual, flavorful sauces, the seafood-packed bouillabaisse and West Indian-style curries are sure-fire winners.

Gumbo Shop

Map 4, F4. 630 St Peter St at Chartres ✆525-1486.

Daily 11am–11pm. Inexpensive.

Touristy, good-natured Creole restaurant housed in an eighteenth-century building lined with murals of old New

Orleans and with a pretty courtyard. Naturally the gumbo –
seafood, chicken and andouille, or z'herbe – is the highlight;
dark, subtly flavored, and excellent value ($3 as an appetizer, $6
as an entrée). Other entrées hover at around $10 – try the
crawfish étouffé, or the succulent grilled redfish smothered with
shrimp Creole. A relaxed, convivial spot for a quick lunch or to
fill up before a night on the tiles.

Johnny's Po-Boys

Map 4, D5. 511 St Louis St at Decatur ℡524-8129.
Mon–Fri 7am–4.30pm, Sat & Sun 9am–4pm. Inexpensive.
A New Orleans institution, this no-frills, checked-tablecloth
joint is heaving at lunchtime with local workers and in-the-
know tourists. It's famed for its po-boys, of course – the
mind-boggling choice of fillings includes pork chop, shrimp,
french fries, oyster, smoked sausage and catfish – but they also
serve breakfast and plate lunches such as red beans and rice,
spaghetti, or fried chicken, all for under $5. Call for deliveries.
No credit cards.

K-Paul's Louisiana Kitchen

Map 4, D5. 416 Chartres St at Conti ℡524-7394.
Mon–Sat 11.30am–2.30pm & 5.30–10pm. Expensive.
Renowned, rustic-smart restaurant serving the "blackened"
cuisine, slathered in butter and spices, introduced to the nation
by Cajun chef Paul Prudhomme in the 1980s. If you like your
food hot and heavy you'll love it here; highlights among the dinner entrées ($20–30) include stuffed smoked soft-shell crawfish,
blackened beef tenderloin with a rich debris sauce, and bronzed
swordfish crusted with roasted pecans, jalapeños and garlic.
Locals long ago left the place to the tourists, who will wait for
hours for a table (reservations are only accepted for the more formal, upstairs room); it's best for lunch, when lines are shorter,
prices are far lower (appetizers start at an unbelievable $2, and
entrées at $7), and you have time to walk it all off afterwards.

La Madeleine

Map 4, G5. 547 St Ann St at Chartres ℂ568-0073.

Daily 7am–9pm. Inexpensive.

Boasting a prime location on Jackson Square, this convenient refueling stop, part of the national chain, fits well in this most French of US cities. The ambience is appealingly rustic, but it's the seductive buttery smells and low prices that pull in the hordes of starving artists and footsore tourists. Specialties include soups (try the wonderfully rich French onion), pizza, pastas and fish, as well as quiches and pies; the boulangerie sells fresh baked bread, French pastries and hot flaky croissants to go. No smoking.

Lucky Cheng's

Map 4, D4. 720 St Louis St at Royal ℂ529-2045.

Mon–Sat 11am–3pm & 6pm till late,
Sun mimosa brunch 11am–3pm. Bar open daily from 10am.
Moderate.

High-camp theme restaurant, where drag queens interrupt their duties serving Asian-Creole fusion to put on a nightly show, draping themselves over tables – and diners – while belting out torch song hits. To see the girls in action (the whole point) you have to spend at least $10 on a meal, which is no hardship for anyone who likes spicy food. Shrimp and crawfish samosas, with shiitake mushrooms and orange sake chile sauce, make a good appetizer, while entrées include fiery chicken with cous-cous and yoghurt. For dessert, Imelda's chocolate shoe, drag-queen sized and filled with raspberry mousse, is a must.

Maximo's

Map 4, J6. 1117 Decatur St at Ursulines ℂ586-8883.

Daily 6pm–midnight. Expensive.

Good Northern Italian food in slick San Francisco-style bistro, with counter seating, booths and moody jazz photos. Service is chatty and enthusiastic, and it's especially buzzy at weekends, when people come to eat late. You can't go wrong with the pasta (from $12), especially penne crawfish diablo, cooked with green onion in a zippy cream sauce, and veal is a specialty, be it cooked with garlic, lemon and wine, or pan-roasted with fresh herbs. There's frothy zabaglione to finish and a list of around 50 Italian wines, many of which are served by the glass.

Mona Lisa

Map 4, J4. 1212 Royal St at Governor Nicholls ℗522-6746.
Daily 11am–11pm. Inexpensive.
Candlelit at night, with brick walls, cobblestone floors and wine coolers made from battered olive-oil cans, the arty – on the point of shabby – decor at this pizza place is a bit bohemian for many tourists, which keeps it a favorite with Quarterites. You can get pasta, sandwiches and salads, but it's best to plump for the robust pizzas, which come with mountainous toppings. A 12in ($9–13) is more than enough for two. There's a wine list, or you can BYOB. Free delivery in the Quarter.

Moon Wok

Map 4, G3. 800 Dauphine St at St Ann ℗523-6910.
Daily 11am–midnight. Moderate.
Chinese food – a rarity in the Quarter – dished up in spruce Art Deco surroundings, with an alternative, trendy feel (the enthusiastic young staff are keen to emphasize that all dishes are prepared without MSG). Entrées include treats such as kung pao shrimp, which comes with peanuts, baby corn and Chinese mushrooms, and they offer good-value specials.

Mr B's Bistro

Map 4, B4. 201 Royal St at Iberville ℗523-2078.
Mon–Fri 11.30am–3pm & 5.30–10pm, Sat 11.30am–3pm & 5–10pm,
Sun 10.30am–3pm & 5.30–10pm. Moderate.
Another Brennans' winner: a casually chic European-style bistro with dark-wood booths, lots of etched glass, a relaxed,

chatty buzz and excellent food. It's difficult to choose from the star-studded contemporary Creole menu: the exquisite garlic chicken is without doubt the city's finest, served with wild rice drowned in a satiny reduction; the same accolade could go to the BBQ shrimp, baked in the shell in a sloppy sauce – you'll need the bib they tie around your neck. Other signature dishes, just as tempting, include coconut- and beer-battered shrimp, pasta jambalaya, and gumbo ya-ya with chicken and andouille.

Napoleon House

Map 4, D5. 500 Chartres St at St Louis ©524-9752.
Food served Mon–Sat 11am–11pm, Sun 11am–6pm.
Inexpensive.

Fabulous old bar (see p.185) and one of the city's best lunch stops. Everyone comes for the muffulettas, but it's worth branching out to try their other Mediterranean sandwiches (the Impastato, say, packed with herby olive salad and melted cheese), gumbos, salads (the Greek variety comes with baby spinach and warm grilled flatbread), freshly grilled chicken and fish. There's also a terrific full-service bistro on site; see *Girod's* (p.154).

Old Coffee Pot

Map 4, F4. 714 St Peter St at Royal ©524-3500.
Mon–Thurs & Sun 8am–midnight, Fri & Sat 8am–1am. Inexpensive.

Homely restaurant in a rambling old building; food is served on the patio or in the cozy parlor complete with fireplace, mirrors, oil paintings and chandeliers. Famed for its ebullient waitresses, it's popular with tourists and locals alike, particularly for breakfast (8.30am–3.30pm): huge affairs, stacked with blintzes, pain perdu or *callas* (rice cakes). Creole lunch specials are just as hearty: try chicken with red beans and rice, or a shrimp étouffé and jambalaya combo, rounding it all off with a fruit cobbler.

Old Dog, New Trick Café
Map 4, B4. 307 Exchange Alley at Bienville ©522-4569.

Daily 11.30am–9pm. Inexpensive.

Laid-back, tiny vegetarian restaurant, with some outdoor tables,
which does creative things with polenta and tempeh, uses lots of
organic produce and even offers vegan options. Entrées include
calzones and pizzas (black bean and veg is good), udon noodles
and burgers. If you're in the mood for something fancy, go for
polenta medici, made with rosemary polenta, black beans and
goat's cheese, grilled veg and pepper sauce. To keep up the
good work, wash it all down with iced hibiscus tea with organic
maple syrup – otherwise, there's a good-value wine list.

Olivier's
Map 4, B6. 204 Decatur St at Iberville ©525-7734.

Daily 11am–3pm & 5–10pm. Moderate.

Mouthwatering Black Creole food, served in smart surroundings in
a charming old building. Family owned, it's very welcoming: the
menu, which describes with relish how each dish is cooked according to the recipe of a different family-member, makes choosing
almost impossible. To start, they offer four gumbos: the Creole variety is fantastic, thick with sausage and shrimp. Entrées are luscious
and not as heavy as they sound: poulet au fromage, baked with five
cheeses, comes with shrimp, while the Creole rabbit is doused in a
dark, herby oyster sauce. They also do an expert crawfish étouffé,
finely flavored and not as gloopy as it sometimes can be.

Peristyle
Map 4, H1. 1041 Dumaine St at N Rampart ©593-9535.

Tues–Sat 6–10pm. Expensive.

Incongruously set on the rougher edge of the Quarter, this
celebrated, elegant restaurant – *very* New Orleans, all choco-
latey dark wood, checkerboard tiled floors and ranks of mismatched mirrors – is one of the hottest places in town to eat
outstanding contemporary French-Creole-New American

RESTAURANTS: THE FRENCH QUARTER

cuisine. It's enjoyably congenial, for all its cachet – young chef Anne Kearney, superstar ascendant, regularly does the rounds to see how diners are enjoying her creations. The menu changes all the time, but typical appetizers include foie gras with polenta, or sweetbreads with puy lentils, while entrées ($18–25) feature offbeat fusions such as curried salmon, along with old favorites like plump seared scallops. Reservations are essential; come early and have a pre-prandial drink in the lovely old bar.

Petunia's

Map 4, E3. 817 St Louis St at Bourbon ℂ522-6440.

Daily 8am–11pm. Moderate.

Casual, gay-run American-Creole restaurant in an attractive, slightly shabby, old house. It's known for its crepes, which are pricey but big – for lunch try the St James, a cheesy mix of crabmeat, shrimp, onions and peppers, and you won't need to eat for the rest of the day. Breakfast, served till 3.30pm, and Sunday brunch are local favorites, featuring grillades and grits, eggs benedict and the more unusual eggs melanzana (fried eggplant topped with shaved ham, tomato, egg and hollandaise). Dinner entrées are competent but overpriced.

Poppy's Grill

Map 4, F4. 717 St Peter St at Bourbon ℂ524-3287.

Daily 24hr. Inexpensive.

Bare-bones diner bang in the center of it all, in the boozy stretch where *Pat O'Brien's* (see p.185) meets Bourbon Street. Owned by the same people as the *Clover Grill* (see p.152), it's in much the same vein, filled in the wee hours with local characters and cholesterol-craving casualties wolfing burgers, omelettes and fries.

Redfish Grill

Map 4, A3. 115 Bourbon St at Iberville ℂ598-1200.

Grill Mon–Sat 11am–3pm & 5–11pm, Sun 10am–3pm & 5–11pm.
Oyster bar daily 11am–midnight. Moderate.

Casual, Ralph Brennan-owned fish restaurant, decorated with
fishy motifs, metallic palm trees and the like. Slightly sterile, it's
not a place to linger, but the food is good value, especially the
raw oysters ($3.75 for 6) and the Bourbon Street sampler –
pecan-crusted shrimp, spring roll (packed with chicken, shrimp,
sausage and red beans), fish beignets and shrimp and shiitake quesadillas – which, at just $10.25, is ample for two. Lunch specials
(around $11) might feature crawfish étouffé or a creamy oyster
stew.

Rita's

Map 4, I5. 945 Chartres St at St Philip ⓒ525-7543.
Daily 11am–10pm. Moderate.

Friendly, functionally furnished, Black Creole restaurant,
brightened up with family portraits, news clippings and photos
of past diners. The New Orleans soul food is substantial, tasty
and good value: for dinner, try the blackened catfish, soft-shell
crabs, or the blow-out "Taste of New Orleans" – gumbo, red
beans and rice, jambalaya, BBQ ribs, crawfish pie, shrimp
Creole, Louisiana yams and bread pudding (which, covered
with a hot praline sauce, you should order anyway).
The cheaper lunch menu includes po-boys.

Royal Café

Map 4, F4. 700 Royal St at St Peter ⓒ528-9086.
Mon–Sat 10am–3pm & 6–10pm. Moderate.

Located in the La Branche House (see p.44), with prime seating on its ornate, wraparound cast-iron balcony, the *Royal Café*
is always full with tourists feasting on reliable Creole food.
Though it looks rather elegant, it's actually a casual place, specializing in excellent barbecued ribs in a good spicy sauce. Fish
fans should go for the trout á la Branche, sautéed and covered
in crawfish and pecans; the salmon with mango is a lighter bet,

RESTAURANTS: THE FRENCH QUARTER

while the shrimp, another winner, comes with a delicious garlicky barbecue sauce.

Shalimar

Map 4, E5. 535 Wilkinson Row at Chartres ℂ523-0099.
Mon–Sat 11am–2.30pm & 5.30–10.30pm. Moderate.
Stylish Indian place, unique in the Quarter, and pulling an appreciative local crowd. The tranquil room, divided by Mughlai wooden screens, is a great backdrop for the beautifully prepared, authentic food, which ranges from Goan dishes, through biryani and tandoori, to creative fusions. Veggie choices are limited to a good thali and a creamy mutter paneer. Entrées start at around $11; the lunch buffet (11.30am–2pm; $6.95) is good value.

Tally Ho

Map 4, D5. 400 Chartres St at Conti ℂ566-7071.
Daily 6am–2pm. Inexpensive.
Tiny diner where worse-for-wear tourists wait in line on weekend mornings for no-frills fry ups with New Orleans flair. If you're not up to wrestling with an alligator sausage, you might try the prawn and pork boudin with grits – and they do all the usual stuff, too, served at a counter or small tables.

FAUBOURG MARIGNY

Adolfo's

Map 4, N5. 611 Frenchmen St at Royal ℂ948-3800.
Mon–Sat 6–11pm. Moderate.
Intimate, easy-going place tucked above the *Apple Barrel* bar (see p.185) and decorated with Christmas-tree lights, red candles and Cubist art on the wood-paneled walls. Food is Italian-Creole, with lots of pasta and Gulf seafood: good choices

include cannelloni stuffed with crabmeat, sweetcorn and ricotta; pan-sautéed soft-shell crab with mirliton and crawfish, and trout with crabmeat and capers.

Café Marigny

Map 4, N5. 1913 Royal St at Frenchmen ©945-4472.
Mon–Thurs 11am–10pm, Fri 11am–11pm, Sat 8am–11pm,
Sun 9am–8pm. Moderate.

Creative Creole cuisine with Southwestern, Mediterranean and Asian accents, served in a tranquil, casually chic corner joint. To start, try a salad (strawberry, walnut, spinach and blue cheese is good), black-bean cakes served with crawfish and salsa, or mussels steamed with garlic and capers. To follow, you can't fail with the ambrosial cheese ravioli, smothered in a savory sauce of crawfish, roasted corn, tomatoes and basil, or the grilled tuna with artichoke hearts, green lentils and yet more fresh basil. Daily specials, including inexpensive veggie options, are invariably excellent and there's good strong espresso and sumptuous pies to finish. Free delivery (minimum order $7) throughout the Faubourg and the Quarter.

Praline Connection

Map 4, M5. 542 Frenchmen St at Chartres ©943-3934.
Mon–Thurs 11am–10.30pm, Fri & Sat 11am–midnight. Moderate.

Waistband-straining soul food served in a bustling, bright restaurant, usually packed with tourists. Entrées include grilled chicken livers with hot jelly, stuffed soft-shell crabs, ribs, seafood étouffés, meat loaf and crispy chicken fried to order, while side dishes – baked macaroni, sugary sweet potatoes, mustard greens cooked in rich stock – are a meal in themselves. There's another branch in the Warehouse District, which does a gospel brunch on Sunday (see p.201).

Siam Café

Map 4, L6. 435 Esplanade Ave at Frenchmen ©949-1750.

Daily 6–11pm. Inexpensive.

Thai restaurant serving mountains of padh thai and zippy green and red curries in funky gamblers' den-cum-opium pit surroundings. The tiny china cups of hot sake are a hit with the hip, very young crowd who usually head upstairs to the *Dragon's Den* club (see p.200) after dining – you can also order food after-hours up there and eat it on cushions on the floor.

THE CBD AND WAREHOUSE DISTRICT

Back to the Garden
Map 3, J5. 920 St Charles Ave at Lee Circle in the YMCA ℂ522-8792.

Mon–Fri 7am–5pm, Sat 9am–4pm. Inexpensive.

Don't be put off by the utilitarian ambience; this bare-bones café is a justified hit with locals – especially those using the Y gym next door – for its cheap, delicious, healthy food. The long breakfast menu (until 11am) features wholegrain pancakes with syrup, while for lunch you can get sandwiches, big salads, or hot dishes like veggie stir fries for around $5. They also do herbal teas, fresh lemonade, smoothies and carrot juice.

Emeril's
Map 3, L6. 800 Tchoupitoulas St at Julia ℂ528-9393.

Mon–Thurs 11.30am–2pm & 6–10pm, Fri 11.30am–2pm & 6–10.30pm, Sat 6–10.30pm. Expensive.

Celebrity chef Emeril Lagasse's flagship restaurant is a noisy, flashy place, filled with delighted tourists and special-occasion locals enthusing over the highly decorative, innovative Creole cuisine. Entrées ($20–30) include roasted rack of lamb with mustard crust, and a "study of duck" – served seared, in a confit, and with its innards whipped up into a rich foie gras, accompanied by wild mushroom bread pudding. For dessert most people go for the chocolate Grand Marnier soufflé or the "dessert storm": a sampler of the pastry chef's best cakes and pies. It's pricey, and service can be haughty, but Lagasse fans will love it.

Metro Bistro

Map 3, M4. 200 Magazine St at Common in the Pelham Hotel ℂ529-1900.
Daily 11am–2pm & 5–10pm. Moderate.
Splendid place that manages to be at once hip, comfortable, buzzy and welcoming. The food is excellent, mostly French-influenced, with lots of duck; you can graze on white-bean dip and warm flatbread while you choose. Appetizers feature grilled shrimp with an onion and tomato risotto cake, and pissaladière, a thin-crusted tart topped with onions, duck confit and olive tapenade; entrées to try ($9–22) include the rich duck cassoulet or Burgundian beef stew with wild mushroom bread pudding. For something lighter, there's grilled fish on corn choux with frizzled sweet potato and a tangy bouillabaisse. The cheaper lunch menu, which features many of the same dishes as at dinner, also includes an oysters Rockefeller crepe, garnished with fried oysters.

Mother's

Map 3, M5. 401 Poydras St at Tchoupitoulas ℂ523-9656.
Daily 5am–10pm. Moderate.
Though tourists go into a tizzy about *Mother's*, thrilled to be eating N'Awlins home cooking in a down-home, authentic ambience (brick walls, concrete floors, counter service, etc), locals are drifting away from the place as prices steadily creep up. That said, the portions are still colossal, the mood friendly and bustling, and the food undeniably good. For a breakfast feast, black ham – the crunchy skin of a cooked ham – is a favorite,

dished up with biscuits and grits or in an omelette, while the debris po-boy is a winner for lunch, dressed with cabbage and pickles. The huge, cholesterol-packed plate lunches – fried chicken, beans and rice with sausage and so on – are not for the faint-hearted. No credit cards.

Palace Café
Map 3, N4. 605 Canal St at Chartres ℗523-1661.
Mon–Sat 11.30am–2.30pm & 5.30–10pm,
Sun 10.30am–2.30pm & 5.30–10pm. Moderate.
Congenial, casually elegant place in the grand old Werlein's music-store building. Always buzzing, with the ambience of a turn-of-the-century European café, it's big and airy, with marble tables, check-tiled floors, a spiral staircase sweeping up to a mezzanine and sunny walls lined with French posters. The food, Creole with a contemporary spin, is first-rate, from the creamy crabmeat cheesecake with mushroom sautée, or the fragrant oyster pan roast, to the crispy oven-roasted duck with white bean and tasso stew. At lunchtime they usually offer fresh fish as a light option – the same can hardly be said of the wonderful white chocolate bread pudding, a warm, sugar-sweet brick soaked in white-chocolate custard.

LOWER GARDEN DISTRICT AND GARDEN DISTRICT

Bluebird Café
Map 3, B4. 3625 Prytania St at Foucher ℗895-7166.
Mon–Fri 7am–3pm, Sat & Sun 8am–3pm. Inexpensive.
Though it looks like a run-of-the-mill diner, the *Bluebird*, on the fringes of the Garden District, is in fact a vaguely hippyish hangout serving good, healthy home cooking. Lines form outside, especially at the weekend, for the huge all-day breakfasts, which include huevos rancheros, corned-beef hash, home-made muffins, pancakes and "power" eggs (with tamari and

yeast). They also do daily plate lunch specials, which you can wash down with virtuous herbal teas and fresh OJ. No reservations; no credit cards.

Café Atchafalaya
Map 3, A6. 901 Louisiana Ave at Laurel ©891-5271.
Tues–Thurs 11.30am–2pm & 5.30–9pm,
Fri 11.30am–2pm & 5.30–10pm, Sat 8.30am–2pm & 5.30–10pm,
Sun 8.30am–2pm. Moderate.
A good lunch-stop during a shopping jaunt on Magazine Street and especially popular for Sunday breakfasts. The food is Deep South, filling and fattening – scrumptious crabcakes with tomato and bearnaise sauce, for example, or pork chop with cornbread-andouille stuffing and a Jack Daniels glaze. On the side, go for the fried green tomatoes, creamy grits and tangy jalapeno cheese bread.

Commander's Palace
Map 3, D5. 1403 Washington Ave at Coliseum ©899-8221.
Mon–Fri 11.30am–1.30pm & 6–9.30pm,
Sat 11.30am–12.30pm & 6–9.30pm,
Sun 10.30am–1.30pm & 6–9.30pm. Expensive.
Exceptional haute Creole cuisine in a Garden District mansion. With a jaunty striped canopy, lovely dining rooms and a tropical courtyard, it's always full with the city's finest, dressed to the nines. The food, most of which comes garnished with lots of adjectives (check the air-dried, oven-roasted, molasses-glazed duck with fennel and caramel potatoes and red cabbage slaw) is heart-thumpingly rich; specialties include roast quail stuffed with crawfish sausage, and an escargot sandwich with "basil-fed" snails, onion bread and a red wine sauce. It's pricey (dinner entrées $25–35), but they offer reasonable prix fixe ($30–35) and all-in jazz brunch ($25–30) menus. Jacket required for dinner and Sunday lunch; no shorts, T-shirts, running shoes or jeans at any time. Reservations are essential.

Magazine Po-Boy Shop

Map 2, M6. 2368 Magazine St at Washington ℂ522-3107.
Mon–Fri 9am–6.30pm, Sat 10am–6.30pm. Inexpensive.
Since the 1940s, this no-fuss place has doled out traditional
Creole breakfasts, hefty shrimp, oyster and roast-beef po-
boys, and satisfying lunch specials – like white beans and rice
with chunky smoked sausage – to an appreciative local
crowd.

The Red Room

Map 3, G5. 2040 St Charles Ave at Josephine ℂ528-9759.
Mon–Thurs 6–11pm; Sat & Sun 6pm–midnight. Expensive.
Swanky dining room, housed in a section of the Eiffel Tower
restaurant, removed during renovations and brought to New
Orleans in 1986. Served in 1940s-evocative supper-club
surroundings, the New American menu is as upscale as you'd
expect, studded with decadent delights like seared foie gras,
duxelles-crusted roasted wild boar and lobster sautéed with
white mushroom glaze. If you don't want to eat, you can have
a drink at the bar (see p.189) or come for the live music
(see p.202); but be sure to dress up. No jeans.

Uglesich's

Map 3, I4. 1238 Baronne St at Erato ℂ523-8571.
Mon–Fri 9.30am–4pm. Moderate.
Shabby seafood joint, two blocks from the streetcar in the
Lower Garden District and firmly on the tourist trail since
locals let slip a jealously guarded secret. Yugoslavians Gail and
Anthony Uglesich ("Yewgle-sitch") draw on Eastern
European traditions to create arguably the best food in the
city, from the oyster brie soup and crawfish macque choux, or
the barbecued oyster stew with buttery new potatoes, to the
phenomenally good "sizzling shrimp Gail", marinated in oil,
crushed red pepper, hot sauce, onions and peppers. Ask the
Uglesichs, or any of their overworked, charming staff, for

recommendations and feast on freshly shucked oysters at the oyster bar while you wait for a table (which can be a long time). No credit cards.

Brigtsens
Map 2, A2. 723 Dante St at River ℃861-7610.
Tues–Sat 5.30–10pm. Moderate.
Convivial, relaxed restaurant, spread across a handful of cozy rooms in an old wooden house near the streetcar line. The long, handwritten menu of imaginative Creole-Cajun dishes changes daily; of the entrées ($15–30) the fish is especially good, be it served in a gumbo or fragrant bisque, blackened, or smothered in creamy sauces; you can't go wrong with rabbit, either, especially when presented on a bed of tasso, parmesan and grits, with Creole mustard and spinach. It's a struggle to leave room for the desserts, which include banana bread pudding and double chocolate cake. Prices are reasonable, especially during early evening specials, but it's at the top end of its range. Reservations advised.

Camellia Grill
Map 2, B2. 626 S Carrollton Ave at St Charles ℃866-9573.
Mon–Thurs & Sun 9am–1am, Fri & Sat 8am–3pm. Inexpensive.
Housed in a genteel, columned Riverbend building, where the streetcar line turns inland, this tiny, characterful diner has become an institution for burgers, omelettes, fries and grilled sandwiches – lines can be long, especially at weekends, but it's worth the wait for the fun of it. The no-nonsense maitre d' seats you on benches until a stool becomes free at the double horse-shoe counter; there, brisk waitstaff, in jackets and bow-ties, bark your orders to the cooks frying and grilling right behind them. The chilli cheese omelette, with potato and onion, packs a punch; round it off with a slab of pecan pie. No credit cards.

RESTAURANTS: UPTOWN

Casamento's

Map 2, I7. 4330 Magazine St at Napoleon ℂ895-9761.

Mid-Sept to May Tues–Sun 11.30am–1.30pm & 5.30–9pm.

Inexpensive.

Spotless, atmospheric neighborhood oyster bar – decorated with dazzling white and floral tiles – that's been here since 1919. Other than the unmissable ice-fresh oysters, shucked at the marble bar and served on the half shell, popular choices include the oyster or trout "loaf", a buttery, overstuffed white bread sandwich, or, when in season, the soft-shell crab. No credit cards.

Dunbar's

Map 2, G4. 4927 Freret St at Upperline ℂ899-0734.

Mon–Sat 7am–3pm & 5–9pm. Inexpensive.

Somewhat off the beaten track, this family-run, absurdly cheap place is worth the trip for its unrivaled Creole soul food. Gut-busting breakfasts – smoked sausage, grits, biscuits – will keep you going all day; alternatively, at lunch or dinner, go for red beans and rice (the specialty of the house) or smothered chicken. Though it's unlikely you'll be able to fit it in, the lemon pudding cake is a perfect finale. Take a cab.

Jacques Imo's

Map 2, B1. 8324 Oak St at Carrollton ℂ861-0886.

Tues–Sat 6–10pm. Inexpensive.

Funky Riverbend restaurant with a colorful patio. The cooking, an inventive Creole-Cajun take on soul food, is astounding and very good value – from the fried oysters and chicken livers to the spicy, buttery blackened redfish and the tender pork chop with wild mushroom sautée. Sides include corn macque choux, sweet potatoes, butterbeans with rice and the like – you'll leave feeling stuffed. It's a great place to fill up before a gig at the *Maple Leaf* (see p.202), and well worth a trip any time.

Jamila's

Map 2, C2. 7808 Maple St at Burdette ℂ866-4366.

Tues–Thurs & Sun 5.30–9.30pm, Fri & Sat 5.30–10.30pm.
Inexpensive.

Service can be slow at this unfussy little North African restaurant, but the quality of the food and the ebullience of the host more than make up for it. The specialty is couscous with fish, veg or meat, but the peppery lamb sausage, served with lentils, is good too, while unusual soups include spinach-crawfish-zucchini and wheat-fish-lemon-capers. There's classical guitar music on Friday evenings and belly dancing on Saturday evenings.

Upperline

Map 2, G6. 1413 Upperline St at St Charles Ave ℂ891-9822.

Wed & Thurs 5.30–9.30pm, Fri & Sat 5.30–10pm, Sun
11.30am–2pm & 5.30–9.30pm. Expensive.

Lovely, bright restaurant filled with fresh flowers and a jumble of local paintings, prints and ceramics. The food, contemporary Creole, is just as attractive, with creative menus based on occasionally outlandish themes – garlic, wine, Claude Monet, Jane Austen. Everything's terrific; try the fried green tomatoes remoulade to start, followed by tender slow-cooked lamb, seared scallops with polenta and lump crabmeat, or a rich duck confit.

MID-CITY AND ESPLANADE RIDGE

Christian's

Map 1, D5. 3835 Iberville St at S Scott ℂ482-4924.

Tues–Fri 11.30am–2pm & 5.30–10pm, Sat 5.30–10pm. Expensive.
In an elegantly restored church near City Park – diners sit at pews – this local favorite, run by a member of the family who owns *Galatoire's* (see p.154), serves superlative, innovative French-Creole food. Highlights include well-prepared, tasty shrimp variations, smoked soft-shell crabs, saffron bouillabaisse, roast duck with blackberry vinegar sauce and trout amandine

Cookery classes

Would-be chefs who want to learn something about New Orleans' distinctive cuisine can choose from a handful of local **cookery schools**. Though the first two listed below are tourist operations, they can be fun, with instructors preparing dishes such as shrimp remoulade, jambalaya, gumbo and pralines while delivering lively, anecdotal patter: the class, who sit at group tables or benches, don't actually do any cooking, but do get to eat the results. Both schools are attached to country store-style **gift shops** selling sauces, herb and spice mixes, crab boils, chicory coffee and cookbooks.

Creole Delicacies Cookin' Cajun, Riverwalk shopping mall (usually daily 11am & 2pm, but call to check; $17.50; ℂ586-8832 or 1-800/786-0941). Lively two-hour classes, brisk and schoolteacherly, geared toward plugging the spices and mixes sold in the shop.

New Orleans School of Cooking, 524 St Louis St at Decatur (Mon–Sat 10am–1pm; $20; ℂ525-2665 or 1-800/850-3008). Convivial classes taught by New Orleans natives.

Spice Inc, 1051 Annunciation St (schedule varies; upward from $35 for 2hr; ℂ558-9995). The foodies' choice: Susan Spicer, of *Bayona* fame (see p.151), and guest chefs lead evening classes on themes such as cooking with wine, comfort food and New World cookery.

meunière. It's not terribly cheap – dinner will set you back about $35 – but ask about their early-evening specials.

Dooky Chase's

Map 1, E5. 2301 Orleans Ave at Miro ℂ821-0600.

Daily 11.30am–10pm. Moderate.
Classy Creole soul food dished up by chef Leah Chase, in a
cozy dining room favored by movers and shakers in the city's
black community. Of the entrées ($8–25), the fried chicken,
oyster-stuffed chicken breast, and filé gumbo with seafood and
okra are all amazing. Side dishes, in soul-food tradition, are
huge; the sweet potatoes are meltingly good. For the best value,
go for the four-course special ($25) or the Creole feast ($38).
Take a cab.

Gabrielle
Map 1, E5. 3201 Esplanade Ave at Mystery ©948-6233.
Oct–May Tues–Thurs & Sat 5.30–10pm, Fri 11.30am–2pm &
5.30–10pm; June–Sept Tues–Sat 5.30–10pm. Expensive.
Chefs Greg and Mary Sonnier serve phenomenal contemporary
Cajun-Creole cuisine in this tiny cube of a restaurant near City
Park. Though there are plenty of traditional-sounding dishes –
lobster and corn bisque; BBQ shrimp pie; braised rabbit with
black-eyed peas, greens and corn bread – all of them come with
some sort of creative spin. Try the whole salt-baked flounder
with roasted garlic and lemon basil butter, or rabbit tenderloin
wrapped in prosciutto with Chinese mustard vinaigrette and
ricotta, and leave room for the stunning desserts. Ask about
early-evening specials.

Japon
Map 1, E5. 3125 Esplanade Ave at Ponce de Leon ©949 6800.
Mon–Thurs 11.30am–2.30pm & 5.30–10pm,
Fri 11.30am–2.30pm & 5.30–11pm, Sat 5.30–11pm, Sun 5.30–9pm.
Moderate.
Serene Japanese restaurant, which is causing a storm on the
Esplanade Ridge dining scene thanks to its outstanding fresh
sushi. They also serve lightly grilled fish and à la carte items
including the outstanding soft-shell crawfish roll and a special
Louisiana roll, filled with crawfish and pickled okra.

RESTAURANTS: MID-CITY AND ESPLANADE RIDGE

Lola's

Map 1, E5. 3312 Esplanade Ave at Ponce de Leon ©488-6946.

Daily 6–10pm. Inexpensive.

Cheerful Spanish place that has become a firm local favorite for mouthwatering, cheap and authentic food. To start, choose from lentil or garlic soup, gazpacho, or lip-licking grilled shrimp; star attractions, however, are the phenomenal paellas, cooked to order in the open kitchen and packed with seafood, meat or veg, or a combo of the three. Be sure to order the fresh bread, which comes warm, with garlic-packed butter. No reservations, so you may have to wait, and BYOB. No credit cards.

COFFEE HOUSES

European-influenced New Orleans has always been *the* American city for **coffee**; drunk in copious amounts, fresh, strong and aromatic, and often laced with chicory, it's been a big part of life here since long before upstart Seattle laid claim to the notion. Most of the coffee houses listed below serve inexpensive **snacks** and pastries, too, and many will rustle up breakfasts and **light lunches**.

Café du Monde

Map 4, G6. 800 Decatur St at St Ann ©587-0833.

Daily 24hr.

Despite the hype, the crowds and the sugar-dusted tabletops, this is an undeniably atmospheric place to drink steaming café au lait, imbued with chicory, and snack on piping hot, sugary beignets for a couple of dollars – apart from orange juice and hot chocolate, they serve little else.

CCs Gourmet Coffee

Map 4, I4. 941 Royal St at St Philip ©581-6996.

Mon–Thurs 6.30am–11pm, Fri & Sat 6.30am–midnight, Sun 7.30am–10pm. Other branches all around town.

Baton Rouge-based chain, serving good strong brews in comfy, if rather sanitized, surroundings. Try the Mochassippi, a creamy iced espresso with a choice of flavors. Also quiches, pastries and muffins. Other branches at 528 St Peter St on Jackson Square and 900 Jefferson Ave at Magazine (©891-4969). No smoking.

Cybercafé @ the CAC
Map 3, K5. 900 Camp St at St Joseph ©523-0990.
Mon, Tues & Sun 7am–8pm, Wed–Sat 7am–11pm.
Small, minimalist café linked to the city's premier contemporary art gallery (see p.72), serving espressos, teas, wines, sandwiches and pastries. Best of all, internet access is free.

Kaldi's
Map 4, I5. 941 Decatur St at St Philip ©586-8989.
Mon–Thurs & Sun 6am–midnight, Fri & Sat 6am–2am.
Spacious coffee house – a haven of calm opposite the French Market – serving fresh brews to a laid-back, bohemian crowd. Sit in weathered wooden surroundings at the open window and watch the world go by, browse through the books and magazines, or head upstairs to surf the net at *Realm of Delirium* (see p.254).

La Marquise
Map 4, E5. 625 Chartres St at Wilkinson Row ©524-0420.
Daily 7am–5.30pm.
Neighborhood patisserie, sister shop to the *Croissant d'Or* (see p.153), serving delectable French pastries, great coffee – the cappuccinos are a work of art – and light lunches. Add to that the friendly staff, interesting clientele and astonishingly low prices and you've got a splendid place to hang out for a couple of hours, either in the cozy interior or in the shady courtyard.

COFFEE HOUSES

PJs Coffee and Tea

Map 4, N4. 634 Frenchmen St at Royal ©949-2292.

Mon–Fri 7am–midnight, Sat & Sun 8am–midnight.

Other branches all around town.

There's nothing special about the decor at this much loved,
twenty-year-old, local chain, but it's a firm favorite for its
expertly made coffee, muffins, bagels and gourmet sandwiches.
Other locations include a Garden District branch at 2727
Prytania (in the Rink; ©899-0335) and one at 5432 Magazine
St at Nashville (©895-0273).

Royal Blend

Map 4, E4. 621 Royal St at Toulouse ©523-2716.

Mon–Thurs & Sun 7am–8pm, Fri & Sat 7am–midnight.

Convenient French Quarter bolthole hidden from the road
behind a courtyard. In addition to coffees, espressos and herbal
teas, they offer a small menu – the gumbo with half a sandwich
makes a good, cheap lunch.

Rue de la Course

Map 4, 6B. 219 N Peters St at Bienville ©523-0206.

Mon–Thurs & Sun 7am–11pm, Fri & Sat 7am–midnight.

Other branches all around town.

With their pressed-tin walls, café-au-lait decor, ceiling fans and
reading lamps, the *Rue* coffee shops have an old Europe
ambience, buzzing with a mixed, local crowd. Liveliest of the
lot, the Garden District branch at 3128 Magazine St at Ninth
(©899-0242) is usually teeming with students pouring over
textbooks or playing Scrabble. The coffee, brewed with beans
from around the world, is great, and there are enough biscotti
and bagels to satisfy the munchies.
Other locations include 1500 Magazine St, in the Lower
Garden District (©529-1455), and a CBD branch at 401
Carondelet (©525-5200).

COFFEE HOUSES

True Brew
Map 3, L6. 200 Julia St at Fulton ℭ524-8841.
Mon–Fri 6.30am–8pm, Sat & Sun 8am–8pm
(bar open later during performances).
Warehouse District coffee house-cum-theater (see p.208) that
serves good espresso, plus healthy, contemporary sandwiches,
soups, salads and quiche (Mon–Fri 11am–3pm).

DELIS, FOOD STORES AND MARKETS

A&P
Map 4, F4. 701 Royal St at St Peter ℭ523-1353.
Daily 24hr.
The largest supermarket in the Quarter and a good bet for
fresh fruit and veg. Its central position keeps it bustling: you'll
rub shoulders with horn players and living statues, bus boys and
maitre d's all "making groceries" between gigs.

All Natural Foods and Deli
Map 2, E7. 5517 Magazine St at Joseph ℭ891-2651.
Mon–Thurs 9am–8pm, Fri 9am–7pm, Sat & Sun 9am–6pm.
Uptown health-food store and grocery, with a deli counter
(from 10am) serving chunky black-bean samosas, vegetarian
tamales, overstuffed sandwiches, falafel, miso broth and fresh-
fruit smoothies, all at low prices.

Central Grocery
Map 4, H6. 923 Decatur St at Dumaine ℭ523-1620.
Mon–Sat 8am–5.30pm, Sun 9am–5.30pm.
Famed for its unfeasibly stuffed muffulettas, this fragrant old
Italian deli, open since 1906, does a range of good picnic sta-
ples, with giant cheeses and salamis hanging from the ceiling
and big tubs of olives marinating in herby oils. Most people
take out, but there is limited counter seating. No credit cards.

Crescent City Market

Map 3, L5. Girod St at Magazine.

Sat 8am–noon.

Neighborhood market in the Warehouse District, with stalls selling fresh herbs, flowers, breads, cheese and organic wines; live music stages and celebrity chef cooking demonstrations.

Martin's Wine Cellar

Map 2, H5. 3827 Baronne St at Napoleon ©899-7411.

Mon–Sat 9am–7pm, Sun 10am–2pm.

Gourmet uptown wine shop offering regular wine tastings, free samples and superior po-boys at the deli counter.

Progress Grocery

Map 4, H6. 915 Decatur St at Dumaine ©525-6627.

Daily 9am–5.30pm.

Old Italian deli, much like the Central Grocery (which is almost next door), but cheaper and less crowded.

Spice Inc

Map 3, K6. 1051 Annunciation St at Howard ©558-9992.

Mon–Fri 9am–7pm, Sat 9am–6pm, Sun 11am–5pm.

Gourmet deli in the Warehouse District owned by chef Susan Spicer of *Bayona* (see p.151). Try the fantastic duck gumbo and garlic soup, or make a picnic from local "artisan" cheeses and fine breads from around the world. Some tables for lunchtime dining.

Verti Marte

Map 4, J4. 1201 Royal St at Gov Nicholls ©525-4767.

Daily 24hr.

Typical French Quarter corner grocery, with the bonus of an astonishingly good 24-hour hot-food take-out deli counter: pick up mountains of baked chicken, stuffed eggplant, macaroni, dirty rice and gumbo for ridiculously low prices. Perfect after a night out on the town. Free delivery in the Quarter and Faubourg.

DELIS, FOOD STORES AND MARKETS

Vieux Carré Wine Shop

Map 4, D5. 422 Chartres St at St Louis ©568-9463.
Mon–Sat 10am–10pm, Sun 10am–7pm.

Huge range of wines – a few of them somewhat obscure –
from around the world. It's something of a meeting place for
local *bon vivants*.

Whole Foods Market

Map 1, E5. 3135 Esplanade Ave at Ponce de Leon ©943-1626.
Daily 8.30am–9.30pm.

Mid-City health-food grocery, with a good, though not all that
cheap, deli counter serving smoothies, salads and sandwiches.
Hot food includes chunky veg soups, crawfish lasagne, baked
eggplant, grilled chicken and the like. You can eat on benches
outside.

DELIS, FOOD STORES AND MARKETS

Drinking

As befits its image as a hard-drinking, hard-partying town, New Orleans has dozens of truly great **bars**. Locals love to drink, and tourists, it seems, even more so, and there are more than enough places to cater to all of them. Gratifyingly, too, in this city of neighborhoods, many establishments are within walking distance of each other, making bar-hopping all the easier. It can be difficult to separate the **drinking scene** from the live-music scene – most bars feature music of some sort, at least one night of the week, and many places now known best as live-music venues started their days as humble local taverns. The establishments listed here tend not to feature live music, or at least are not primarily known for it – check the Live Music chapter (see p.191) for bars that do.

If you've run out of cash and there's no ATM in sight, there's a very good chance of finding one in the nearest bar – designed, of course, to get you to spend as much money as possible on drink.

Despite the popular misconception, there's more to drinking in New Orleans than the French Quarter, and there's more to drinking in the French Quarter than **Bourbon Street**. A boozy enclave of beer stalls, karaoke

Cocktails

It is said that the **cocktail** was invented in New Orleans in the 1790s. Operating from 437 Royal St, Haitian pharmacist Antoine Peychaud served medicinal tonics of brandy and bitters in little china egg-cups called *coquetiers*, which Anglo-Americans translated as "cocktails". Since then, several potent concoctions have been dreamed up in New Orleans, many of them the signature drinks of the city's classier establishments.

Hurricane The boozathon out-of-towner's favorite, a headache-inducing concoction – made with sugar, fruit juice and rums – which many bars refuse to serve. It's traditionally drunk, in reckless quantities, by the tourists at *Pat O'Brien's* (see p.185), but in fact *Lafitte's* (see p.184) shakes up a better one. If you're feeling really down on yourself, you can buy chemical-laced Hurricane mixes in plastic packs from the tourist stores.

Pimm's Cup The specialty of the *Napoleon House* (see p.185), served simply in a long cool glass with a slice of cucumber.

Ramos Gin Fizz A frothy swirl of gin, lemon juice, milk, egg-white, powdered sugar and orange-flower water, invented by barman Harry Ramos at the turn of the century. It was later perfected at the *Sazerac Bar* in the swanky *Roosevelt Hotel*, now the *Fairmont* (see p.187) – still the best place to order one.

Sazerac Another drink associated with the *Roosevelt*, and its *Sazerac Bar*: a caramel-colored mix of rye whiskey, bitters, lemon, and ice, stirred together in a glass rinsed out with aniseed liqueur.

clubs, strip joints and daiquiri bars – and even the odd jazz venue – Bourbon is usually heaving by nightfall, along with many of its guests, leaving plenty of room in a host of great bars elsewhere in the Quarter. That said, it's a pretty unusual first-time visitor who doesn't spend at least an hour or so on Bourbon Street, stumbling through the hollering crowds with a lurid cocktail to go – perhaps in a pink plastic goblet molded into the form of a nubile woman, or a neon-green alien-shaped beaker – before dipping out again to find more atmospheric haunts nearby. The bedlam of dance music and shrieking revelers at the gay clubs *Oz* (see p.238) and *Parade* (see p.236), on the 800 block, where Bourbon meets St Ann, heralds the **gay** stretch of Bourbon Street. Beyond here, the further you head toward Esplanade Avenue, the quieter and more residential the street becomes. Once you've crossed Esplanade you're in the **Faubourg Marigny**, where Frenchmen Street features a handful of bars and music venues that attract a stylish, arty and increasingly young crowd.

**For a rundown of gay and lesbian bars,
most of which welcome straights, see p.236.**

Bars in the **CBD** and **Warehouse District** tend to be after-work drinking holes – not bad for a quick beer, but little competition for the atmospheric places in the **Garden District** and uptown, many of which are accessible from the streetcar line along St Charles Avenue.

While many tourists come to New Orleans intending to drink the place dry of **cocktails**, the city also offers some interesting **beers**. Abita is the local brew, with varieties including the caramelly Amber, raspberry-flavored Purple Haze, and the seasonal Christmas Ale. *The Acadian Beer Garden*, based in Mid-City at 201 N Carrollton Ave, also brews its own pilsner, which is served all over town.

Though **24-hour drinking licenses** are common, don't expect every bar to be open all night – even on Bourbon Street many places close whenever they empty, which can be surprisingly early during quiet periods. It's legal to drink on the streets, though not from a glass or

DRINKING

bottle – simply ask for a "**to go**" cup in any bar and carry it around with you. You'll be expected to finish your drink before entering another bar, however. The **legal drinking age** is 21; you should carry ID, though few bartenders bother asking for it.

THE FRENCH QUARTER

Bombay Club
Map 4, C3. 830 Conti St at Dauphine ℗586-0972.
Swanky cocktail bar, a favorite with power-brokers and martini-sipping uptown belles. The atmosphere evokes a colonial English gentlemen's club, with paintings of Winston Churchill and sleek thoroughbreds on the wall, plump leather chairs, secretive curtained-off booths and lots of dark wood.
Pianist Wed–Sat.

Carousel Bar
Map 4, B4. *Monteleone Hotel*, 214 Royal St at Iberville ℗523-3341.
Gimmicky hotel bar, favored by a high-spirited conventioneer and tourist crowd. The central bar is kitted out like a fair-ground carousel, with the stools set on a revolving floor; it takes fifteen minutes to do one full rotation. Drinks are a little pricey, but you get free snacks, and it's a fun stop on a bar crawl. If you're feeling dizzy you can settle at stationary booths illuminated by a trompe l'oeil starlit sky, but that's missing the point somewhat.

Crescent City Brewhouse
Map 4, E5. 527 Decatur St at Toulouse ℗522-0571.
Trailblazing microbrewery (opened in 1991), with a big balcony overlooking Decatur. Though it could be anywhere in the US, it's a favorite spot for large groups of noisy yuppies and tourists who plump for the 3-beer samplers. The food – crabcakes, gumbo and the like – isn't bad either.

The Dungeon

Map 4, E4. 738 Toulouse St at Bourbon ⓒ523-5530.

Gloomy Goth hideout, hidden away down a spooky side-alley.
It's said to appeal to visiting rock stars, who enjoy anonymity in
the murky web of nooks and crannies, and features good
specials, such as 3-for-1 drinks on Fridays from 1am to 4am.
Open Tues to Sun from midnight; $3 cover on weekends.

Keuffer's Bar

Map 4, E5. 540 Chartres St at Toulouse ⓒ523-8705.

Though it's smack bang in the heart of the Quarter, this
unpretentious neighborhood bar lacks any New Orleans
atmosphere, which, perversely, is part of its charm. A good
place to stop off for a couple of quiet beers and a game of pool.

Lafitte's Blacksmith Shop

Map 4, H3. 941 Bourbon St at St Philip ⓒ523-0066.

Dim, ancient wooden bar frequented by artists and writers
(how they see by the candlelight remains a mystery), and a few
stray tourists. One of the oldest buildings in the Quarter,
bought by notorious pirate Jean Lafitte in 1809 (see p.52),
it's a tumbledown shack with beamed ceilings and a blackened
brick fireplace (where Lafitte's treasure is said to be stashed).
In the evenings, a gloriously cheesy piano player pounds out
cocktail-lounge standards to a gaggle of drunken reprobates –
there's a pretty patio for those who want a quieter time.

Molly's at the Market

Map 4, J5. 1107 Decatur St at Ursulines ⓒ525-5169.

Once famed for being a genuine local Irish bar, haunt of
politicos and media stars, *Molly's* has been cleaned up and now
pulls in a younger, bored-looking crowd. Still, it has its
moments, and stays open during hurricane alerts, which says
something. There's a photobooth, and belly-filling greasy
Chinese food from the *China Dragon* restaurant around the back.

Napoleon House

Map 4, D5. 500 Chartres St at St Louis ℗524-9752.

Exuding a classic, relaxed New Orleans elegance, the *Napoleon House* is quite simply one of the best bars in the United States. The venerable building was once the home of Mayor Girod, who schemed with Jean Lafitte to rescue Napoleon from exile (see p.37); the shadowy interior is romantic in the extreme, its crumbling walls lined with ancient oil paintings and the old, well-stocked wooden bar dominated by a marble bust of the frowning emperor. The clientele, an interesting mix of tourists and regulars, dally for hours, either indoors, where the burble of chat mingles with the classical music on CD, or in the gorgeous courtyard, fringed with lush, green plants. The bar food (see p.158) and restaurant (see p.154) are superb, too. Closes at 7pm on Sun.

Pat O'Brien's

Map 4, F4. 718 St Peter St at Bourbon ℗525-4823.

One of the most famous bars in New Orleans, spilling over with drunken tourists and bellowing frat packs, most of them guzzling the requisite Hurricane cocktail, served in 29-oz hurricane-lamp glasses ($2 deposit). You can also get a Magnum of the stuff, three gallons-worth, served with a handful of straws. The three drinking areas include an outdoor patio and a raucous singalong "dueling" piano bar. If you love Bourbon Street you'll want to make a beeline for *Pat's*; if you don't, keep well away.

FAUBOURG MARIGNY

Apple Barrel

Map 4, M5. 609 Frenchmen St at Chartres ℗949-9399.

Tiny place beneath *Adolfo's* restaurant (see p.162). Its cozy, pub-like atmosphere (there's even a darts board) seems a little out of place on this supercool stretch, but it holds its own with a core group of laid-back regulars and drop-ins from hipsters on the Frenchmen bar-hop circuit.

DRINKING: FAUBOURG MARIGNY

Checkpoint Charlie's

Map 4, L5. 501 Esplanade Ave at Decatur ℗949-7012.
Boozy, dingy laundromat/bar, which occasionally hosts
unknown rock bands and serves sandwiches and burgers until
late. The young, grumpy crowd makes more of the pool tables,
slot machines and pinball than the incongruous lending library.

R-Bar

Map 4, M4. 1431 Royal St at Kerlerec ℗948-7499.
Friendly, attitude-free bar whose quirky, thrift-store decor –
Buddhist prayer flags, peeling bordello mirrors on the red walls,
1970s armchairs and the like – announces its bohemian creden-
tials. The pool table is played by some of the coolest sharks in
town, while the superb, eclectic jukebox features Elvis, the
Pogues, Al Green, klezmer and local boys the Soul Rebels,
among others. Popular with a youngish, convivial set, which
includes visitors staying at the guesthouse upstairs (see p.139).

THE CBD AND WAREHOUSE DISTRICT

Ernst Café

Map 3, M5. 600 S Peters St at Lafayette ℗525-8544.
Friendly, no-frills blue-collar joint – said to be a favorite of
honorary New Orleanian John Goodman – with pressed-tin
walls and a fine old wooden bar. Quiet during the day, it fills in
the evening with an older, mellower set of regulars than you'll
find in the CBD's other after-work haunts. Happy hour Fri
4–7pm.

Lucy's Retired Surfers' Bar

Map 3, L5. 701 Tchoupitoulas St at Girod ℗523-8995.
Gimmicky Warehouse District bar – something of a 20- and
early 30-somethings pick-up joint – heaving after office hours
with a winding-down, white-collar clientele. Trying to evoke
a West Coast scene, the walls are lined with surf boards, beach

DRINKING: FAUBOURG MARIGNY

movies flicker on the video and chirpy bar staff dole out
garish, frosted cocktails. It also serves decent Tex-Mex food.
Happy hour Mon–Fri 4–7pm.

Sazerac Bar

Map 3, 3N. *Fairmont Hotel*, 123 Baronne St at Canal ©529-4733.
Classy Art Deco bar in the grand old hotel that was, until
1965, the *Roosevelt* – check out the 1930s "Caribbean-Cubist"
murals by artist Paul Niñas. Serving champagne, fine wines,
tip-top cocktails and desirable desserts, it attracts a well-dressed
uptown and business traveller clientele – a very different scene
from the tumbledown French Quarter haunts, but just as much
part of the New Orleans landscape. It's the best place in town
to sip their signature cocktails (see p.181). Closed Sun.

Top of the Mart

Map 3, N5. *World Trade Center*, Canal St at the river ©522-9795.
The world's largest revolving cocktail bar, high in the sky on the
33rd story of the World Trade Center. Though you pay over
the odds for a drink, the ambience is appealingly kitsch, stuck
somewhere in the 1960s with its tired red and gilt decor, chandeliers and bored waitresses. Mostly, however, you come here
for the unbeatable views: one 90-minute revolution spans the
startling bend in the river across to the west bank, the tiny, congested grid of the French Quarter, the drab roofs of the CBD
high rises, and the poker-straight channel of Canal Street.

Vic's Kangaroo Cafe

Map 3, L5. 636 Tchoupitoulas St at Girod ©524-4329.
Just across the street from *Lucy's* (see opposite), *Vic's* is another
popular after-work Warehouse District joint, this one appealing
to a yuppier crowd. Its theme, unsurprisingly, is antipodean –
a mural showing flip-dry and drip-dry "dunnies" sets the tone.
The small mezzanine is almost entirely consumed by its pool
table; you can also retire up there to play darts.

LOWER GARDEN DISTRICT AND GARDEN DISTRICT

Audubon Hotel

Map 3, I5. 1225 St Charles Ave at Erato ©568-1319.

Not for the faint-hearted, this Lower Garden District flop-house-cum-techno-rave venue attracts a wild, eccentric band of lost souls, downing fatal cocktails as if their lives depended upon it.

Bayou Bar

Map 3, G5. *Pontchartrain Hotel*, 2031 St Charles Ave at St Andrew ©524-0581.

Civilized bar on the fringes of the Garden District. The ambience is very uptown New Orleans, all exposed brick walls and glossy dark wood, with a classy set sipping cocktails and spirits. It's said to be a favorite of local author Anne Rice, who has used it as a location in a number of her novels.

The Bulldog

Map 3, B5. 3236 Magazine St at Toledano ©891-1516.

Standard American bar with a youngish after-work crowd and lively, local scene at night. The appeal here is the wide range of beers – some 50 on tap and more than 200 in bottles – from around the world. Video trivia games are hugely popular, as are the occasional acoustic music sets.

Columns Hotel

Map 2, J6. 3811 St Charles Ave at General Taylor ©899-9308.

Gorgeous, atmospheric hotel (see p.141) on the edge of the Garden District, with a louche old bar, richly decorated in dark wood and faded velvets. You can drink in a number of rooms, all of which seep faded grandeur, with chandeliers, baroque mirrors, and vases of plump pink roses; on warm evenings, people make for the columned verandah, which overlooks the St Charles streetcar line. Tony Green and his gypsy jazz band play regular sets of fado, tango and French waltzes for a cover of around $6.

The Red Room
Map 3, G5. 2040 St Charles Ave at Josephine ℂ528-9759.
The Garden District's swanky restaurant/music venue (see pp.168 & 202) is also a very scarlet, very sexy bar. There's no better place if you're in the mood to dress up and sip on glamorous cocktails like the Red Passion – brandy, chambord, champagne, OJ and raspberries, served in a decadent goblet. No jeans.

UPTOWN

Carrollton Station
Map 2, C1. 8140 Willow St at Dublin ℂ865-9190.
Welcoming, laid-back neighborhood bar opposite the streetcar barn, near *Jimmy's* and the *Maple Leaf* (see p.202). Lots of good beers on draft, plus darts, and live music at weekends, when there's a small cover charge.

F&M Patio Bar
Map 2, G8. 4841 Tchoupitoulas St at Lyons ℂ895-6784.
Friendly, drunken, local hangout – a favorite on the post-*Tipitina's* (see p.203) circuit since the 1960s – with pool tables, a patio, great jukebox and cholesterol-packed snacks served till the wee hours. Traditionally it's *de rigueur* to guzzle Bloody Marys and dance on the pool table, but no one will mind if you don't.

Snake and Jake's Christmas Club Lounge
Map 2, D2. 7612 Oak St at Hilary ℂ861-2802.
Tumbledown shack, with perennial, Yuletide decorations fading fast in the gloom. Nothing much happens before 2am, when it fills up with a jubilant local crowd of musicians,

journalists and students. The jukebox is one of the best in town, with a playlist of New Orleans music, classic soul and r'n'b.

ELSEWHERE IN THE CITY

Ernie K-Doe's Mother-in-Law Lounge

Map 1, E6. 1500 N Claiborne Ave at Columbus, in Tremé ℗947-1078.

Stop by after 6pm to be served a beer by eccentric r'n'b veteran Ernie, who, along with his wife Antoinette, has simply fixed his home up with a bar and a few chairs, opened it to the public and called it a lounge. Sporadic music performances, usually on the weekend, often star the strutting, self-styled "Emperor of the World" himself (see p.203) and are an experience not to be missed. Take a cab there and back.

Saturn Bar

3067 St Claude Ave at Clouet, in the Bywater ℗949-7532.

Atmospheric, junk-filled neighborhood dive (it's an electrical repair shop by day), with a funky retro New Orleans cachet. The easy-going regulars – artists, intellectuals, and off-duty service industry workers – are often joined by hip out-of-town celebs (Nicolas Cage, Sam Shepard and the like). Take a cab there and back.

Live music

New Orleans is quite simply one of the best places in the world to hear **live music**. From lonesome street musicians, through the shambling, joyous brass bands, to international names like Dr John and the Neville Brothers, music remains integral to the Crescent City, the thread that keeps the whole place together. At any time of year – especially during the **festivals** – the sheer quantity, variety and quality of what's on offer is staggering.

For a history of New Orleans' music, with a discography of essential CDs, see p.284.

While the French Quarter has its share of atmospheric clubs and bars, there are plenty of good venues elsewhere. To decide **where to go**, check the listings papers *Offbeat* or *Gambit* (see p.8), and keep an ear cocked to local radio station WWOZ (90.7FM; see p.10), which announces local events and offers ticket competitions. You could also take pot-luck: most clubs have an eclectic booking policy, but as a rule you can be pretty sure of getting **brass bands** at *Donna's*, **modern jazz** at *Snug Harbor*, **trad jazz** at the *Palm Court* and *Preservation Hall*, rambunctious **blues** and **r'n'b** at the *Maple Leaf*, and a **mixed bag** at *Funky Butt* and both branches of *Tipitina's*.

Visitors making a beeline for **Bourbon Street**, hoping to find it crammed with cool, smoky jazz clubs, however, will be disappointed by the string of 3-for-1 cocktail stands, drab strip joints and karaoke bars. That said, even this tawdriest of streets has a couple of good places to hear jazz and blues, and at any time of day you may well stumble upon superb musicians playing happy-hour sets in even the dingiest alcohol-swilled dives.

As for timing your night out: with **24-hour drinking licenses** common (see p.182), the music often doesn't get going until around midnight, even if the show is listed as starting at 10pm. A number of places put on **two sets** a night, often by different performers, so with a little creative club-hopping you could easily see three outstanding gigs in one evening. Bear in mind also that **club hours** are always open to change, especially during Mardi Gras and JazzFest, when many places get started early and stay open for all-night jams.

....

Many musicians, especially those in the brass bands, get the bulk of their income from playing for tips. When in a club, always have a dollar or so ready for when the bucket is passed around.

....

Another distinctive feature of New Orleans' nightlife is that many shows can be seen – and heard – from the street. If you hear something you like, but don't want to pay the **cover charge** – low or nonexistent in bars, but as much as $20 in some clubs – it's perfectly acceptable to stand outside with a "to go" cup (see p.183), moving on when the fancy takes you.

Oddly, for a city so defined by its music, it can be difficult to predict how big a **crowd** will turn up to a gig. New Orleans is a small place, with a lot of clubs, and occasionally, especially during quiet times, you may find yourself in

LIVE MUSIC

the extraordinary position of sitting with just two or three others, listening to a local legend who has sold out the place the night before.

JAZZ

Jazz in New Orleans remains a living, evolving art form, and you're spoiled for choice for places to see it. Local, world-class musicians, including the multi-talented **Marsalis** family, **trumpeters** Terence Blanchard, Irvin Mayfield and Nicholas Payton, and **scat** singer Charmaine Neville (of *the* Nevilles) all play regularly. Of the **pianists**, don't miss Henry Butler – whose superb, superfast modern jazz is matched by his mean r'n'b and blues repertoire – or Davell Crawford, who infuses traditional New Orleans piano with heartfelt gospel.

Jazz funerals – decorous affairs, with dirges and hymns expressing grief, followed by a burst of musical joy at the prospect of eternal life – now occur only occasionally, in the poorest neighborhoods, and are by no means tourist attractions.

Two of the city's best-loved performers, trumpeters **Kermit Ruffins** and younger pup James Andrews, can always be counted on for a good show. Both cut their teeth in local **brass bands**, the ragtag groups of musicians who blast out New Orleans' homegrown party music, born from the city's long tradition of street parades. Regulars on the circuit include the **ReBirth** (Ruffins' old crew); the **Lil Rascals**, **New Birth** and **Hot 8** brass bands, whose ear-splitting spin on traditional tunes is as big a hit in the parades as in the jazz clubs; and the fresh "street" sounds of the **Soul Rebels** and **Coolbone**, who mix a fabulous cacophony of horns with hard funk, hip-hop and reggae.

On any given night you'll find at least one brass band playing at least one club, but it's even more fun to catch them at
neighborhood bars, parades and festivals, when they really
let rip, surrounded by the community that supports them.
These are some of the hardest-working musicians in town:
don't be surprised to find that the crowd of horn-blasting
buskers in Jackson Square is made up of the phenomenal
musicians you paid $5 to see the night before.

For details of Dixieland **jazz cruises** along the
Mississippi, see p.89.

THE FRENCH QUARTER

Donna's
Map 4, G1. 800 N Rampart St at St Ann ℗596-6914.
Mon & Wed–Sun from 8pm.
Run by the formidable Donna and husband Charlie, *Donna's*
feels like a locals' place – there's no stage, you have to fight your
way through the blasting horns to get to the bathroom, and
they fire up regular barbecues out on the street – but it attracts a
big out-of-town crowd, who tend to get hooked after one visit.
With a varied roster of acts – old timers, newer young bands,
Afro-Caribbean nights – it's a must-see, especially during
JazzFest and Mardi Gras. Cover varies; one drink minimum.

Fritzel's European Jazz Pub
Map 4, F3. 733 Bourbon St at Orleans ℗561-0432.
Daily 5pm–2am.
Hokey-looking German-themed bar that showcases some of
the best trad jazz on Bourbon Street, with late shows Friday to
Sunday and after-hours jams. No cover; one drink minimum.

Funky Butt
Map 4, G1. 714 N Rampart St at Orleans ℗558-0872.
Daily 9pm–2am.

Stylish, intimate and atmospheric club named after an early haunt of jazz legend Buddy Bolden. The eclectic decor resembles an Art Deco bordello-cum-Seventies pad, while the music – mostly contemporary jazz and r'n'b – is consistently exceptional, and they serve pasta, po-boys and gumbo upstairs. On a good night many people drift between here and *Donna's* (see opposite). Cover varies, rising to $15, but you can drink in the bar for free.

John Wehner's Famous Door

Map 4, C3. 339 Bourbon St at Conti ©522-7626.
Daily 8pm–2am.
Venerable trad jazz club, open since 1934. A plaque by the door lists the many celebrities who have performed here – including Louis Armstrong and Harry Connick Jr (who played the club when he was just 13); today you'll hear sets by the polished house band and occasional big names.
No cover; one drink minimum.

Palm Court Jazz Café

Map 4, J5. 1204 Decatur St at Gov Nicholls ©525-0200.
Wed–Sun 7–11pm.
The jazz aficionado's favorite: top-notch trad jazz played in elegant supper-club surroundings. New Orleans jazz memorabilia adds atmosphere, and they sell collector's items and records. Reservations are recommended for dinner.
Cover varies, but a seat at the bar costs nothing.

Preservation Hall

Map 4, F4. 726 St Peter St at Bourbon ©522-2841.
Daily 8pm–midnight.
Shabby old room – with no seats, bar, air conditioning or toilets – long lauded as the best place to hear trad jazz in New Orleans. Though the ersatz dereliction (contrary to popular belief, it's only been open since the 1960s) and over-reverent

JAZZ: THE FRENCH QUARTER

tourist audiences can be off-putting, the music, played by old pros, is unquestionably good. The Hall is always bursting at the seams, with lines forming well before the doors open. Sets are at 9pm and 11pm; you can stay for both. Cover $4.

Storyville District
Map 4, A3. 125 Bourbon St at Iberville ©410-1000.
Daily noon–3pm & 5.30pm–1am; food served 11.30am–3pm & 5pm–midnight.
Swish "entertainment complex", with bars, dining areas (it's part-owned by Ralph Brennan of the city's famous restaurant clan) and two stages featuring live music, from ragtime through big bands to modern jazz. Geared toward tourists, it feels rather sanitized, with admittedly superb acts turning out trad jazz background music for a low or non-existent cover charge.

ELSEWHERE

....

Call a cab (see p.12) to get to and from any of the music venues outside the French Quarter.

....

Joe's Cozy Corner
Map 1, F6. 1030 N Robertson St at Ursulines, in Tremé; no phone.
Daily 24hr.
Few tourists head out to this friendly local bar, where on Sunday evenings Kermit Ruffins plays a jubilant end-of-the-week set to a noisy crowd of friends and family. Tremé, just a few blocks from the Quarter, can be dangerous, and it may be difficult to get a cab to pick you up; book one in advance, and check *Offbeat* first to make sure there'll be live music. Cover varies.

Snug Harbor
Map 4, N5. 626 Frenchmen St at Royal ©949-0696.

Daily 5pm–2am.

Excellent Faubourg Marigny jazz club, in a small, vaguely nautical-looking space packed tight with tables and chairs. Shows start at 9pm and 11pm, but the restaurant (serving pasta, burgers and the like) and bar stay open after the music stops. Regulars include Astral Project, who play cool modern jazz, Charmaine Neville, and Ellis Marsalis. Cover $5–25.

Vaughan's

4229 Dauphine St at Lesseps, in the Bywater district ℂ947-5562.
Daily 11am–3am.

Tiny neighborhood bar that fills to bursting on Thursday, Kermit Ruffins' night. It's all very convivial, with the band crammed right up against the hard-dancing audience – a mixed bunch of locals, high-spirited students and the players' friends and family; between sets, help yourself to all-you-can-eat beans and rice from a massive pot. Cover $5.

OTHER LIVE MUSIC

There's far more to New Orleans than jazz. Though the "**New Orleans sound**", an exuberant, carnival-tinged hybrid of blues, parade music and r'n'b, had its heyday in the early 1960s, many of its greatest stars are still going strong. Check listings papers for gigs by the Neville Brothers; the fabulous Ernie K-Doe, of the shiny suits, big hair and lung-bursting vocals; Eddie Bo, who hots up traditional barrelhouse piano with funk and soul; and "soul queen of New Orleans" Irma Thomas, whose classics *Breakaway*, *It's Raining* and *Ruler of My Heart* send shivers down the spine every time. Super-talented songwriter-producer Allen Toussaint, who gave many of them their big breaks, is still hard at work, too, showcasing new acts in his weekly sets at *Tipitina's French Quarter*.

In recent years, the **swing** revival has taken off in a big way in New Orleans: jumping and jiving Johnny Angel dominates the scene, dragging behind him a die-hard following of hip young things dressed to the nines and sipping fancy cocktails. **Latin** music is popular, too, along with **funk** – the funky Meters, Art Neville's old group, still play regularly, as do the supercharged Galactic. If you want to see New Orleanians really let rip, try to catch a rare gig by longtime local heroes The Radiators, whose noisy blend of r'n'b, funk and rock brings the house down. **Blues** fans should look out for guitarists Snooks Eaglin and Walter "Wolfman" Washington, the younger, Delta blues-influenced John Mooney and, for powerful gospel-blues, the formidable Marva Wright.

Though many people associate New Orleans with **Cajun** music, it's not indigenous to the city: that said, locals do love to *fais-do-do* (the Cajun two-step), and there are a couple of fantastic places to dance to **zydeco**, its bluesier black relation. The city has also taken **klezmer** to its heart, and in particular the local Klezmer Allstars, who bang out a frenzied blend of Yiddish folk, jazz and funk. Finally, for something totally unique, scour the listings for **Mardi Gras Indians** (see p.274) such as the Wild Magnolias or Golden Eagles, whose rare gigs – you're most likely to catch them around Mardi Gras or JazzFest – are some of the funkiest, most extraordinary performances you're ever likely to see.

THE FRENCH QUARTER

House of Blues
Map 4, B5. 225 Decatur St at Iberville ©529-2583.
Daily 8pm–3am; food served 11am–midnight.
Enormous, slick venue, part of the national chain, with Southern folk art-themed decor. While the high prices and un-New Orleans attitude (the bouncers and wrist tags led early

detractors to nickname it "House of Rules") can be off-putting, they book the best in everything from blues, funk, reggae and zydeco to rap, hip-hop and rock. Big names have included Bob Dylan, Ray Charles and Johnny Cash, as well as local stars like the Nevilles and Dr John. Gospel brunch on Sun (10am & 1pm; call to reserve) and DJ nights on Mon, Thurs and Fri. Cover varies.

Levon Helm's Classic American Café
Map 4, C6. 300 Decatur St at Bienville ℅592-2582.
Daily 6pm until late.
Squeaky clean, newish place, owned by the former drummer of The Band, who books high-caliber rock, blues and r'n'b. The café serves burgers, gumbo and the like. Free swing and jazz daily from 1pm; cover varies after 8pm.

To glimpse Bourbon Street bawd at its old-fashioned best, check out Chris Owens' one-woman variety show. Glitzy, spangly and unashamedly camp, Chris has been high-kicking and grinding for years; you'll find her at 500 Bourbon St.

Tipitina's French Quarter
Map 4, B6. 233 N Peters St at Iberville ℅566-7095.
Daily 11am–2am.
Geared toward tourists who've heard of the famed uptown venue (see p.203) but don't want to leave the Quarter, this newer branch of *Tip's* lacks the atmosphere of its older sibling and can feel oddly empty, even when it's rocking with a "gonna-have-fun-if-it-kills-me" crowd. It features a great line-up, though, with weekly gigs from Harry Connick Sr, Henry Butler and Kermit Ruffins (who hosts a swing brunch on Sunday), along with Allen Toussaint and Cyril Neville, both of whom showcase new talent. Cover varies.

FAUBOURG MARIGNY

Café Brasil
Map 4, M5. 2100 Chartres St at Frenchmen ©947-9386.
Mon–Thurs & Sun 6pm–2am, Fri & Sat 6pm–4am.
Minimalist, arty club at the heart of the Faubourg scene,
with eclectic live music (Latin, jazz, klezmer, reggae,
world), poetry readings and a small adjoining bar (where
they crank the CD player up loud in order to drown out
the bands). The young, gorgeous crowd often spills onto
Frenchmen Street, mingling with the fallout from the
Dream Palace opposite to create a lively block party. Cover
varies.

Dragon's Den
Map 4, L6. 435 Esplanade Ave at Frenchmen ©949-1750.
Daily 6pm–3am.
Bohemian, opium-den style bar/club above the *Siam Café*
(see p.163), where bright young things loll on velvet floor
cushions eat at the low tables, or dance like demons to r'n'b,
blues, jazz and brass bands. Some seating on the perilously
decrepit balcony. There's a wild poetry slam on Thursday;
Monday is 2-for-1 sake night. Low or no cover.

Dream Palace
Map 4, M5. 534 Frenchmen St at Chartres ©945-2040.
Daily 8pm–2am.
One of the longest established Faubourg clubs and still one
of the best, usually packed with friendly, enthusiastic locals
dancing to hot reggae, Latin and world music, local funk and
brass bands. Hop between this and the *Brasil*, opposite, for a
great New Orleans night out. Cover varies.

THE CBD AND WAREHOUSE DISTRICT

Howlin' Wolf
Map 3, L6. 828 S Peters St at Julia ⓒ523-2551.
Mon–Sat 3pm till late.
Big, bare-bones Warehouse District club that attracts a mixed
bunch of cool young locals and tourists. Mostly alternative
rock, with some funk and r'n'b, and open mike nights.
Cover varies.

Mermaid Lounge
Map 3, J6. 1102 Constance St at John Churchill Chase
ⓒ524-4747.
Tues–Sat 9pm–3am.
Hidden away down a dead-end alley in the Warehouse District,
this tiny, noisy local bar features a mixed bag of garage, punk,
klezmer, Cajun (the ancient Hackberry Ramblers always go down
a storm with the college crowd), blues and funk. Cover varies.

Mulate's
Map 3, L6. 201 Julia St at Convention Center Blvd ⓒ522-1492.
Daily 11am–11pm.
Very touristy Cajun restaurant, filled with conventioneers
determinedly two-stepping to first-rate live bands (from 7pm).
Good fun, but not a patch on *Tipitina's* weekly *fais-do-do*
(see p.203) or *Mid-City Lanes'* zydeco nights (see p.204).

Praline Connection Gospel and Blues Hall
Map 3, L6. 907 S Peters St at St Joseph ⓒ523-3973.
Mon–Thurs 11am–10.30pm, Fri & Sat 11am–midnight,
Sun gospel brunch 11am & 2pm.
Black Creole restaurant that puts on a gospel brunch with an
all-you-can-eat soul-food buffet, and from Thursday to
Saturday offers live music while you dine. It's especially lively
during JazzFest, when it hosts official festival concerts.

OTHER LIVE MUSIC: THE CBD AND WAREHOUSE DISTRICT

201

LOWER GARDEN DISTRICT AND GARDEN DISTRICT

Le Bon Temps Roulé
Map 2, H7. 4801 Magazine St at Bordeaux ©895-8117.

Daily 11am–3am.

Long-running, convivial neighborhood bar – the name comes
from the Cajun phrase meaning "let the good times roll" –
with occasional live music (blues, acoustic, brass, zydeco and
rock), food specials (free red beans and rice, oysters for 25¢),
a wide selection of beers and a patio. Clientele is a spirited mix
of locals and hard-drinking students. Low or no cover.

The Red Room
Map 3, G5. 2040 St Charles Ave at Josephine ©528-9759.

Mon–Sat 6pm–2am.

Smooth cocktail bar (see p.189), restaurant (see p.168) and
music venue, on the fringes of the Garden District. At the fore-
front of the city's swing revival, with regular sets from locals'
sweetheart Johnny Angel, it also features jazz and Latin bands,
attracting a supercool uptown set. Cover varies; no jeans.

UPTOWN

Jimmy's
Map 2, C1. 8200 Willow St at Dublin ©861-8200.

Tues–Sat 8pm–3am.

Long-established rock club, with a big dance floor, usually
commandeered by raucous students; it also books Latin,
hip-hop and reggae bands. Cover varies.

Maple Leaf Bar
Map 2, B1. 8316 Oak St at Dante ©866-9359.

Daily 3pm–4am.

Friendly old bar with pressed-tin walls, a dance floor and a
patio. Open for 25 years, it's much beloved of locals, who fill

the place – and the sidewalk outside – for a nightly menu of fantastic Cajun, zydeco, r'n'b, brass bands (ReBirth play every Tues) and blues (don't miss Walter "Wolfman" Washington). There's chess and pool, too, and poetry on Sunday afternoons. Cover varies.

Neutral Ground Coffeehouse

Map 2, G5. 5110 Danneel St at Soniat ©891-3381.

Tues–Thurs & Sun 8pm–midnight, Fri & Sat 8pm–1am.

Tucked away, grungy co-op featuring live acoustic, folk and wistful country music, plus regular poetry readings. The earnest crowd is mostly below-drinking age, sipping coffee and playing chess and backgammon. No cover.

Tipitina's Uptown

Map 2, I8. 501 Napoleon Ave at Tchoupitoulas ©897-3943.

Daily 6pm–2am.

Legendary venue, named for a Professor Longhair song and sporting a banner with his likeness above the stage. Though there's a smaller branch in the Quarter (see p.199), this is the original and still the best, with a consistently good funk, r'n'b, brass and reggae line-up, spanning the range from local favorites to national acts. The Cajun *fais-do-do* (Sun 5–9pm) is great fun, too, with free red beans and rice. Cover varies.

ELSEWHERE

Ernie K-Doe's Mother-in-Law Lounge

Map 1, E6. 1500 N Claiborne Ave at Columbus, in Tremé ©947-1078.

Daily 6pm till late.

Difficult to categorize venue – bar/club/living room – in the home of flamboyant r'n'b veteran Ernie K-Doe. A great place for a drink (see p.190), it's even better during one of Ernie's shows, when he invariably belts out the eponymous 1950s hit to a motley crew of die-hard fans, family and thrill-seeking hipsters. Unmissable. Call to ask about music; cover varies.

Lion's Den

Map 1, D6. 2655 Gravier St at Broad Ave, in Mid-City ℗822-4693.
Days and hours vary.

Tiny club part-owned by r'n'b legend Irma Thomas, who performs occasionally, especially during festivals (check listings magazines, or call), when she may even prepare beans and rice for her devoted fans. The neighborhood is desolate; take a taxi. Cover varies.

Mid-City Lanes Rock'n'Bowl

Map 1, D5. 4133 S Carrollton Ave at Tulane, in Mid-City ℗482-3133.
Daily noon–2am.

Eccentric bowling alley-cum-live music venue in an unprepossessing mall. Though it's especially heaving on Wednesday and Thursday – when zydeco greats Beau Jocque and Boozoo Chavis stir the crowd into such a frenzy that you can barely hear the clanging of the bowling balls – they also book good local r'n'b, blues and swing. There's another stage downstairs at Bowl Me Under; on 2-for-1 nights you can dash from floor to floor, in between trying to get a strike. Fantastic fun, especially if you're in a group. Take a taxi. Cover varies.

Theater and the arts

—

Despite the city's long association with the **performing arts** – from the earliest years of the French colony, when short dramas were performed in private drawing rooms, through to the nineteenth-century golden era, when theaters, ballrooms, and the glorious French Opera House were packed every night – few visitors come to New Orleans for opera or the ballet. However, while the high-arts scene poses little competition for bigger, wealthier cities – arts funding is pitifully low – New Orleans does have respected **operatic** and **orchestral** companies, a small **ballet** company, a couple of **rep theaters** and a handful of places showcasing **avant-garde** and experimental works. There's little in the way of comedy, but **spoken word** performances have a loyal, if small, following in local bars – the *Maple Leaf* (see p.202) and the *Dragon's Den* (p.200) feature regular poetry readings and open mike nights.

Though America's first purpose-built cinema opened on Canal Street in 1896, it's long since been torn down, and New Orleans today aren't great film-goers.

Nonetheless, the city does have its fair share of mainstream cinemas and a few places to catch independent and art-house **movies**.

For a filmography of movies made in or about New Orleans, see p.293.

One of the best things about the high-art scene in New Orleans is the **Louisiana Philharmonic Orchestra** (℃523-6530), owned by its members, which puts on fine classical concerts at the grand old Orpheum Theater; tickets cost between $15 and $50. The highly regarded **New Orleans Opera Association** (℃529-2278) and the **New Orleans Ballet Association** (℃522-0996) both stage short, well-received seasons at the Mahalia Jackson Theater of the Performing Arts; tickets start at $30.

To check what's happening on any particular night, check the **listings** pages of *Gambit*, or the *Lagniappe* supplement of the *Times-Picayune* (see p.8).

THEATERS AND PERFORMANCE VENUES

Contemporary Arts Center
Map 3, K5. 900 Camp St at St Joseph ℃523-1216.
Modern gallery and performance space in the Warehouse District, hosting touring and one-off art exhibitions, dance, performance art, video installations, art-house movies and experimental theater. For more on the CAC, see p.72.

Mahalia Jackson Theater of the Performing Arts
Map 4, G1. Louis Armstrong Park, Rampart St at St Ann ℃565-7470.
Large, lavish setting for touring musicals, classical concerts, opera and ballet, ice spectaculars, fights and so on.

Municipal Auditorium
Map 4, G1. Louis Armstrong Park, Rampart St at St Ann
Ⓒ565-7470.
Another large venue for touring companies and big concerts.

Orpheum Theater
Map 3, M3. 129 University Place at Canal Ⓒ524-3285.
Historic venue, built in 1918 as a vaudeville theater and movie
house. Today, seeping faded grandeur, it makes a characterful
base for the Philharmonic Orchestra.

Petit Théâtre du Vieux Carré
Map 4, F5. 616 St Peter St at Chartres Ⓒ522-2081.
The nation's longest-running community theater, formed in
1919 by the Drawing Room Players, who first trod the boards
in private homes. Nowadays, the building, on the corner of
Jackson Square in the French Quarter, is a pretty setting for
middle-of-the-road musicals, comedies and drama, and an
atmospheric venue for the annual Tennessee Williams
Literary Festival (see p.249).

Saenger Theater
Map 4, A1. 143 N Rampart St at Canal Ⓒ524-2490.
Beautifully restored 1920s movie theater, replete with classical
statuary, glittering chandeliers, and, best of all, a star-spangled
night-sky ceiling. It's a lovely, special-occasion venue for
touring Broadway productions and big-name concerts.

Southern Rep Theater
Map 4, A7. Canal Place shopping mall, 333 Canal St Ⓒ861-8163.
Conveniently situated, intimate venue in one of downtown's
best malls (see p.211). For most of the year, it features the work
of Southern playwrights – up-and-coming and established –
performed by local actors; it also doubles as a movie theater
during the annual film festival (see p.251).

THEATERS AND PERFORMANCE VENUES |

State Palace Theater

Map 4, A1. 1108 Canal St at N Rampart ☏522-4435.
Gorgeous old theater hosting big-name rock concerts and
notorious for its occasional raves.

Superdome

Map 3, K2. Sugar Bowl Drive ☏587-3800.
Gargantuan stadium variously used for Saints' football games,
teeming trade shows and overblown rock concerts. For more
on the building and its history, see p.72.

True Brew Theater

Map 3, L6. 200 Julia St at Fulton ☏522-2907.
Eighty-seat theater in a Warehouse District coffee house
(see p.177). Shows, usually on the weekend, tend to be short
dramas or comedies of local interest, and there's some
stand-up comedy.

Zeitgeist Alternative Arts Center

Map 3, G7. 2010 Magazine St at St Andrew ☏524-0064.
Avant-garde arts center on lower Magazine Street, with two
movie screens (lots of gay, lesbian and world cinema),
performance space and a gallery.

CINEMAS

For details of the **New Orleans Film and Video
Festival**, held each October, see p.251.

Joy

Map 3, N2. 1200 Canal St at Elk Place ☏522-7575.
Downtown cinema screening the latest mainstream releases.

Landmark Cinemas at Canal Place

Map 4, A7. Canal Place shopping mall, 333 Canal St ☏581-5400.

Conveniently located in a high-quality downtown mall (see p.211), this four-screen cinema features the best mainstream releases along with independents and world cinema. In October, it's the main venue for the film festival (see p.251).

Movie Pitchers
Map 1, D5. 3941 Bienville St at N Pierce ℂ488-8881.
Four-screen Mid-City cinema, a must for cinephiles for its interesting program of independent and art-house movies.

Prytania
Map 2, F6. 5339 Prytania St at Leontine ℂ891-2787.
Atmospheric, if shabby, old uptown movie theater showing art-house, Hollywood and independent movies. Also a venue for the city's annual film festival (see p.251).

CINEMAS

Shopping

Shopping in New Orleans, where mega-malls play second fiddle to small, stylish stores, can be a lot of fun. In a place where hanging out is a priority, most visitors spend a lot of time browsing and window shopping, whether their budget extends to a framed WeeGee original or to funky one-of-a-kind crafts by local designers.

The **French Quarter** has its share of tacky tourist shops hawking T-shirts, ersatz voodoo *gris-gris* and cheap little ceramic masks – but beyond these are some superb antique shops (concentrated on Royal Street, the "Main Street" of the old Creole city), and individualistic places to buy art, clothes, books and music.

On Saturdays, when the Quarter can get choked with tourists, you're best off heading for the antique shops, thrift stores and workshops along six-mile **Magazine Street**, which starts at Canal in the CBD and runs through the Warehouse and Garden Districts to Audubon Park. You could also spend a weekend browsing in the Riverbend area around **Maple Street**, the student uptown district on the streetcar line. If you've got serious money to spend on contemporary art, head for the galleries of the **Arts District** (see p.66).

Sadly, the fine old department stores that once graced **Canal Street** are slowly disappearing; the elegant buildings

Shopping categories

Antiques	p.212
Art, prints, posters and maps	p.216
Books	p.219
Clothes and accessories	p.222
Costumes, masks and disguises	p.225
Food and drink	p.227
Gifts	p.228
Health and beauty	p.231
Malls	p.211
Music	p.232

are filled today with questionable electrical stores, luggage stores, fast-food outlets, and sportswear chains. If you're looking for a department store, head for the **malls**.

....

**For details of Louisiana's Tax Free shopping scheme,
whereby the state's nine percent sales tax is
reimbursed to foreign visitors, see p.256.**

....

MALLS

Canal Place
Map 4, A7. 333 Canal St at N Peters ©522-9200.
Mon–Wed 10am–6pm, Thurs–Sat 10am–7pm, Sun noon–6pm.
Tranquil and upmarket, featuring the deli/kitchen store Williams Sonoma, Pottery Barn, Laura Ashley, Saks Fifth Avenue, Jaeger, Gucci and the shop of local jewelry designer Mignon Faget. It also has a **cinema** showing independent movies (see p.208), **rep theater** (see p.207) and **gym** (see p.254). The food court isn't bad, but you're near enough to the Quarter to give it a miss.

SHOPPING: MALLS

211

Jackson Brewery (JAX)

Map 4, E6. Decatur St between Toulouse and St Peter ℂ566-7245.
Mon Sat 10am–9pm, Sun 10am–7pm.

More than fifty stores housed in restored 1891 brewery buildings dominated by Planet Hollywood and the Virgin Megastore (see p.233). Among the ubiquitous pralines, hot sauces, T-shirts and crawfish-emblazoned neckties, you'll find branches of Gray Line, Denim Depot, The Limited and Sunglass Hut.

Riverwalk

Map 3, M7. 1 Poydras St, on the Mississippi ℂ522-1555.
Mon–Sat 10am–9pm, Sun 11am–7pm.

Bustling, touristy mall running half a mile along the river from the Convention Center to the Plaza d'España, providing an easy conduit from the Warehouse District to the French Quarter. Its three stories (still undergoing repair since a boat plowed into the side in 1996) feature some 150 shops, including DeVille Books (see p.221), Disney Store, Banana Republic, The Gap, Warner Bros, Victoria's Secret, Body Shop, Crabtree and Evelyn, Tie Rack and Cookin' Cajun cooking school (see p.172). There's also a *Café du Monde* (see p.174) and a good food court where you can eat outside above the river.

ANTIQUES AND VINTAGE STORES

New Orleans is a world-class **antiques center**. You'll need serious money if you want to buy from the places on elegant **Royal Street**, many of which have been trading since the late 1800s. If your budget doesn't stretch to Persian rugs or eighteenth-century armoires, check out the vintage stores along the 1100 and 1200 blocks of **Decatur Street**: great for bric-a-brac and funky retro furniture. Or go store-hopping along **Magazine Street**, where thrift stores sit alongside classy antiques warehouses.

Let's go antiquing

If you're short of time, or simply overwhelmed by the choice, Macon Riddle at **Let's Go Antiquing** (☏899-3027; *hillrid@aol.com*) leads customized shopping expeditions. She'll take up to six people in one trip, but doesn't mix groups, and charges upwards of $50 an hour for a minimum of three hours. Simply tell her what you want and she'll take you where you can find it; if you're looking for a particular piece, give her details and measurements and she'll come up with a range of choices.

For antique **maps** and **prints** see p.216; for rare and antique **books**, see p.219.

Animal Arts
Map 4, E5. 617 Chartres St at Wilkinson Row ☏529-4407.
Mon–Sat 10am–5pm.
Animal themed antiques – oil paintings, ceramics, upholstery, Majolica, Palissy. Also large pieces of wooden furniture.

Barakat
Map 4, H4. 934 Royal St at Dumaine ☏593-9944.
Mon & Thurs–Sun 11am–5pm.
Funky junk, Fifties furniture, coffee sets and the like, along with a host of primitive rural furniture, textiles and old postcards.

James H. Cohen
Map 4, D4. 437 Royal St at Conti ☏522-3305.
Daily 9.30am–5.15pm.
Musty specialist store dealing in rare coins and antique weapons; though the bulk of the stuff dates from the Civil War (flags, photos, swords, cannonballs, muskets), there are also presidential buttons, vintage magazine ads and ancient coins.

SHOPPING: ANTIQUES AND VINTAGE STORES

Dixon and Dixon

Map 4, B4. 237 Royal St at Iberville ©524-0282.
Mon–Sat 9am–5.30pm, Sun 10am–5pm.
Huge, friendly, long-established store selling seventeenth- to
nineteenth-century English, French and Dutch antiques,
oil paintings, jewelry, tall case clocks and Persian rugs.

Jon Antiques

Map 2, H7. 4605 Magazine St at Valence ©899-4482.
Mon–Sat 10am–5pm.
Established store offering choice antiques in a homely
environment: they specialize in eighteenth- and nineteenth-
century English and French furniture, Staffordshire pottery,
glass, porcelain, lighting and bric-a-brac.

Gerald D. Katz

Map 4, D4. 505 Royal St at St Louis ©524-5050.
Daily 10am–5.30pm.
Gorgeous old store, with banks of antique jewelry (mostly
nineteenth-century), plus fine china and oil paintings.

Keil's

Map 4, C4. 325 Royal St at Conti ©522-4552.
Mon–Sat 9am–5pm.
Trading since 1898, with an imposing double storefront
opening onto a showroom of eighteenth- and nineteenth-
century French and English furniture, chandeliers and jewelry.
Some good prices.

Lucullus

Map 4, E5. 610 Chartres St at Wilkinson Row ©528-9620.
Sept–May Mon–Sat 9.30am–5.30pm;
June–Aug closed Mon.
Intriguing collection of dining-related antiques – coffee pots,
table linens, earthenware jars, cut-glass decanters, oyster

SHOPPING: ANTIQUES AND VINTAGE STORES

214

forks, candlesticks – dating from the 1600s onwards. It's
named for the Roman general who held notoriously lavish
banquets. There's another branch at 3932 Magazine St
(©894-0500).

Manheim Galleries
Map 4, D4. 409 Royal St at Conti ©568-1901.
Mon–Sat 9am–5pm.
Run by the same family for generations, in a building designed
as a bank by Benjamin Latrobe. Famed for their collections of
jade and porcelain Boehm birds, they also have paintings,
wooden furniture, tapestries and Oriental pieces.

Moss Antiques
Map 4, D4. 411 Royal St at Conti ©522-3981.
Mon–Sat 9am–5pm.
A favorite with serious buyers seeking out eighteenth-
and nineteenth-century French and English furniture and
decorative arts, including porcelain and Baccarat crystal.
Also walking sticks and precious and semi-precious jewelry.

Nineteenth-Century Antiques
Map 2, H7. 4838 Magazine St at Lyons ©891-4845.
Mon–Sat 10am–5pm.
Established store selling a jumble of smaller, quality pieces,
including a fantastic selection of unusual clocks and watches,
china and cut glass.

Orient Expressed Imports
Map 2, I7. 3905 Magazine St at General Pershing ©899-3060.
Mon–Sat 10am–5pm.
Eclectic, sprawling shop that sells unusual antiques and imports
including Mexican wooden *santo* figures, masks and icons, and
antique Chinese ancestors. Also contemporary gifts, including
cushions, candles and children's clothes.

M.S. Rau

Map 4, E4. 630 Royal St at Toulouse ✆523-5660.

Mon–Sat 9am–5.15pm.

Third-generation-owned store, specializing in nineteenth-century American antiques, with chandeliers, silver, ironwork, Cartier and Tiffany jewelry, and pieces by Prudence Mallard, New Orleans' foremost nineteenth-century cabinet maker.

Royal Antiques

Map 4, C4. 309 Royal St at Bienville ✆524-7403.

Mon–Sat 9am–5pm.

French and English eighteenth- and nineteenth-century furniture and chandeliers. Also a good selection of brass work.

Vintage 429

Map 4, D4. 429 Royal St at St Louis ✆529-2288.

Mon–Thurs 10am–6pm, Fri & Sat 10am–6.30pm.

Stylish store, specializing in autographs – from local boy Kermit Ruffins through Mohammed Ali and Elvis to Greta Garbo (whose autographed and framed photo will set you back close to $4000). Cheaper stuff includes 1950s cocktail sets, cigarette cases and concert posters, plus pens and postcards.

ART, PRINTS, POSTERS AND MAPS

There are scores of places to buy **art** in New Orleans, from the cheapest poster to the classiest antique painting, and a whole lot of distinctive, interesting stuff in between. It seems that every second shop in the Quarter, especially along Decatur and Royal, sells **posters** and **prints** – the overload can be enervating, especially as the same, tired images come up time and time again. Best buys include official and unofficial JazzFest and Mardi Gras posters, reproduction historical prints, and old maps.

Don't overlook the artists who display their work in **Jackson Square** – along with portraits and caricatures, usually at very low prices, you'll find abstracts, quirky local scenes, and folk art (look out for Big Al Taplet, whose humorous, boldly colored ads for his shoe-shine service, painted on slates, have become collectibles). All works are originals.

If your budget for artworks runs to **fine oil paintings**, see the antiques stores listed on pp.212–16. And if you're in the market for **cutting-edge works**, check the Arts District galleries on p.67.

Bergen Galleries
Map 4, F4. 730 Royal St at Orleans ©523-7882.
Daily 9am–9pm.
Huge print and poster store, featuring local artists Michalopoulos (vivid, dreamlike streetscapes) and Rodrigue (whose little blue dog pops up everywhere), along with Vargas and Erté, etchings, and the best JazzFest and Mardi Gras posters. They ship worldwide.

Berta's and Mina's Antiquities
Map 2, I7. 4138 Magazine St at Jena ©895-6201.
Daily 10am–6pm.
Misleadingly named store crammed full with the inventive folk art of Nicaraguan-born Nilo Lanzas, who started painting at the age of 63. Brash dioramas, many of them painted on old wooden window frames, his works show quirky biblical and rural scenes, or depict life in the imaginary town of Niloville.

Cassel Gallery
Map 4, G4. 818 Royal St at St Ann ©524-0671.
Daily 10am–6pm.
A warren of prints, posters and old illustrations, hanging on every inch of wall space, in piles on the floor and on racks.

SHOPPING: ART, PRINTS, POSTERS AND MAPS

There's the whole gamut of New Orleans stuff, along with old
magazine illustrations, fashion plates and collectible stamps.

The Centuries
Map 4, D5. 517 St Louis St at Decatur ℗568-9491.
Mon–Thurs & Sun 10.30am–6pm, Fri & Sat 10.30am–6.30pm.
Antique prints and maps, engravings and etchings. The print
bins are well labeled, and the laid-back staff are happy to let you
browse. Categories include architecture, towns and countries.

A Gallery for Fine Photography
Map 4, C4. 322 Royal St at Bienville ℗568-1313.
Daily 10am–6pm.
Superb place, more of a gallery than a store. Many prices are in
four figures, and rare platinum prints go for at least $12,500.
Works date from as early as 1839 and include pictures by
Edward S. Curtis, Jacques-Henri Lartigue, WeeGee, Diane
Arbus, Helmut Lang and David Bailey. Look out for Walker
Frans' photos of the 1930s French Quarter, a host of jazz
portraits, and Clarence White's ghostly double-exposed images.
The books section includes rare nineteenth-century titles.

Historic New Orleans Collection
Map 4, E4. 533 Royal St at St Louis ℗523-4662.
Tues–Sat 10am–4.45pm.
Excellent French Quarter museum (see p.43) shop with a great
collection of old maps and prints, on subjects including New
Orleans, the Civil War, Napoleon, and Audubon's "botani-
cals". It's also worth checking their postcards (early city plans,
paintings of the Quarter in the 1930s, old photos, etc) and used
books.

Peligro
Map 4, C4. 305 Chartres St at Bienville ℗581-1706.
Mon–Thurs 10am–6pm, Fri & Sat 10am–8pm, Sun noon–6pm.

The French Market

New Orleans' **French Market**, a restored arcade taking up five blocks of Decatur Street downriver from Jackson Square, has been a marketplace since the Choctaw traded here in the 1700s. Today, along with the tourist shops selling T-shirts, Cajun and jazz music, cookbooks, Mardi Gras beads, masks, pralines and posters, there's a 24-hour **Farmers Market**, which starts at the 1100 block of N Peters St, selling fresh seasonal produce, sacks of beans and nuts, coffee, pyramids of spices and the like. The 1200 block is taken up by a **flea market**, a jumble of plants, jewelry, junk, and used and new clothes, with some interesting Latin American and African crafts among the tourist trinkets. It's open daily, but busiest at weekends; haggling is acceptable.

Southern folk art of varying quality, with Mexican tin boxes, bottle-top saints, glittery fridge magnets and the like, along with more expensive paintings and sculpture.

Shadyside
Map 2, K7. 3823 Magazine St at Peniston ⓒ897-1710.
Mon–Sat 10am–5pm.
Studio for the pottery of Charles Bohn, who uses the "raku" process – whereby high-sand content earthenware is fast fired and cooled – to create gorgeous turquoise and copper, emerald green, or ethereal white "crackle" hues. Prices range from $25 to $450. Call for details of the occasional classes.

BOOKS

For **used non-fiction**, you could also try the record stores (p.232) and the Historic New Orleans Collection (opposite).

Arcadian Books

Map 4, F4. 714 Orleans St at Royal ℗523-4138.

Mon 10.30am–6.30pm, Tues–Sat 10am–6.30pm, Sun noon–5pm.

Small, friendly store in the center of the Quarter, with a good selection of used books including local and regional history, fiction, New Orlean's classics, travel guides and French-language titles.

Beaucoup Books

Map 2, F7. 5414 Magazine St at Jefferson ℗895-2663.

Mon–Sat 10am–6pm, Sun noon–5pm.

Good selection of new fiction, including many titles by local authors. Also cookbooks, art books, travel guides, Granta periodicals, and cards and postcards. Frequent author readings.

Beckham's Books

Map 4, B6. 228 Decatur St at Iberville ℗522-9875.

Daily 10am–6pm.

Rambling, two-story bookstore with thousands of old editions, rare and out-of-print titles, and vintage magazines at good prices. You could browse here all day. There's a sister branch, Librairie Books, at 823 Chartres St at St Ann (daily 10am–8pm).

Bookstar

Map 4, D6. Riverfront Marketplace ℗523-6411.

Mon–Thurs 9am–11pm, Fri & Sat 9am–midnight, Sun 9am–10pm.

Excellent bookshop with wide range of local and regional titles, plus books on travel, cookery, literature and music and lots of magazines. Many discounts, particularly on hardbacks.

Dauphine Street Books

Map 4, D3. 410 Dauphine St at Conti ℗529-2333.

Mon & Thurs–Sun 11am–7pm.

Superb store with a varied stock of used books, especially strong on local fiction, history, photography and Latin American translations.

SHOPPING: BOOKS

DeVille Books

Map 3, M6. Riverwalk mall ©595-8916.
Mon–Sat 10am–9pm, Sun 11am–7pm.
Very good selection of local titles, history, mysteries and
thrillers, travel guides, avant-garde works and sections dedicated
to blacks and women. The branch at 334 Carondelet St
(Mon–Fri 9.30am–5.30pm) also sells used paperbacks.

Faubourg Marigny Bookstore

Map 4, M5. 600 Frenchmen St at Chartres ©943-9875.
Mon–Fri 10am–8pm, Sat & Sun 10am–6pm.
Established (since 1977) gay and lesbian bookstore, selling
travel guides, regional titles, postcards and calendars.

Faulkner House Books

Map 4, F5. 624 Pirate's Alley at Chartres ©524-2940.
Daily 10am–6pm.
Tiny store tucked away in the building where the novelist lived
while writing *Soldier's Pay*, his first book, in 1925. Along with
Faulkner's publications, it stocks works by other Southern writers
and many local-interest titles, including first editions. The
owners, who are a good source of information on local literary
events, organize their own annual literary festival (see p.251).

Garden District Bookshop

Map 3, D5. The Rink, 2727 Prytania St at Washington ©895-2266.
Mon–Sat 10am–6pm, Sun 11am–4pm.
Strong selection of local titles, new fiction and limited editions.
Anne Rice does many of her signings here – it's next door to
her own store (see p.229) – and they stock rare editions and
autographed copies of her books.

George Herget Books

Map 2, L7. 3109 Magazine St at Louisiana ©891-5595.

Mon–Sat 10am–5.30pm, Sun 11am–5pm.

Cool, musty store, good for rare and out-of-print titles. They stock more than 20,000 used books, with categories including fiction, music, art, Louisiana, New Orleans, the Civil War, Americana, travel and cookery.

Kaboom Books

Map 4, K2. 901 Barracks St at Dauphine ℗529-5780.
Daily 11am–6pm.

Excellent store: the floor plan helps you negotiate the narrow aisles, which are stuffed full of used books including fiction, drama, travel, movie books, biographies and photography. It's strong on history, especially of the South, and has a good African-American section.

Maple Street Book Shop

Map 2, C3. 7523 Maple St at Cherokee ℗866-4916 or 862-0008.
Mon–Sat 9am–9pm, Sun 10am–6pm.

Excellent neighborhood store in an old house in the Riverbend area. Lots of local titles, classic and contemporary, and a great art/photography selection. They host frequent autograph parties and can do searches for hard-to-find titles. The same people own the children's bookshop next door at no. 7529.

CLOTHES AND ACCESSORIES

Though not famed as a fashion city, New Orleans is certainly a stylish one. Locals adore dressing up, be it in haughty haute couture or flamboyant secondhand gladrags – **vintage clothes**, in particular, are a hit with a population that not only revels in nostalgia and drama, but is also made up of an inordinate number of penniless musicians and artists.

Many of the clothes stores listed here also sell **jewelry** – look out especially for the work of local designer Mignon

Faget, whose striking metal pieces are inspired by local wildlife and architecture – and other accessories, and if you crave a hep-cat hat to top that sharp suit there are a couple of serious **hat stores**.

We've listed here only one-off, local stores; for **chain stores**, check the malls listed on pp.211–12. And for **sportswear**, head for Canal Street.

See also **costume**, on p.225. And for more jewelry, check out the **antique shops** listed on pp.212–16.

Grace Note
Map 4, H4. 900 Royal St at Dumaine ℂ522-1513.
Mon–Sat 10am–6pm, Sun 11am–5pm.
Fabulous hats, vintage and designer women's clothes, jewelry and gloves – all very New Orleans, with lots of velvets, satins, embroidery and fringing. Check out the floaty 1930s dresses; perfect for debauchery on a wrought-iron balcony.

Hemline
Map 4, E5. 609 Chartres St at Toulouse ℂ529-3566.
Daily 10am–7pm.
Funky women's clothes, hats, jewelry and shoes. There's a second branch at 7916 Maple St (Mon–Sat 10am–6pm), while Simplicity by Hemline, 838 Royal St (daily 10am–6pm), sells a more casual range, including shoes, jackets and sweaters.

Meyer the Hatter
Map 3, N4. 120 St Charles Ave at Canal ℂ525-1048.
Mon–Sat 10am–6pm.
Traditional, characterful old store for traditional, characterful old hats, along with baseball caps and Kangols.

New Orleans Hat Company
Map 4, D5. 402 Chartres St at Conti ℂ524-8792.
Mon–Thurs 10am–5pm, Fri–Sun 10am–6pm.

SHOPPING: CLOTHES AND ACCESSORIES

Classy store that takes millinery very seriously, selling everything from straw hats to felt trilbys and genuine Panamas from Ecuador. The annex sells designer garb by Comme des Garçons.

Rapp's Luggage
Map 3, N4. 604 Canal St at St Charles ⓒ568-1953.
Mon–Sat 10am–6pm.
The most reputable baggage store on Canal Street, with a good, reasonably priced selection including Samsonite, Tumi and Jans backpacks. Also briefcases and purses, and a repair service.

VINTAGE CLOTHING

Creative Native
Map 2, L7. 3116 Magazine St at Louisiana ⓒ899-6485.
Daily 10am–6pm.
Smallish vintage clothes store, with a particularly good selection for men, including gaudy, frilly, lounge-lizard cocktail shirts. Check out also the Forties necklaces.

Fiesta
Map 2, L7. 3322 Magazine St at Louisiana ⓒ895-7877.
Mon & Thurs–Sun noon–5pm, Tues & Wed 2–5pm.
Hawaiian shirts, denim jackets, Fifties dresses and seersucker swimsuits, evening gowns and Mardi Gras costumes. Also shoes, shades and jewelry, a small selection of retro lamps, and ever-so-useful luminous Virgin Marys.

Jazzrags
Map 4, K6. 1215 Decatur St at Gov Nicholls ⓒ523-2942.
Thurs–Sun noon–6pm.
Cheap, reliable vintage-clothes store – one of the longest standing on this thrift-store row – its rails packed tight with a variety of styles from the 1930s to the 1970s, including jeans. Also jewelry, shoes and hats, but not much choice for men.

Mariposa
Map 3, F6. 2038 Magazine St at Jackson ✆523-3037.
Mon–Sat 11am–6pm, Sun noon–5pm.
Very cool vintage clothes on the lower, slightly funkier end of
Magazine. Good prices for styles from the 1940s to 1970s,
including shoes, bags and sunglasses.

Paisley Babylon
Map 4, J6. 1129 Decatur St at Ursulines ✆529-3696.
Wed–Mon 1–5pm.
Friendly store for second-hand jeans, party frocks and the like,
with a good selection of men's sharp suits and Hawaiian shirts.
Not always that cheap, but there's something for everyone.

Ragin' Daisy
Map 2, L7. 3125 Magazine St at Louisiana ✆269-1960.
Mon–Sat 11am–6pm.
Clothing from the Fifties to the Seventies, along with new
spandex, crushed velvet and pvc ensembles. Also costume jewelry, nippy hats for boys and girls, beatnik accessories, bags
and shoes.

Trashy Diva
Map 4, G5. 829 Chartres St at St Ann ✆581-4555.
Mon–Sat noon–7pm, Sun 1–6pm.
Pricey, top-of-the-range vintage clothes; beautiful 1940s suits,
1930s evening wear and a wide range of sexy antique corsets.

COSTUMES, MASKS AND DISGUISES

Orleanians love **costumes**, and, so, it seems, do the
tourists. Scores of shops sell cheap T-shirts, feather boas and
whacky hats to satisfy exhibitionist impulses, but for serious
costuming – at Mardi Gras, say, or Halloween – head for
the specialist shops listed below. Even off season they're

SHOPPING: COSTUMES, MASKS AND DISGUISES

225

worth a browse: the older, deliciously shabby, Mardi Gras suppliers in particular are full of treasures.

See also Fifi Mahony's for **wigs** and super-cool **accessories** (p.231) and all the stores listed under **Vintage Clothing** on pp.224–25.

Accent Annex
Map 4, E4. 633 Toulouse St at Royal ℂ592-9886.
Daily 10am–6pm.
Contemporary Mardi Gras suppliers with a large selection of glittery masks, hats, costumes, T-shirts and souvenirs. It's good year round for wigs, fancy dress and stage make-up.

Little Shop of Fantasy
Map 4, H5. 523 Dumaine St at Decatur ℂ529-4243.
Mon, Tues & Thurs–Sat 11am–6pm, Sun 1–6pm.
Fabulous little shop that showcases extraordinary designer masks. What with these, and the big velvet hats, cloaks, satin flowers and angel wings, you'll be playing dress-up here for hours. They also sell soaps, aromatherapy oils and off-beat jewelry.

Mardi Gras Center
Map 4, G5. 831 Chartres St at St Ann ℂ524-4384.
Mon–Sat 10am–5pm.
Traditional store for inexpensive costumes, plumes, wigs, jewelry, masks (satin, sequined, feathered, gruesome, animal, celebrity), hats, glitter, stage make-up and magic tricks. It's one of the only costume stores open on Mardi Gras itself.

MGM
Map 3, H5. 1617 St Charles Ave at Euterpe ℂ581-3999.
Tues–Fri 9.30am–5.30pm, Sat 9.30am–5pm.
Elaborate stage and film costumes, worn by the stars, from the Hollywood studio renowned for its big-budget movie extravaganzas. Rental only, from $25 to $500 a day.

SHOPPING: COSTUMES, MASKS AND DISGUISES

Royal Rags

Map 4, H5. 627 Dumaine St at Chartres ℭ566-7247.
Wed–Mon 11am–6pm.

Closet-sized store selling handmade outfits: angel wings and
wild headdresses, ball gowns and satin opera gloves, hoop skirts,
drag gear, feathery antennae and the like. The staff are happy
to let you rifle before making that crucial decision between
sequinned leggings or shocking pink tutu. They'll custom
design, too, given enough notice.

Uptown Costume and Dance Company

Map 2, E7. 5533 Magazine St at Joseph ℭ895-7969.
Mon–Fri 10am–6pm, Sat 10am–5pm.

Unusual selection of inexpensive wigs, masks, costumes, hats,
shoes and sunglasses. Always busy at Mardi Gras (when krewe
members and marching bands come here to dress themselves
up) and Halloween (stage make-up and hideous latex heads are
particularly popular), when opening hours are extended.

Vieux Carré Hair Store

Map 4, G4. 805 Royal St at St Ann ℭ522-3258.
Mon–Sat 10am–5pm.

Old theatrical supplier that takes its business seriously, despite
the shrieking doormat and "we have warts" sign. It's a surreal
place, with shelves of polystyrene heads sporting off-center
wigs, rubber masks, sideburns and beards, bald heads and false
noses. They also sell stage make-up, much of which is hidden
behind the old-fashioned glass-fronted counter.

FOOD AND DRINK

A glut of tourist stores in the Quarter do a rapid turn-
around in easily transportable **foodie gifts**, from café au
lait and beignet mixes to red beans and rice and jambalaya
spices. Other buys include cans of Community blend coffee

laced with chicory, filé (for gumbo), peppery crab-boil and sugary pralines, along with hundreds of brands of hot sauce – some of them emblazoned with flaming toilets, burning butts and such in an effort to seem hotter than the next – and make-your-own Hurricane mixes (see p.181), inexplicably popular concoctions of sugar and artificial additives.

For **picnic food**, head for the neighborhood groceries and delis reviewed in our Eating chapter, on p.177, or the Farmers Market, covered on p.219.

N'Awlins Cajun and Creole Spices
Map 4, J6. 1101 N Peters St, in the Farmers Market ©566-0315.
Daily 24hr.
One of the better stops for hot sauces, coffee, spices and mixes – everything imaginable in a packet.

Old Town Pralines
Map 4, E4. 627 Royal St at Toulouse ©525-1413.
Mon–Sat 10am–5pm.
The best, creamiest and sweetest pralines in town, sold in a characterful old building with a subtropical patio.

Orleans Coffee Exchange
Map 4, F4. 712 Orleans St at Royal ©522-5710.
Mon–Fri 8am–6pm, Sat 9am–6pm, Sun 10am–6pm.
Hundreds of teas and coffee beans for sale, in a quiet little coffee bar in the heart of the Quarter.

GIFTS

While you could buy souvenirs in many of the stores listed in this chapter, there's also a host of hard-to-categorize places selling well-made, good-looking objects that are perfect to give as **gifts**. The best finds are in the Quarter and along Magazine Street.

Amazed and Amused

Map 4, H5. 612 Dumaine St at Chartres ©524-2443.

Daily noon–8pm.

Fun store for would-be Houdinis: how-to-amaze-your-friends books; coin tricks; magic ropes; jokes; and crucial accessories (hankies, dice, cups and balls, gimmick playing cards and the like). As soon as you enter you'll be treated to card tricks and illusions: if you've always wanted to learn the "pen through anything" or "arm chopper" trick, this is the place to come.

The Anne Rice Collection

Map 3, D5. The Rink, 2727 Prytania St at Washington ©899-5996.

Mon–Sat 10am–6pm, Sun 11am–4pm.

Gift shop in which everything is either designed or personally chosen by Rice. There's something for everyone, from black candles and tote bags featuring Stefan, Arnaud or Claudia, to Lestat wine and cologne ("A Scent to Die For") and a Lestat doll for around $300. Also Catholic icons, signed items of Rice's clothing, and artworks by husband Stan.

Big Life Toys

Map 2, L7. 3117 Magazine St at Louisiana ©895-8695.

Mon–Sat 11am–6pm.

Not just for kids, though the piles of tricks and games will keep them happy. Hip not-so-young things can enjoy the "expanding dates" (male and female: drop them in water and watch them grow) Mexican icons, powder-pink chokers emblazoned with pin-up girls, and retro furnishings. There's a children's branch down the street at no. 5430 (©899-8697).

Casa del Corazon

Map 4, H5. 901 Chartres St at Dumaine ©569-9555.

Daily 10am–5pm.

Small store crammed with colorful, kitsch Mexican stuff: icons, Jesus gear-stick knobs, glittery Frida Kahlo boxes, tin mirrors, Day of the Dead skeletons, plastic wrestlers and nightlights.

The Living Room

Map 4, H4. 927 Royal St at Dumaine ©595-8860.
Mon, Tues & Thurs–Sat 10am–6pm, Sun noon–6pm.
Quirky, individualistic crafts with a Southern folk-art feel: glittery jewelry boxes, pop shrines studded with plastic dolls and found objects, Elvis art, cool jewelry, retro-style glasses and ceramics. Also some antiques, including religious icons.

Le Monde Creole

Map 4, E4. 624 Royal at Toulouse St ©568-1801.
Daily 10am–5pm.
Excellent, eclectic little store set back from the street in a courtyard. It's run by the people who lead the superb city and plantation tours (p.15), and sells a selection of books, ceramics, games, furniture and antiques, all related to the Creoles.

RHINO

Map 4, A7. Canal Place mall ©523-7945.
Mon–Wed 10am–6pm, Thurs–Sat 10am–7pm, Sun noon–6pm.
Interesting, varied work – jewelry, ceramics, collages, greeting cards, textiles, hats, glassware, sculpture, clothing – produced by a local co-op that also runs workshops and exhibitions.

Scriptura

Map 2, F7. 5423 Magazine St at Jefferson ©897-1555.
Mon–Sat 10am–6pm.
Exquisite store selling delicate handmade notebooks, art papers, wax seals, rich inks, classy writing paper and designer cards. Also butter-soft leather diaries and address books and the like. They'll make up invitations, letterheads and business cards, too.

SHOPPING: GIFTS

Thomas Mann Design
Map 4, G4. 829 Royal St at St Ann ℗523-5041.

Daily 11am–6pm.

Modern, inventive lighting, photo frames and mirrors, and furniture made from found objects. Prices can be high ($250 for a mirror) but well worth it. The branch at 1804 Magazine St (℗581-2113) specializes in Mann's striking metal jewelry.

Three Dog Bakery
Map 4, G4. 827 Royal St at Dumaine ℗525-2253.

Daily 10am–6pm.

High-camp concept for the pampered pooch – home-baked doggy treats including truffles, petit fours and birthday cakes. Best sellers include "bark'n'fetch" cookies – try fat-free apple, oatmeal or carob. Also bowls, photo albums and gift packs.

UFO
Map 2, L7. 3324 Magazine St at Louisiana ℗891-1191.

Thurs–Sun 11am–5pm.

One-off and limited edition furnishings: "rocket" lamps made from electrical objets trouvés; coffee tables made from street signs; hubcap bedposts; and space-age lampshades assembled from rock'n'roll singles and Mardi Gras beads.

HEALTH AND BEAUTY

For a list of **pharmacies**, see p.255. For **day spas** (perfect for post-debauchery detox), see p.254.

Fifi Mahony's
Map 4, G5. 828 Chartres St at St Ann ℗525-4343.

Mon–Sat 11am–7pm, Sun noon–6pm.

Fabulous make-up and wig store, staffed by friendly, gorgeous boys and girls with neon hair and sparkling eyelids. All manner of nail polish, hair mascara and eye jewels and the like, with brands from Urban Decay and Cookiepuss to Fifi's own.

Hové Parfumeur

Map 4, G4. 824 Royal St at St Ann ©525-7827.

Mon–Sat 10am–5pm.

Elegant parfumier, with a distinctly old-world ambience. Best seller is the Tea Olive, made from the sweet olive blossom, common in New Orleans gardens; sniff out too the Magnolia, Carnaval and musky Rue Royale. Staff manage to be haughty without being unfriendly. They also do mail order.

MUSIC

There are plenty of places to buy good **music** in New Orleans. Prices tend to be lower at the used record stores, but though these are excellent for rare and collectible stuff, they may not have as wide a choice of new releases as the well-stocked superstores.

For a history of New Orleans music, with a discography, see p.284.

Jim Russell Records

Map 3, G7. 1837 Magazine St at St Mary ©522-2602.

Mon–Sat 10am–7pm, Sun 1–6pm.

Large collection of rare vinyl, along with singles, cassettes and CDs, specializing in soul, r'n'b and blues.

Louisiana Music Factory

Map 4, B6. 210 Decatur St at Bienville ©586-1094.

Daily 10am–10pm.

A great source of local music at low prices: especially strong on jazz, r'n'b, Cajun and zydeco. Some vinyl and hard-to-find secondhand music books. Staff are expert and friendly, and they also host frequent live performances. There's a second branch in the Old US Mint on Esplanade Avenue (see p.35).

Magic Bus
Map 4, D5. 527 Conti St at Chartres ℂ522-0530.
Daily 11am–8pm.
Established warehouse–type record store with new, used and rare CDs and vinyl. Strong on classic jazz and blues, with a small selection of contemporary local music.

Rock and Roll Collectibles
Map 4, K6. 1214 Decatur St at Gov Nicholls ℂ561-5683.
Daily 10am–10pm.
Shambolic old store selling secondhand blues, jazz and soul, mostly on vinyl. Prices can be steep ($80 for a rare Dr John LP, say) but are often negotiable.

Tower Records
Map 4, D6. Riverfront Marketplace, N Peters St ℂ529-4411.
Daily 9am–midnight.
Wide selection, especially good on releases by local musicians, as well as rock, pop and classical. Also books – with the emphasis on alternative, grungy titles – and videos, and a Ticketmaster stand (see p.256). Prices are slightly lower than at Virgin.

Virgin Megastore
Map 4, E6. Jackson Brewery mall ℂ671-8100.
Mon 10am–12.30am, Tues–Sat 10am–midnight.
Three floors of CDs, tapes and videos. The local selection is small but well-judged, and there's a good books section, with regional and local titles, music books and photography. The café, with a terrace overlooking the river, is one of the few places you can sip espresso while watching the activity on the Mississippi.

Gay New Orleans

New Orleans is one of the easiest and most enjoyable cities in the US for **gay travelers**. The French Quarter has a large gay community and a host of gay-owned restaurants, hotels, bars and businesses to serve it. In the anything-goes atmosphere of the Quarter, however, it can be hard to distinguish between gay-only and straight establishments – most places accept most people.

If you're after a wild time, try to plan your visit to coincide with one of New Orleans' **festivals** – especially those that involve dressing up, like Halloween (see p.251) and, of course, Mardi Gras (see p.240) – when the French Quarter bars and clubs are particularly lively. One of the biggest gay festivals is the cross-dressing, heavy-drinking extravaganza known as **Southern Decadence** (see p.250), held in the Quarter the weekend before Labor Day. In the fall, there's a **Gay Pride** parade (see p.250), with partying in Louis Armstrong Park, but perhaps because there are so many other opportunities for gay celebration and expression it's neither as outrageous nor as well-attended as Pride festivals in bigger cities.

PUBLICATIONS

Free publications, available at clubs, cafés and record stores, include *Impact*, which reports local gay-relevant news

Gay accommodation

Although gay travelers will feel comfortable staying in most places in the city, the following gay-run or -owned **guesthouses**, concentrated in the French Quarter and Faubourg, are particularly welcoming.

The Frenchmen, 417 Frenchmen St ℡948-2166; see p.138.
Lafitte Guest House, 1003 Bourbon St ℡581-2678; see p.135.
Maison Esplanade, 1244 Esplanade Ave ℡523-8080; see p.138.
Melrose Mansion, 937 Esplanade Ave ℡944-2255; see p.138.
Rue Royal Inn, 1006 Royal St ℡524-3900; see p.137.
St Peter Guest House, 1005 St Peter St ℡1-800/535-7815; see p.137.
Hotel St Pierre 911 Burgundy St ℡524-4401; see p.137.
Ursuline Guest House 708 Ursulines St ℡525-8509; see p.137.

stories and includes a campy listings supplement, *Eclipse*, and *Ambush*, heavy on club listings. Both hit the stands every two weeks, on alternate Thursdays. The smaller, ad-heavy *Weekly Guide* has good bar, club, restaurant and business listings. The useful **Web site** *gayneworleans.com* has numerous links to local gay publications, attractions, bars and clubs. Look out, too, for the *Gay and Lesbian Yellow Pages*, which although primarily aimed at residents, does include listings for accommodation, coffee houses, restaurants and, usefully, dungeons.

SHOPS AND RESOURCES

Alternatives
Map 4, H3. 907 Bourbon St at Dumaine ℡524-5222.
Mon–Thurs & Sun 11am–7pm, Fri & Sat 11am–9pm.
Gift shop selling cards, clothes, toys, condoms and lubricants.

Faubourg Marigny Bookstore

Map 4, M5. 600 Frenchmen St at Chartres ©943-9875.

Mon–Fri 10am–8pm, Sat & Sun 10am–6pm.

Established gay and lesbian bookstore, filled with travel guides, regional titles, fiction, postcards and calendars.

Lesbian and Gay Community Center

Map 4, G1. 816 N Rampart St at St Ann ©522-1103.

Mon–Fri noon–7pm, Sat & Sun 9.30am–5.30pm.

Information on current events, plus up-to-date resource listings.

GAY TOURS

Run by the exemplary Bienville Foundation, who lead a number of alternative walking tours (see p.14), the **Gay Heritage Tour** (2hr 30min; $18; ©945-6789) is a lively, informative scoot around the French Quarter, concentrating on the gay characters – and homophobes – who have contributed so much to its rich cultural life. Tours leave from outside Alternatives (see p.235), but schedules vary; call to check and reserve a place.

GAY BARS AND CLUBS

Most of New Orleans' **gay bars and clubs** are in the Quarter or the Faubourg: the majority of them attract a mixed crowd. They all have a dizzying series of daily happy hours and special deals – for the latest check the "dollar stretcher" pages in the *Weekly Guide*.

Bourbon Pub/Parade

Map 4, G3. 801 Bourbon St at St Ann ©529-2107.

Pub daily 24hr; Parade Mon–Sat from 9pm, Sun from 5pm.

Noisy, sweaty video-bar and club. *Parade*, upstairs, is the biggest and liveliest of the city's gay dance clubs, especially on Sunday nights, when it keeps hopping long after other places have emptied out. Frequent happy hours, plus a popular tea dance with free draft beer (Sun 5–10pm). Cover at *Parade* $2–6.

Café Lafitte in Exile
Map 4, H3. 901 Bourbon St at Dumaine ©522-8397.
Daily 24hr.
Rambunctious gay men's bar in the heart of the Bourbon Street hustle, with a pool table and heaving balcony. It's the HQ for Gay Pride day. Happy hour daily 4–9pm.

Golden Lantern
Map 4, K4. 1239 Royal St at Barracks ©529-2860.
Daily 24hr.
Established neighborhood gay/drag bar, the HQ for the Southern Decadence festival, usually full with a crowd of devoted regulars. Happy hour daily 5–9am & 5–9pm.

Good Friends and Queen's Head Pub
Map 4, G3. 740 Dauphine St at St Ann ©566-7191.
Daily 24hr.
Friendly bar in the quieter part of the French Quarter and at the heart of the gay community. It's got a cozy, neighborhood feel, with a real coal fire and a pool table. Daily happy hour 4–9pm; drinks specials on Sunday. The *Queen's Head*, upstairs, is quieter, with a mock-English ambience and a much-played darts' board.

The Mint
Map 4, L5. 504 Esplanade Ave at Decatur ©525-2000.
Mon–Fri noon till late, Sat 10am till late.
Raucous revues, burlesque and drag shows, served up to a mixed crowd. Happy hour daily 5–9pm.

GAY NEW ORLEANS: BARS AND CLUBS

MRB

Map 4, I5. 515 St Philip St at Decatur ℂ524-2558.

Daily 24hr.

Boys' dance club with cabaret and dancers – the initials stand for Mississippi River Bottom.

Oz

Map 4, G3. 800 Bourbon St at St Ann ℂ593-9491.

Daily 24hr.

Noisy, hi-tech disco opposite the *Bourbon Pub* (see p.236) and very similar. Special drag nights, go-go boys, cabaret and hard-house nights. Happy hour Sun 5pm–midnight. Cover $4–6.

Rawhide 2010

Map 4, G2. 740 Burgundy St at St Ann ℂ525-8106.

Daily 24hr.

Hard-core leather and denim bar, with brutalist garage decor, that keeps going around the clock. On Mardi Gras, the Bourbon Street awards – the biggest, most flamboyant gathering of costumed revelers in the city – is staged on the sidewalk outside.

The Roundup

Map 4, D3. 819 St Louis St at Dauphine ℂ561-8340.

Daily 24hr.

Relaxed neighborhood haunt, favored by drag queens and transsexuals. The c'n'w jukebox is said to be a favorite of Ashley Judd when she's in town.

Rubyfruit Jungle

Map 4, N5. 640 Frenchmen St at Royal ℂ947-4000.

Mon–Wed 4pm–1am, Thurs & Fri 4pm till late, Sat 2pm till late, Sun 2pm–1am.

Very friendly lesbian bar, all chrome and neon, in the Faubourg Marigny. Themed nights – c'n'w, swing, hip-hop,

hi-NRG, drag and the like – and cheap food deals.
Daily happy hour 4–8pm; Bloody Marys $2 all day Sat.

Wolfendale's
Map 4, H1. 834 N Rampart St at Dumaine ©596-2236.
Daily 5pm–5am.
Black gay bar, with drag and cabaret performances.
Thurs–Sun $3 cover.

Festivals

As befits this party-loving, parade-crazy, multicultural city, New Orleans' calendar is packed with **festivals**. The big one, of course, is the pre-Lenten bacchanalia of **Mardi Gras** – closely followed by the superb **JazzFest** – but whenever you come you're bound to coincide with some celebration or other, be it a saint's day or a sinner's beanfeast. Whatever the festivity, music and food feature prominently, as do **street parades**, which occur at the drop of a hat throughout the year. Parades are particularly important in the black neighborhoods, where local social clubs organize noisy, jubilant processions featuring the city's best **brass bands**, followed by a "second line" of dancing crowds.

If you're planning to come to New Orleans for
Mardi Gras or JazzFest, be sure to reserve a
hotel room several months in advance.

MARDI GRAS

New Orleans' **carnival season** – which starts on Twelfth Night and runs for the six weeks or so until Ash Wednesday – is unlike any other in the world, bringing together the traditions, obsessions and desires of countless disparate groups in quite extraordinary ways. Though the name is used to define the entire season, **Mardi Gras** itself, French for "Fat Tuesday", is simply the culmination of a whirl of parades, parties, bohemian street revels and secret masked balls, all inextricably tied up with the city's labyrinthine social and political structures. While it's by far the busiest **tourist season**, when the city is invaded by millions of people, Mardi Gras is still very much an event for New Orleanians, with tourists welcomed as unofficial guests.

Mardi Gras is always the day before Ash Wednesday: in 2000 it falls on March 7, in 2001 on February 27, and in 2002 on February 12.

Much of the "official" carnival revolves around the members-only **krewes** (see p.271), who, in tandem with organizing the public **parades**, also hold elite society **balls**, glittering, arcane affairs that are strictly invitation-only. But Mardi Gras is equally defined by its spontaneous events: a whirlwind of superb **live music** and all-night jamming sessions, plus crazy, satirical shindigs thrown by the unofficial, **alternative krewes** (see p.246) and abundant spur-of-the-moment carousing in the French Quarter and the Faubourg. And of course, there's also the heavy drinking, stripping off and throwing up on **Bourbon Street**, should that be your bag.

You need stamina to survive carnival season, which gets increasingly frenzied as it progresses. To have the most fun, you'll need to go with the flow: catch a couple of the big parades, rifle the thrift stores and costume outlets (see p.225) for fabulous **disguises** and **masks** (you'll feel left out if you don't), keep an eye out for flyers, and listen to the local radio (WWOZ; see p.10) for news of the best gigs and parties. Official events and parade routes are advertised in the press and in the glossy handbook **Arthur Hardy's Mardi Gras**

Guide; for a more portable guide, pick up the invaluable folding **Mardi Card**, which has a daily schedule of the best official and off-beat happenings, with maps of parade routes and some background history.

For a history of Mardi Gras and the krewe system,
see p.271.

The parades

More than sixty krewes organize major **parades** during Mardi Gras; huge overblown events, featuring colorful, motorized floats and masked riders hurling "throws" (see opposite) to the shrieking hordes that throng the sidewalks. Though they occur all over the city, the biggest parades head downtown and attract audiences of hundreds of thousands. The busiest parade days are the two weekends before Mardi Gras itself.

Parades follow routes of up to six or seven miles and can take at least two hours to pass any one point, their multitiered floats joined by strutting high-school marching bands, masked horsemen, stilt walkers and the **second liners**, who dance behind. Night parades may also be accompanied by black **flambeaux carriers**, whose nerve-wracking swirling and leaping is rewarded by the crowds throwing quarters at them.

Some visitors pay for places on **stands**, often linked to a particular hotel or restaurant, where $10 or so gets you a good view and an elevated vantage point for catching throws. In the less congested areas outside downtown, families colonize whole swathes of sidewalk with picnic boxes, folding chairs and step ladders. Others hop around, dipping in and out of side streets to catch up and overtake the rumbling floats. Good **viewing areas** include Canal Street, which sees the densest crowds, and St Charles Avenue, especially

Beads and throws

Enjoying a **Mardi Gras parade** is as much about participation as simply spectating. While marveling at a particularly inventive, elaborate or just plain funny float (and bitching about the lame ones) is part of the fun, most people are out to catch "**throws**". Strings of beads, toys, beakers and doubloons (toy coins marked with krewe insignia) are flung into the crowds by masked float-riders, towering above the hoi polloi. Competition among spectators is fierce, and the krewe members milk the hysteria for all it's worth, teasing and taunting the screeching masses. Souvenirs vary in worth: the bright, cheap strings of beads that adorn balconies everywhere are the most common, while the bizarrely garbed **Zulu coconuts** – handed down rather than thrown, as hurling coconuts can be hazardous – have become the most prized. While old-guard krewes – including Rex – tend to be more restrained with their throws, the **super krewes** (see p.276) are the most excessive. In particular, both **Endymion** and the scatalogically humorous **Tucks** shower the streets with plastic-bagfuls of beads and a rainstorm of doubloons.

An offshoot of the tradition of parade throws is the citywide **bead-bartering** system, where strangers, already heavily laden with the things, approach each other in the street begging to swap some particular string in exchange for another. Over the years the stakes have become higher, giving rise to the famed "**show your tits**" phenomenon – young co-eds respond to the challenge, chanted by goggling mobs, by pulling up their shirts in exchange for strings of beads and roars of boozy approval. New Orleanians leave these antics to the tourists: anyone desperate to see the show should head for Bourbon Street – a tacky strip at the best of times, but especially grim during Mardi Gras.

MARDI GRAS: BEADS AND THROWS

between Melpomene and Jackson avenues, where there's more of a local scene. Bear in mind when staking your place that **timings** quoted in parade schedules are approximate – Zulu, in particular, who parades first thing on Mardi Gras itself, is notorious for setting off two or three hours late.

Lundi Gras

Lundi Gras, the day before Mardi Gras, is one of the most feverish of the season. From mid-morning, some of the city's best musicians play at **Zulu**'s free party, held at Woldenberg Park by the river. Featuring two stages, food stalls and crafts areas, it climaxes at 5pm with the arrival of the king and queen by boat. Following this, you can head just around the corner, to the **Plaza d'España**, where, in a formal ceremony, unchanged for over a century, the mayor hands the city to Rex, King of Carnival. The party continues with more live music and a fireworks display, after which people head off to watch the big **Orpheus** parade or start a frenzied evening of clubbing. Most clubs are still hopping well into Mardi Gras morning.

For more about the Mardi Gras krewes, see p.271.

Mardi Gras

The fun starts early on Mardi Gras day, with **walking clubs** striding through uptown on their ritualized bar crawls. Meanwhile, on the other side of town, the fabulously costumed **Mardi Gras Indians** (see p.274) gather to parade, preparing for their afternoon standoffs in Tremé. **Zulu**, scheduled to set off at 8.30am – but usually starting much later – heads from uptown to Canal Street, its float-riders daubed in war paint and dressed in grass skirts. Their wild burlesque is trailed by the motley **Krewe du Jieux** walking parade, organized by members of the Klezmer Allstars (see p.198); though they follow Zulu's route, as an unofficial parade they're not licensed to do so and often have to disperse to avoid the police. The refined **Rex** parade, dominated since its debut in 1872 (see p.272) by the colossal Boeuf Gras, arrives on Canal Street in the afternoon.

Ironically, by the time Rex turns up, many people have had their fill of the official parades. The wildest party is going on in the **French Quarter**, which is teeming with masked, costumed merrymakers, bead-strung tourists, strutting drag divas, and banner-carrying Baptists preaching hellfire and brimstone. The surreal **St Ann walking parade**, a fairytale procession of the most extraordinary costumes, gathers outside the *R-Bar* (see p.186) at around 11am, while the flamboyant gay costume competition known as the **Bourbon Street awards** (see p.238) gets going at noon. At 3pm, a noisy skirmish begins between the grim-faced religious zealots standing sentry outside St Louis Cathedral and a debauched **mock-pope**, his taunts met with howls of approval by a rabble of dissolute followers.

In the late afternoon, hipsters head to the Faubourg, where **Frenchmen Street** is ablaze with bizarrely costumed carousers, whose bohemian street party evokes the irreverent misrule of medieval carnival. The fun continues throughout the Quarter and the Faubourg until **midnight**, when a siren wail heralds the forceful arrival of mounted police who sweep through Bourbon Street and declare through megaphones that carnival is officially over.

....

Throughout carnival, New Orleanians feast on
King Cake, which is served all over the city. A ring of
brioche, iced in the carnival colors of gold, green and
purple, each cake is baked with a small plastic baby
inside; traditionally, whoever gets the baby has to host
the next party, or at least buy the next cake.

....

Alternative krewes

The spirit of old Mardi Gras, when maskers took to the streets
to create their own parades and parties, is kept alive today in
the city's many alternative, or **unofficial krewes**. Chief among
them is the anarchic **Krewe du Vieux** (from Vieux Carré,
another name for the French Quarter), whose irreverent "ball"
(a polite term for what tends to be a wild party, open to all) is
the first of the season, starting with a weird and wonderful
march that weaves its way from the Faubourg Marigny
through the French Quarter. Ragtag costumes and bizarre
mini-floats satirize current local affairs and scandals, while the
funkiest brass bands provide musical accompaniment.
Uptown, the *Maple Leaf* bar (see p.202) is the headquarters of
the **Krewe of OAK** ("Outrageous And Kinky"), whose
"parade" is more of a bar crawl, ending up back at the *Maple
Leaf* for live music and food. And then there's the **Mystic
Krewe of Barkus**, made up of dogs, a thousand or so of
whom trot proudly through the French Quarter – all spiffed up
on some spurious theme – before ending up, with owners and
onlookers, at the *Good Friends* gay bar (see p.237). To find
out the movements of these and other alternative krewes,
check the usual sources (see p.8).

JAZZFEST

The internationally acclaimed **New Orleans Jazz and
Heritage Festival** (**JazzFest**) is held during the last weekend (Fri–Sun) in April and the first weekend (Thurs–Sun)
in May, at the Fair Grounds racetrack near City Park.
Started in 1969 as a small-scale celebration of local roots
music, it has mushroomed into an enormous affair, rivaling
Mardi Gras in size and importance. Detractors complain

that it has suffered as a consequence, but gripes about over-crowding and occasional poor acoustics apart, it's still an extraordinary show, attracting a mellower audience than Mardi Gras; the "jazz" of the title is taken as a loose concept, with ten **stages** hosting r'n'b, gospel, funk, blues, African, Caribbean, Latin, Cajun, folk, bluegrass, reggae, country, Mardi Gras Indian and brass band music. Here, more than at any other of New Orleans' festivals, the **food** is as big a deal as the music, with dozens of stalls dishing up truly spectacular local and international cuisine.

The Fair Grounds site stays open from 11am to 7pm. While some people book up for all seven days, others prefer to pace themselves and take time out for a breather; there's plenty going on in town throughout the festival, including free in-store performances by JazzFest acts at local record stores. The second Thursday at the Fair Grounds, traditionally one of the quietest days of the festival, before the week-enders have hit town, is a favorite with locals; the second Saturday, on the other hand, has been known to draw some 100,000 spectators. In the **evenings**, in addition to the official big-name concerts, usually staged at the Municipal Auditorium and the Praline Connection Gospel and Blues Hall, **clubs** all over town feature superb line-ups and unofficial jam sessions into the early hours.

Festival **schedules** are listed on the **official Web site** (*www.nojazzfest.com*), in *Times-Picayune* and *Gambit*. The best program, however, comes free with the music listings paper *Offbeat*, whose Web site (*www.offbeat.com*) also features a JazzFest preview page and messageboard.

Tickets, available from Ticketmaster (©522-5555 or *www.ticketmaster.com*), cost $14 per day; you can also buy them for $18 on the day, at the Ticketmaster stand in Tower Records (see p.233) but you may have to wait in a long line. The official evening concerts, which book up fast, cost between $20 and $35. To **get to the Fair Grounds**, hop on one of the shuttle buses from downtown ($8 round-trip; $5 one-way), or try your luck finding a taxi; they hike their rates during the festival and drop off at two designated ranks near the Fair Grounds.

For more **details**, call ℂ522-4786 or check the festival's Web site (*www.nojazzfest.com*).

A FESTIVAL CALENDAR

The following list covers a wide spread of festivals, but is by no means exhaustive; for a **full rundown**, including details of sporting events such as New Year's **Sugarbowl** game (see p.73), contact the **New Orleans CVB** (ℂ1-800/672-6124 or 566-5011; *www.nawlins.com*). **Neighborhood events** are announced on WWOZ radio station (see p.10).

Jan 6 to the day before Ash Wednesday
Mardi Gras See p.240.

March 17
St Patrick's Day New Orleanians celebrate the Irish saint's day in fine, high-spirited style, beginning the Friday before with a parade that sets off from *Molly's at the Market* bar (see p.184) and weaves through the French Quarter. The next day, another parade heads along Magazine Street and the Irish Channel – the blue-collar neighborhood that spreads below the Garden District toward the river – with float-riders throwing carrots, onions and potatoes to a raucous bunch of roisterers swathed in green beads and swigging green beer. On March 17 itself, there's a big street party in the Irish Channel, organized by *Parasol's Bar*, 2533 Constance at Third (ℂ897-5413), plus drinking events all over town.

March 19
St Joseph's Day The Italian saint's day, which falls roughly

at the mid-point of Lent, is a big deal in this most Catholic of North American cities. Families all over town build massive, elaborate altars of food in their homes, taking out newspaper ads inviting the general public to come and admire them and to share meals, in exchange for a small donation. The Sunday closest to St Joseph's ("Super Sunday") is also the only time outside Mardi Gras that the Mardi Gras Indians (see p.274) take to the streets.

End of March

Tennessee Williams Literary Festival Superb festival, attracting internationally known actors and writers – recent attendees have included Richard Ford, Alec Baldwyn, Margaret Atwood and John Berendt. Based in the French Quarter's Petit Théâtre du Vieux Carré (see p.207), it fills four days with lively discussions – on subjects as varied as presidential speeches, Elvis, and the gothic elements of jazz – master classes, a book fair, concerts, walking tours and performances of Williams' plays. The *Streetcar named Desire* shouting contest, in which overwrought Stanleys compete in Jackson Square to holler "Stellaaaa!" as loudly as they can, has become a cult (watch out for practice runs in the gay bars). Check the festival's official Web site at *www.gnofn.org/~twfest* or contact the organizers on ©581-1144.

March/April (week after Easter)

Spring Fiesta Perfect for nosy parkers and decorative-arts fans alike – a five-day festival during which the general public are invited to ogle the interiors of many of the loveliest private homes in the French Quarter and Garden District. It's all rather genteel, with guides rigged up in hooped skirts, a classical concert series and special tours of the River Road plantations. For full details, call the organizers on ©581-1367.

Early April
French Quarter Festival Lively free music festival that in its own quiet way has come to rival JazzFest (see p.246) for the quality and variety of music on offer. For three days the Quarter is even more vibrant than usual, with music stages and superb food stalls along Bourbon Street and in Woldenberg Park, a giant jazz brunch in Jackson Square, tours of private patios, free evening gigs, parades and talent contests. Contact ©522-5730 or *www.frenchquarterfestivals.org*

End of April/beginning of May
JazzFest See p.246.

Mid-June
Reggae Riddums Inspired by Jamaica's Sunsplash, this three-day festival in City Park features big names in reggae, African and Caribbean music, along with food and crafts stalls. Contact the organizers on ©367-1313.

First Sunday in September
Southern Decadence New Orleans' biggest gay extravaganza, held on the first Sunday before Labor Day, is celebrated in the gay bars and clubs of the French Quarter. It culminates in a huge, flamboyant costume parade on the Sunday afternoon, organized by the *Golden Lantern* bar (see p.237), from where a Grand Marshall leads a flock of thousands along a secret parade route.

End of September
New Orleans Gay and Lesbian Pride Surprisingly, with its significant gay population, New Orleans' Pride event is a relatively small affair, based in Louis Armstrong Park. Contact *NGaypride@aol.com*

Faulkner Society Literary Festival Week-long event, focusing on the work of Faulkner and other Southern writers, with panels, workshops, readings and parties. It's organized by Faulkner House Books, in the French Quarter at 624 Pirate's Alley (℃524-2940).

Early October
Swampfest Jubilant festival held in Audubon Zoo over the first two weekends in October. Celebrating the music and food of Southern Louisiana, it features big-name Cajun and zydeco bands, some truly fantastic food stalls, and crafts demonstrations. Contact the organizers on ℃581-4629.

Art for Art's Sake The city's major art event, held on the first Saturday in October. Highlights include gallery receptions in the Arts District and on Magazine Street, a block party along Julia Street, and the closing gala at the Contemporary Arts Center (see p.206; ℃523-1216).

Early/mid-October
New Orleans Film and Video Festival Well-regarded, week-long festival, showcasing big-name independent features and short experimental works. The major premieres are screened at the Landmark (see p.208) and Prytania cinemas (see p.209), while independent shorts show at the Southern Rep Theater (see p.207). Call ℃523-3818 for details.

October 31
Halloween Thanks to its long-held fascination with all things morbid, and the local passion for partying and costuming, New Orleans is the perfect place to celebrate Halloween. Pale-faced Goths start descending during the week or so before the big day, attending wannabe vampire conferences and covens held in the big hotels; Haunted

A FESTIVAL CALENDAR

Houses pop up in the parks, and music clubs all over town host costume competitions. The best public events include the wild, arty "Decadence" bash, held in a different location every year, and Anne Rice's Memnoch Ball (see p.84); on the night itself, get dressed up and head to the Faubourg, to join the scariest, most bizarre-looking street party in town.

For details of the city's best costume stores, see p.225.

December

Creole Christmas The French Quarter pulls out all the stops for the festive season, with tours of patios and private homes; candlelight caroling in Jackson Square, the Plaza d'España and on riverboat cruises; a tree-lighting ceremony by the *Café du Monde*; and special feasts, known as *reveillons*, put on by the finest Creole restaurants. Contact *www.frenchquarterfestivals.org*

December 31 New Orleans, which always throws a good party, is beginning to rival New York as a New Year's destination. Festivities are concentrated around Jackson Square, with fireworks over the river and a whole lot of reveling throughout the French Quarter.

Directory

AIRLINES Aeroméxico ℰ1-800/237-6639; American ℰ1-800/433-7300; British Airways ℰ1-800/428-4322; Continental ℰ581-2965; Delta ℰ1-800/221-1212; Northwest ℰ1-800/225-2525; Southwest ℰ1-800/435-9792; TWA ℰ529-2385; United ℰ1-800/241-6522; USAir ℰ428-4322.

AMERICAN EXPRESS 158 Baronne St (Mon–Fri 9am–5pm; ℰ586-8201).

AREA CODE The telephone area code for New Orleans is ℰ504.

ATMS Most of New Orleans' banks, and many of its bars, have ATMs; international visitors can withdraw cash from machines displaying the Cirrus or Plus symbols (which most do), for a fee of between $1.25 and $2 per transaction.

BANKS AND EXCHANGE New Orleans has few bureaux de change, though there is one at the airport (daily 6am–7pm). To change currency you're better off heading for a bank (Mon–Fri 9am–5/6pm, Sat 9am–noon); bring photo ID.

EMERGENCIES ℰ911; police non-emergency ℰ821-2222.

GYMS AND DAY SPAS Day membership ($10) to the friendly Downtown Fitness Center, in the Canal Place mall (see p.211), gives you access to classes, weights, a sauna and steam room (Mon–Fri 6am–10pm, Sat & Sun 9am–6pm; ℂ525-2956), plus the rooftop swimming pool at the *Meridien Hotel* on Canal St (Mon–Fri 6am–9pm, Sat & Sun 7am–9pm). The atmospheric 125-year-old New Orleans Athletic Club, 222 N Rampart St, is filled with antique weights and equipment, as well as state-of-the-art machines and a lovely sky-lit marble pool ($20 per day; Mon–Fri 6am–10pm, Sat 6am–6pm, Sun 8am–6pm; ℂ525-2375). For a range of alternative treats, including massage and aromatherapy, Belladonna, 2900 Magazine St (Mon–Fri 9am–8pm, Sat 9am–6pm, Sun noon–5pm; ℂ891-4393), is a gorgeous, upmarket day spa; Earthsavers, in the French Quarter at 434 Chartres St (Mon–Wed, Fri & Sat 10am–6pm, Thurs 10am–8pm, Sun noon–5pm; ℂ581-4999) is slightly cheaper.

HOSPITALS New Orleans' Charity Hospital, 1532 Tulane Ave (ℂ568-3723), has one of the best emergency rooms in the US.

INTERNET ACCESS The cybercafé at the Contemporary Arts Center (see p.175) offers free internet access. Others to try include *Realm of Delirium* (Mon–Thurs & Sun 10am–midnight, Fri & Sat 10am–2am; ℂ586-8989) upstairs at *Kaldi's* coffee bar (see p.175), and for 24-hour access, Kinko's, 762 St Charles Ave (daily 24hr; ℂ581-2541).

LAUNDROMATS The friendly, efficient Washing Well Laundryteria, 841 Bourbon St (Mon–Fri 7.30am–6pm, Sat 7.30am–2pm), offers same-day laundry and dry cleaning. *Checkpoint Charlie's*, the 24-hour rockers' bar in the Faubourg Marigny (see p.186), has a coin-operated laundromat at the back.

LIBRARIES New Orleans Public Library, 219 Loyola Ave
(Mon–Thurs 11am–6pm, Sat 11am–5pm; ✆596-2570).
In the French Quarter, the Williams Research Center,
410 Chartres St (Tues–Sat 9am–5pm; ✆598-7171), linked to
the Historic New Orleans Collection (see p.43), is a superb
resource for anyone interested in local history.

OPTICIAN Orleans Optical, in the old D.H. Holmes department store building, 819 Canal St (Mon–Fri 9.30am–5.30pm;
✆523-3385), sells frames and lenses and does on-the-spot repairs.

PHARMACIES Rite Aid has branches all over the city:
those at 3401 St Charles Ave (✆895-0344) and at 4330
S Claiborne Ave (✆895-6655) are open 24hr. There's also a
Walgreen's at 900 Canal St (Mon–Fri 7am–9pm; ✆568-1271)
and the Royal Pharmacy at 1101 Royal St (Mon–Sat
9am–6pm; ✆523-5401) – a lovely old-fashioned place
complete with traditional soda fountain.

PHONE CARDS Semans House, just off Canal St at
115 Royal St (✆529-6000), sells cheap national and
international phone cards.

PHOTO PROCESSING Avoid the cowboy outfits along
Canal Street and the first blocks of the French Quarter;
try Walgreen's, 134 Royal St (✆522-2736), or French Quarter
Camera, 809 Decatur St (✆529-2974).

POLICE STATION There's a police station at 334 Royal St
in the French Quarter. In emergencies call ✆911;
in non-emergencies ✆821-2222.

POST OFFICE The main post office is at 701 Loyola Ave
(Mon–Fri 7am–11pm, Sat 7am–8pm, Sun noon–5pm; ✆523-
4638;

zip code 70140 for General Delivery). An equivalent service, along with fax, photocopying, cellular phone rentals and the like, is offered by French Quarter Postal Emporium, 940 Royal St (Mon–Fri 9.30am–6pm, Sat 10am–3pm; ✆525 6651). The nearby Royal Mail Service, 828 Royal St (✆522-8523), is similar.

TAX New Orleans' sales tax is 9 percent, and 11 percent on hotel bills. For foreigners, the **Louisiana Tax-Free shopping** scheme reimburses the sales tax on all goods that you can take out of the country. Most participating businesses display a sticker, but if you don't see one at the bigger stores it's still worth asking. Show your passport when buying, and they'll give you a voucher, redeemable at the booth opposite the American Airlines desk at the airport (daily 7am–6pm). Refunds of less than $500 are given out in cash on the spot; higher sums will be mailed as a cheque. There's a small handling fee.

TICKETS Ticketmaster (✆522-5555) has an outlet in Tower Records on N Peters St (see p.233).

TIME New Orleans is on Central Standard Time, six hours behind GMT. Daylight Savings Time, when clocks go forward an hour, runs from the first Sunday in April to the last Sunday in October.

TIPPING New Orleans' economy is based on tourism and the service industry, yet wages tend to be low. Wait staff in restaurants expect tips of around 17.5 percent, higher if you've had particularly good service. Bar staff should get 15 percent, or a dollar per round, whichever is higher; taxi drivers 15 percent; hotel porters about $1 per piece of baggage; and housekeeping staff $1 per night.

CONTEXTS

A history of New Orleans

The history of New Orleans is inextricably tied up with that of the mighty **Mississippi River**, which has been its *raison d'être*, the source of its fortunes and its potential destroyer. In 1543, **Hernando de Soto**, exploring the Gulf of Mexico as part of the relentless Spanish quest for gold in the Americas, encountered the river somewhere close to Natchez, in today's state of Mississippi; he died of a fever before he could establish any claim to the land, however, and more than a century passed before another expedition was despatched to the Gulf. This time it was **France**, the most powerful nation in Europe, who hoped to establish a permanent foothold on the shoreline, and thus form a link between the burgeoning French territories in Canada and the West Indies.

The French colony

In 1682, Robert Cavalier, **Sieur de la Salle**, journeyed down the Mississippi from Canada. Reaching the mouth of the river, he planted a cross claiming the entire Mississippi valley for France and named it **Louisiana** in honor of his monarch, Louis XIV, the Sun King. La Salle returned to France a hero and was sent back two years later, hoping to build a city; he lost his way, however, landed on the coast of Texas, and was eventually assassinated by his men as they headed overland toward Canada in a vain search for the river.

Under Quebecois brothers Pierre le Moyne, **Sieur d'Iberville**, and Jean-Baptiste le Moyne, **Sieur de Bienville**, in 1698 the French sent a second expedition to establish a colony from where they could trade with the Spanish in Mexico and block the westward expansion of the British. Settlement was originally concentrated along the coast, although inland trading posts were also set up at

Natchez and Natchitoches; the capital was Biloxi, in present-day Mississippi.

In 1717, preoccupied with the war in Europe, Philippe, duc d'Orleans – regent for the five-year-old Louis XV – handed over responsibility for the development of Louisiana to Scottish financier **John Law**. Through a clever boosting campaign, Law's Company of the West engineered a major investment scam, in which shareholders were sold stakes in a promised gold- and silver-filled paradise peopled with friendly natives who would work for free. This so-called **Mississippi Bubble** inevitably burst in 1720, bankrupting many of its investors; by then many of them had already upped and left Europe for Louisiana, only to be stranded without the wherewithal to return.

Meanwhile, Bienville, now governor of the colony, was under orders to establish a city near the mouth of the Mississippi. As it was almost impossible to navigate the treacherous lower reaches of the river, tangled with snags and impeded by swamps and sandbars, he chose a site some hundred miles upriver, on a portage that led to Lake Pontchartrain. Seeing the twin potential for defense and trade afforded by this convenient route between the river and the Gulf, Bienville had high hopes for his city, and named it **La Nouvelle Orleans** for the French regent.

Progress was slow for the early settlers, who, in the face of hurricanes and yellow fever epidemics, painstakingly cleared the canebreak and set about building levees in an attempt to protect the banks from annual flooding. In 1721, French engineer **Adrien de Pauger** laid out a military-style grid-plan on the morass – a layout that remains intact to this day in the French Quarter. A year later, Bienville persuaded the French to shift the colonial capital from Biloxi to New Orleans; within five years or so the population doubled, more streets were built and drainage vastly improved.

The first **colonists** were a mixed bunch: convicts and aristocrats from France, French-Canadian adventurers and, between 1719 and 1730, a massive influx of **slaves** from Africa and the West Indies. These were joined by the **free people of color**, educated and wealthy Francophones, most of whom were slave-owners from the West Indian colonies. Because of the city's large slave population, in 1724 Bienville adopted the **Code Noir**, drawn up by the French in 1685 to govern the slaves in Saint-Domingue (today's Haiti). While placing restrictions on slaves – including a ban on mixed marriages and the death penalty for anyone who attempted to escape bondage – the Code also afforded them rights unknown in Anglo colonies, including the possibility of buying their freedom and the liberty to take Sundays off. From this latter privilege grew the gatherings in **Congo Square**, a patch of land behind the city where the slaves danced, drummed and traded. The only place in the United States where Africans were permitted to gather freely, Congo Square has been credited with being a breeding ground for jazz music and also for the spread of voodoo throughout New Orleans; although the Code Noir pronounced **Catholicism** to be the official religion of the colony, slaves were able to use the gatherings to maintain and develop their own rituals and beliefs.

The first European women in Louisiana were jailbirds sent over from Paris. These were joined in 1727 by the French **Ursuline nuns**, who, invited to establish a hospital, also went on to open schools for Native American, black and white children. Between 1728 and 1750 they also harbored the **filles de cassette**, the virginal daughters of respectable French families who, carrying their dowries in caskets, or *cassettes*, were brought over as suitable marriage material for the settlers.

Due to internal wrangling, Bienville was recalled to France in 1725. Almost immediately, relations with the

THE FRENCH COLONY

local Native Americans – with whom Bienville had been on reasonably good terms – deteriorated, climaxing in 1729 with an alliance between the Natchez and a group of slaves that led to a massacre at **Fort Rosalie**, some 150 miles upriver from New Orleans; 250 colonists were murdered and 450 women, children and slaves kidnapped before the French executed the rebels and virtually decimated the Natchez tribe.

Although he returned to govern in 1731, Bienville resigned for good in 1743 under pressure from his rivals, who held him personally responsible for the floods, droughts, epidemics and Native American uprisings that blighted the colony. His replacement, the **Marquis de Vaudreuil**, brought to this shabby outpost the fashions, customs and corruption of the French court; under his governorship New Orleans' first theatrical production was staged, dueling became commonplace and balls and parties began to stud the calendar. Meanwhile, as Bienville had predicted, the city steadily grew to become a major **market** for the lumber, bricks, tar, tobacco, indigo, hide and sugar being taken from the interior to the West Indies, the eastern seaboard and Europe, and the cargoes of silk, wines, cocoa, spices and silver coming in from overseas.

The Spanish era

In 1754, the **French-Indian War** (which merged with what became known in Europe as the Seven Years' War) broke out between the French and English, grappling over their American colonies. After England seized Canada in 1760, Louis XV signed the secret **Treaty of Fontainebleu**, handing New Orleans and all Louisiana west of the Mississippi over to his cousin, Carlos III of Spain, for safekeeping. Carlos, for his part, was keen to establish a buffer between the encroaching British and his colony in Mexico. In 1763, the **Treaty of Paris**, which ended the Seven Years' War and effectively marked the end of France's involvement in North America, handed England all French territory east of the Mississippi except New Orleans – which only then did Louis XV reveal he had passed over to the Spanish.

The citizens of New Orleans were not happy with their new Spanish status. Some attempted to form a republic, calling for the overthrow of the first Spanish governor, **Antonio de Ulloa**. In October 1768, Ulloa fled to Cuba and was replaced by **Alexandro O'Reilly**, an Irish soldier of fortune who had worked his way up the Spanish ranks. Arriving with some three thousand troops, O'Reilly promptly executed the rebels in the Place d'Armes.

Despite early resistance, however, New Orleans benefited greatly from its period as a Spanish colony; sensibly, the Spanish maintained French as the official language and allowed French culture to remain intact. They also adopted an open **immigration** policy, which led to the city's population trebling in size; newcomers included Anglo-Americans escaping the American revolution being fought to the east, French Acadians banished by the British from Canada and aristocrats fleeing revolution in France. New Orleans also became a haven in the 1790s for refugees – whites and free blacks, along with their slaves – escaping the slave revolts against the French in **Saint-Domingue**; as in the West Indies, the Spanish, French and free people of color in New Orleans associated and formed alliances to create a distinctive **Creole** culture. The Creoles, known for their love of dancing and partying, were also amassing great fortunes; after 1795, the year that local planter Etienne de Boré perfected the sugar granulation process, the **sugar plantations** boomed and their owners, the wealthiest men in the colony, came to dominate the political scene. Meanwhile, inspired by the events in Saint-Domingue, slaves instigated a revolt at Pointe Coupé, one hundred

THE SPANISH ERA |

miles upriver from the city; though its perpetrators were executed immediately, the Spanish were not able to rid the colony entirely of revolutionary ideas, and the threat of further **slave insurrection** was never far away.

Over in Europe, **Napoleon**, as part of his strategy to reassert French presence in the New World, offered the Spanish a kingdom in Tuscany in exchange for Louisiana. The Spanish, mindful that this could leave their territory in Mexico vulnerable, agreed only on the express understanding that he would not turn it over to another power, and in 1800 the countries signed the secret **Treaty of San Ildefonso**. In 1803, however, Napoleon, busy fighting the British in Europe, realized that any attempt to hang on to his New World possessions would require him to spread his armies too thinly. Imminent bankruptcy left him with little choice but to sell.

The Louisiana Purchase and "Americanization"

US President Thomas Jefferson, for his part, had been keeping a close eye on New Orleans for some time, keen to control the full length of the Mississippi River, which was fast developing as the nation's major commercial waterway. In 1803, under the terms of the **Louisiana Purchase**, he bought from Napoleon all French Louisiana, which stretched from the mouth of the river up to Canada and west to the Rocky Mountains, for $15 million – doubling the size of the United States and nearly bankrupting the nation in the process.

The Americans had bought a city of some eight thousand people – a mixture of French, Spanish, Caribbean, Latin American, African and German settlers, of whom more than four thousand were black slaves or free people of color. Almost immediately after the purchase, traffic using the port doubled by fifty percent. Redneck boatmen – derisively called "Kaintocks" by the Creoles – poured into the city on cumbersome, slow-moving flatboats, bringing goods from the interior to be traded or exported on great sea-going vessels, while fortune-seeking Anglo-Americans settled upriver from the French Quarter in a district that became known as the **American sector**. In 1804, fearing the further spread of revolutionary ideas from the West Indies – where the ultimate success of the Saint-Domingue slave revolts had led to the formation of the independent black state of Haiti – the Americans revoked the Code Noir and **banned the external slave trade**. Instead, slaves were bought from other states, literally "sold down the river" to New Orleans.

An exception was made in 1809 and 1810, however, when yet more French-speaking refugees from Saint-Domingue – ten thousand of them – were invited to the city and allowed to bring their slaves with them. This influx doubled New Orleans' free black population and maintained the dominance of French culture; the arrival of the slaves also gave a firmer foothold to **voodoo** and led to another **slave revolt**. In January 1811, hundreds of slaves, led by Haitian Charles Deslondes, marched toward the city from forty miles upriver, razing plantations as they went. They were met eighteen miles out by US troops; most of the slaves were killed in battle, while the others were beheaded and their heads displayed on spikes along the River Road.

In 1812, the same year that Louisiana achieved **statehood**, the US declared war on the British; on January 8, 1815, the **Battle of New Orleans** was fought about two miles downriver of the city by General Andrew Jackson and a motley volunteer crew of Creoles, Anglo-Americans, free men of color, Native Americans and pirates. The battle made Jackson a hero; soon afterward, however, news reached the city that the Americans had already won the war and that a peace treaty had been signed two weeks before the battle took place.

THE LOUISIANA PURCHASE AND "AMERICANIZATION"

The year 1812 also saw the first **steamboat** puff its way down the Mississippi. This revolution in river traffic – steamers, able to travel both upriver and downriver, took three days to travel distances that had taken the earlier flat-boats three months – marked the beginning of the city's greatest days as a port.

The antebellum years

The **antebellum years**, between 1820 and the outset of the Civil War, are known as New Orleans' **golden era**. In this period the city grew to become the major **slave-trading** center in the south and its **port** boomed, exporting cotton and sugar and importing luxury wares from Europe, the Caribbean and the northeastern states. By 1840, expanding commerce had made New Orleans the fourth largest city in the nation, bursting at the seams with a varied mix of Creoles, Anglo-Americans and ever more arrivals from throughout Europe.

Though it's easy to exaggerate the antipathy between the Creoles and the Anglo-Americans, it is true that cultural and language barriers led to bad feeling between the two, and the Creole-controlled city government made conspicuously little effort to aid the progress of the new American districts. Thus, in 1836, the Americans called for a division of the city into three **municipalities** – the Vieux Carré, the American sector, and the outlying areas – each governed by its own council. The arrangement lasted until 1852, when the Anglo-Americans, who now dominated the legislature, called for the city to be reunited.

Not all was golden in the golden era, however. The city was still prone to hurricanes and drastic **floods**, which periodically wiped out entire sugar plantations. Antebellum New Orleans was also the nation's unhealthiest place to live, plagued with fatal **epidemics** of yellow fever, typhoid and cholera – in the summer of 1853 alone some 8000 people were felled by disease. Between June and November, those who could afford it left for the nearby plantations or to visit family in Europe, leaving the poor and the weak to die.

Even so, this was also a time of great cultural and **recreational activity**. New Orleans was famed for its theaters and ballrooms, many of which featured European-trained musicians and hosted the notorious **quadroon balls**, where, under a system known as plaçage, white men would take young quadroon girls (one-quarter black) as their mistresses, sometimes setting them up in homes of their own. And in the 1850s **Mardi Gras**, celebrated since the earliest days of the colony, took on a new, organized form with the appearance of a night-time parade of Anglo-Americans calling themselves the "Mistick Krewe of Comus".

The Civil War

By 1860, New Orleans, the largest **cotton** market in the world, had a lot to lose from joining the **Confederacy**. The wealthiest Anglo-Americans had familial, social and commercial ties with the north, while the free men of color, though many of them owned slaves, were ambivalent about fighting for a system that denied them the right to vote. However, because the slave economy was crucial to the city's wealth, there was little choice for New Orleans but to join the Confederate states, and Louisiana seceded from the Union on January 26, 1861. Just three months later, New Orleans' General Pierre Gustave Beauregard ordered the first shots of the Civil War at **Fort Sumter** in Charleston Harbor.

By May 1861, the Union fleet had blockaded the mouth of the Mississippi and a year later the city was under **military rule**. White New Orleanians didn't react well to the occupation and were particularly displeased with **Major Benjamin "Beast" Butler**, who seized the property of families who remained loyal to the Confederacy, hanged a

THE CIVIL WAR

man for tearing down the Union flag and passed the notorious Order 28, declaring that any townswoman who taunted his soldiers should be seen as no better than a prostitute. Newly freed slaves, however, felt differently, joining forces with free men of color to demand electoral and civil rights; in 1862 they started a Francophone newspaper, *L'Union*, which proposed full emancipation in order to maintain the union.

Reconstruction and its aftermath

In April 1865, Lee's **surrender** at Appomattox ended the Civil War and the Thirteenth Amendment pronounced the emancipation of all slaves. While the Northern states embarked upon a period of industrialization and expansion, the defeated South was left to deal with a disintegrating social structure and a destroyed economy. In New Orleans, race riots were commonplace, culminating in the **massacre of 1866**, when a mob attack on a meeting called to discuss black voting rights resulted in the murder of 34 black men.

In 1867, the federal government passed the **Reconstruction** laws, placing the South under military rule until political stability could be achieved. There followed in New Orleans an unprecedented period of violence when, as in the rest of the South, anyone working to transform the city came under attack as a "carpetbagger" (a Northern opportunist out for political and financial gain) or a "scalawag" (a Southern collaborator). Returned Confederates, having lost their property, were further humiliated by not being able to hold political office; their former slaves, meanwhile, had new voting rights, were involved in government and played a central role in the new Metropolitan police force. Supremacist whites promptly formed militia such as the **White League**, who undertook brutal campaigns against the government and the newly integrated schools, and who, enraged by the seizure of a boatload of their weapons, fought a pitched battle with the police at the **Battle of Liberty Place** in 1874. In the face of systematic abuse, New Orleans' **black population**, backed by a few relatively liberal whites, used the political machine as best they could, eventually winning more rights than anywhere else in the South. But they never achieved real power and when Reconstruction ended, in 1878, the previously free blacks of New Orleans were worse off than they ever had been.

Though a continuing demand for cotton and sugar meant that New Orleans was able to survive as a distribution center, it nonetheless faced serious economic decline in the late nineteenth century, due in part to the arrival of the **railroads**, which diminished river traffic, and to heavy debts incurred during the Civil War and Reconstruction. The city had also been culturally and socially ravaged by the lawless, violent Reconstruction years, and in 1896, the Supreme Court ruling in **Plessy vs Ferguson**, which upheld the conviction of Homer Plessy, a black New Orleanian, for attempting to sit in a whites-only train carriage, proved the death knell for the ideals of the post-Civil War government. Allowing for "separate but equal" facilities for blacks and whites, the ruling effectively legalized segregation throughout the South, a state of affairs that was to exist for more than sixty years.

The twentieth century

In the early years of the twentieth century New Orleans achieved a certain notoriety nationwide for its red-light district, **Storyville**, the spectacular parades and balls of **Mardi Gras** and its indigenous musical form, **jazz**. And although the **Depression** hit here as hard as it did in the rest of the country, it also heralded the resurgence of the French Quarter, which had disintegrated into a slum since the Civil War. The **Vieux Carré Commission**, the first organization of its type in the nation, was established to preserve the architecture of the old quarter, and under President Roosevelt's New Deal, the **Works Progress Administration** (WPA) restored a number of its most important buildings. Meanwhile, the local political arena was dominated by Roosevelt's avowed enemy, the quasi-fascist Governor **Huey Long**, whose radical "Share the Wealth" programs were funded by strong-arm tactics, political patronage and financial corruption. Wildly popular with the state's poor sharecroppers and despised by the old-guard elite, Long was assassinated outside the Baton Rouge capitol in September 1935 by Dr Carl Weiss, just one of the many people who held a grudge against him.

By the 1950s a rash of **petrochemical** plants along the river had almost entirely wiped out the old sugar plantations; two decades later the **oil** boom saw corporate towers and the gargantuan Superdome shoot up in the Central Business District (CBD). After the oil bust of the mid-1980s, however, the second half of that decade was a particularly gloomy period for New Orleans, with office buildings standing empty, a sky-high crime rate that frequently won it the label of nation's number-one murder city and a notoriously corrupt police force. In the early 1990s, the on-off prospect of an enormous land-based **casino** and the city council furore over an ordinance that demanded the **desegregation** of the Mardi Gras krewes summed up the city's political divisions and racial tensions. Now that the dust has settled, New Orleans finds itself with a strong, popular, black-dominated city government. Mayor Marc Morial, son of the city's first black mayor, "Dutch" Morial, was voted in for a second term in 1998; his administration's highly publicized police force clean-up program, in the context of a relatively stable economy based upon tourism, seems set to lead the city into the new millennium with renewed confidence.

A history of Mardi Gras

Mardi Gras was introduced to New Orleans in the 1740s, when **French** colonists brought over the European custom, established since medieval times, of marking the imminence of Lent with partying, masking and feasting. Their slaves, meanwhile, continued to celebrate **African** and **Caribbean** festival traditions, based on musical rituals and elaborate costumes, and the three eventually fused.

For the practicalities of visiting New Orleans during Mardi Gras, see p.240.

While street revels had been a feature of carnival since its earliest days, when party-loving Creoles would join loosely organized **parades** that careered through the city to end up at designated ballrooms, it was only in the mid-nineteenth century that Mardi Gras took its current form. In 1857, a mysterious torchlit procession, calling itself the "Mistick Krewe of **Comus**, Merrie Monarch of Mirth", took to the streets, initiated by a group of wealthy, white Anglo-Americans. Their parade, on the theme of Milton's *Paradise Lost*, with decorated floats and masked riders dressed as the demon actors of the epic poem, was more elaborate than anything so far seen during Mardi Gras – a very different experience from the earlier processions, which tended to descend into rowdy affairs, with masked revelers flinging flour, mud and even bricks into the crowds. Almost immediately, the concept of the "**krewe**", a secret carnival club whose mythological name afforded it a spurious gravitas, was taken up enthusiastically by the Anglo elite. More and more krewes were formed, each electing their own "king" and "queen" – usually an older business man and a debutante – who, costumed and masked, and attended by a fairytale court, would reign over a themed parade and a closed tableau ball.

A HISTORY OF MARDI GRAS

Though this "organized" carnival trailed off during the Civil War, it gathered strength during the city's violent **Reconstruction** era. In 1872, newspapers published an arcane announcement heralding the imminent arrival of a so-called "**King of Carnival**", and ordaining that the city be closed down for the day and handed over to him. On Mardi Gras morning, the masked **Rex** arrived by river-boat, to preside over a brilliantly executed parade that fea-tured a huge fatted ox called the Boeuf Gras. Composed of leading civic figures, the Krewe of Rex was formed partly to greet the Russian Grand Duke Alexis Romanoff, who was visiting the city for Mardi Gras that year. Rex himself, despite his claim to be "king" of carnival, always bowed to the venerable Comus; while Rex's motto is *pro bono publico* ("for the good of the public"), Comus' is *sic volo, sic iubeo* ("as I wish, I command"). Comus and Rex, along with newly formed krewes **Proteus** and the satirical **Knights of Momus**, came to dominate organized carni-val, their self-appointed monarchs sweeping through crowds of subjects on stately parades that wallowed in romantic, exotic and exalted themes. Dominated by the white supremacists whose resistance to the Reconstruction government often exploded into violence (see pp.60 & 268), the krewes also used their parades to savagely attack the Republicans, representing the newly liberated blacks as simian fools. The general populace, however, didn't always submit to this appropriation of carnival: a number of smaller, informal groups satirized the pomposity of the big krewes and more than once the Comus parade was blocked by jeering hordes.

Throughout much of the nineteenth century, the role of black New Orleanians in official carnival was limited to that of torch-carrier, float-hauler, or band-player. In the 1880s, however, as post-Reconstruction racism became entrenched, groups of black men began to organize themselves into

Mardi Gras Indian tribes, or gangs (see p.274), leading their own processions through local neighborhoods. **Zulu**, the first official **black krewe**, was established in 1909, when, so the story goes, a black man mocked Rex by dancing behind his float with a tin-can crown and a banana-stalk scepter. While Zulu lampooned white carnival – in 1917 the king arrived in a tugboat along the New Basin Canal, parodying Rex's arrival on the Mississippi – it also continued African-derived carnival traditions, and by the 1940s the "Zulu Social Aid and Pleasure Club" had become one of the most important black organizations in the United States. In 1949, local boy **Louis Armstrong**, who had left the city as a young man, rode as King of the parade, thrusting Mardi Gras, and the city, into the public eye – less publicized, however, was his post-carnival avowal that he would never return to his home town, sickened by its segregation and racism. Today Zulu is one of New Orleans' biggest krewes and its parade, a raucous cavalcade of black-face savages setting off on Mardi Gras morning, is among the most popular of the season.

After a hiatus in World War I, when masking was banned as potentially subversive and the organized krewes stopped parading, carnival was revived during the **Jazz Age**. By 1925 Rex, Comus, Momus and Proteus were parading once more, while crowds of ordinary citizens took to dancing in the streets, accompanied by small jazz bands on motorized trucks. Many of the official parades also featured brass bands, followed by "**second liners**" who danced, twirled umbrellas, and created their own freewheeling procession. Seen as a boost to morale, carnival was in full force during the Depression, and in 1941 the **Krewe of Venus** became the first female krewe to parade. The 1950s saw the first **gay carnival ball**, a pastiche of straight carnival, which was raided by the police. In 1969, **Bacchus** emerged on the scene – a very different kind of krewe, less concerned with exclusivity and lofty aspirations than with cheerful excess.

The Mardi Gras Indians

New Orleans' **Mardi Gras Indians** are not, in fact, Native
Americans, but working-class black men who organize
themselves into tribes, or "gangs". Today there are more
than twenty tribes, each with between ten and fifty members, who, on Mardi Gras morning ("that day" in Indian
parlance) parade through local neighborhoods in fabulous,
extravagant **costumes** and headdresses. The tradition of
"masking Indian" is said to have originated in the 1880s,
when Becate Battiste, of mixed Native American and
African blood, turned up in a bar in Tremé with a bunch of
friends who announced themselves as the Creole Wild
West. Why they did so, and why the tradition spread, is
unclear. Some say it harks back to the early days of the
settlement, when indigenous tribes harbored and inter-
married with African slaves, but it's more likely that it
developed in response to the hugely popular **Buffalo Bill
Wild West** show, which stopped in the city during its
nationwide tour of 1884.

   The first Indians dressed relatively simply – copying
the apparel of local tribes and Caribbean Amerindians –
and fought gang wars on designated "battlefronts". Since
the 1950s, however, they have competed instead with
dances and chants and for the "prettiest" costume.
Today's costumes, or "**suits**" – which are worn in layers,
so sections can be revealed one by one to the admiring
crowds – can weigh as much as 100lb, their tunics, leggings and moccasins heavy with beads, rhinestones and
sequins. The ensemble is topped with a towering feather
headdress known as a **crown**; the one worn by the **Big
Chief** reaches colossal proportions. Though suits weren't

traditionally recycled, more recently, in the face of diminishing tribe numbers and the huge expense involved – an outlay of thousands of dollars – more and more are handed down by older tribe members to younger ones.

The gangs set out early on **Mardi Gras morning**, led by the spy boy, on the look out for other tribes, and the flag boy, who alerts Big Chief when his rivals come into view. When tribes meet, they gather on opposite sides of the street and communicate with hand gestures, percussion-rattling and improvised calls-and-responses. Influenced by Native American, Haitian and African chants, the songs lament lost tribe members, recall past battles and brag about their fine suits. Mardi Gras Indian **music** has long been a major influence on the New Orleans sound and many famous records, including the much-covered favorites *Iko Iko* and *Hey Pocky Way*, were originally Indian compositions. In 1976, the Nevilles' recording with the **Wild Tchoupitoulas** (see p.290), whose Big Chief Jolly was an uncle of theirs, brought Indian music to the public eye.

At Mardi Gras the various tribes roam through local neighborhoods where tourists, although tolerated, aren't particularly welcome, before assembling in Tremé. General spectators are likeliest to see them on the Sunday closest to the Italian St Joseph's day (see p.248), known as **Super Sunday** – which happens to coincide with a voodoo festival – when the Indians take to the streets in a more structured parade. Also, many of the more famous groups – the **Wild Magnolias**, in particular, headed by the formidable Big Chief Bo Dollis – play gigs around town in the run-up to Mardi Gras and during JazzFest (see p.246). Don't miss these performances if you have the chance; the Indians' supercharged blend of funk, danceable African beats and New Orleans party music is nothing short of astonishing.

The Bacchus parade boasted the biggest ever floats, a widely trumpeted celebrity king (Danny Kaye) and, in place of the invitation-only, hush-hush ball, a public extravaganza open to anyone who could afford the ticket. Thus began the era of the "**super krewes**", with members drawn from the ranks of New Orleans' new wealth – barred from making inroads into the gentlemen's-club network of the old-guard carnival krewes – and parades characterized by expensive, flashy floats and generous throws (see p.243). Other super krewes include **Endymion** and **Orpheus**, established by Harry Connick Jr in 1993, which usually features a well-known musician as king and whose parade boasts the 120ft-long Leviathan float, emblazoned with a constellation of flashing lights.

In 1992, after months of widely publicized and bitter wrangling, the city government instigated a **non-discrimination policy** for all parading krewes, requiring that, in order to be granted a parade license, they sign affidavits confirming their organizations to be open to all people, regardless of race or religion. While the super krewes, who in any case were held to be more democratic, agreed to the new conditions – as did Rex – Comus, along with Momus and Proteus, refused to comply, insisting that their membership be kept secret. Since 1992, none of them has paraded, though they continue to stage their elaborate balls, as exclusive and white as ever.

Comus' parade slot, the final one of the season, was filled in 1998 by the controversial **Krewe of America**, whose membership is open only to non-residents. Its appeal to big-spending out-of-towners was seen as a travesty by many New Orleanians, but the big-spending out-of-towners proved in any case to be too busy getting drunk on Bourbon Street to be bothered with riding on floats, and the krewe suffered heavy losses.

Books

Few cities in the United States have inspired as many stories as New Orleans. Since its earliest days, many of its greatest writers – Kate Chopin, George Washington Cable, Sherwood Anderson, Tennessee Williams et al – have been **outsiders**. Inspired by the stirring, sensual city, so unlike the rest of America, echoing with centuries of memories and ghosts, they composed some of their best works while living here. Others, **locals** like John Kennedy Toole and Anne Rice, capture perfectly the essence and spirit of their home town in a range of styles as diverse as the city itself.

Though a definitive modern **history** of New Orleans has yet to be written, many authors have dealt with its key themes, including the free people of color, Reconstruction and Mardi Gras. Some of the liveliest histories available today were written in the 1930s, by figures such as Lyle Saxon and Robert Tallant, leading lights in the regeneration of the French Quarter.

For details of New Orleans' literary festivals, see p.248.
For bookstore listings, see p.219.

Most of the following titles, all of which are in print, should be readily available in North America and the UK. Unless otherwise stated, all publishers listed are based in the US.

Fiction, poetry and drama

Brooke Bergan, *Storyville: A Hidden Mirror* (Asphodel Press).
Punctuated by E.J. Bellocq's haunting photographic plates of the prostitutes of Storyville, New Orleans' nineteenth-century red-light district, Bergan's lyrical quest to find truth, meaning, and

beauty in the past weaves together poetry, oral reminiscences and folklore.

George Washington Cable, *The Grandissimes* (Penguin UK). In the nineteenth century, Cable was regarded as one of the finest writers in America and *The Grandissimes* was his masterpiece. A labyrinthine, romantic saga of Creole family feuds, it's a superb evocation of the complex relations between the city's free men of color and Creoles, its voodooists and slaves; written in the late 1800s, during Reconstruction, but set in the years following the Louisiana Purchase in 1803, even at the time of publication it read like a nostalgic evocation of a lost era. One of Cable's chief aims, to represent faithfully the dying Creole culture, also informs the short stories of *Old Creole Days* (Pelican), in which the patois can take some getting used to.

Kate Chopin, *The Awakening* (The Women's Press UK). Subversive story of a married Creole woman whose fight for independence ends in tragedy. Swampy turn-of-the-century New Orleans is portrayed as both a sensual hotbed for her sexual awakening and as her eventual nemesis.

William Faulkner, *Mosquitoes* (Dell). Faulkner fans will delight in the poetry, the pace and the vision of this satiric account of the wealthy bohemian set in the 1930s French Quarter; detractors dismiss it as a work of overblown hubris.

Ellen Gilchrist, *In the Land of Dreamy Dreams* (Little, Brown & Co). Brittle, diamond-sharp short stories about betrayal, lust and loss among New Orleans' uptown elite, penned by one of the modern city's finest chroniclers.

John Miller and Genevieve Anderson (eds), *New Orleans Stories* (Chronicle). Superb collection of extracts from some of the best writers on the city, including John James Audubon, Mark Twain, Lyle Saxon, Tennessee Williams, Ellen Gilchrist and Anne Rice.

Michael Ondaatje, *Coming Through Slaughter* (Picador). Extraordinary, dream-like fictionalization of the life of doomed cornet player Buddy Bolden, written in a lyrical style that evokes the rhythms and pace of jazz improvisation.

Walker Percy, *The Moviegoer* (Vintage). Much-lauded novel, in which movie buff Binx Bolling cracks under the strain of a privileged uptown New Orleans upbringing. Profound tale of the search for meaning and redemption in an essentially empty world, or an existentialist drone in which too little happens. Take your pick.

Jewell Parker Rhodes, *Voodoo Dreams* (Picador). Populist and absorbing fictionalization of the life of nineteenth-century voodoo queen Marie Laveau, portraying her as an unsung heroine.

Anne Rice, *Interview with the Vampire*; *The Witching Hour*; *Lasher*; *Memnoch the Devil* (all Ballantine) and many more. Rice's Gothic tales of vampires, witches and evil spirits make good use of the city as a location; the vampire chronicles, featuring the brooding Lestat, are the most psychologically complex. Perhaps her finest novel, however, is the lesser-known *Feast of All Saints* (Ballantine), a fascinating historical saga set among the Creoles and free people of color of antebellum New Orleans, dealing sensitively and intelligently with issues of race, sexuality and gender.

Julie Smith, *New Orleans Mourning*; *The Axeman's Jazz* and many more (all Ivy Books). Pacey detective novels featuring misfit New Orleans cop Skip Langdon sleuthing her way through the city's myriad social strata. The first in the series, Edgar Award-winning *New Orleans Mourning*, is by far the best, a tale of uptown murder set against a backdrop of carnival, corruption and cross-dressing.

John Kennedy Toole, *A Confederacy of Dunces* (Penguin UK). The quintessential New Orleans novel, an anarchic black tragicomedy

BOOKS: FICTION, POETRY AND DRAMA

in which the pompous and repulsive antihero Ignatius J. Reilly
wreaks havoc through an insalubrious and surreal New Orleans.

Tennessee Williams, *A Streetcar Named Desire*; *Vieux Carré*
(New Directions). *Streetcar*, an overwrought tale of perverse
desires and brutality in the sultry city, has become one of the
seminal works in American drama; its film version (see p.296),
though iconic in itself, doesn't do the play justice, however.
Written thirty years later, *Vieux Carré*, a semi-autobiographical
account of Williams' early years in a dilapidated New Orleans
boarding house, is as bleak in its vision as *Streetcar*, if somewhat
lower-key.

History and biography

Christopher Benfey, *Degas in New Orleans* (Knopf). A slightly mis-
leading title for an engaging history that draws upon the novels of
George Washington Cable and Kate Chopin, as well as the
paintings of Edgar Degas – who stayed in the city in 1872 – to
draw a memorable picture of Creole experience during
Reconstruction.

John W. Blassingame, *Black New Orleans 1860–80* (University of
Chicago). Scholarly, accessible survey of the political and social
life of blacks in the city during Reconstruction, covering both the
experience of the educated, urban free men of color and the
newly freed plantation slaves.

Garry Boulard, *Huey Long Invades New Orleans* (Pelican). Gripping
account of one of the most dramatic moments in New Orleans'
twentieth-century history, when, in 1934, the "Kingfish",
Louisiana's populist and notoriously corrupt governor, sent in
troops to wrest control of the city from its old-wealth, old-guard
elite.

John Churchill Chase, *Frenchmen, Desire, Good Children and
other streets of New Orleans* (Touchstone). Chatty, fast-paced

and highly readable, if occasionally inaccurate, popular history of the city, using its weird and wonderful street names as a lynchpin.

Frank de Caro (ed), *Louisiana Sojourns* (Louisiana State University). Chunky collection of travelers' tales; the chapters on the Mississippi River and New Orleans include extracts from Mark Twain, Frances Trollope and Simone de Beauvoir, among many others. Perfect background reading.

Mary Gehman, *The Free People of Color of New Orleans* (Margaret Media). Clearly laid out, concise history of the city's free black population, from the first days of the colony, via the ravages of Civil War and Reconstruction, up to the advent of "Jim Crow" segregation laws in the 1890s.

James Gill, *Lords of Misrule* (University of Mississippi). Excellent, informed exploration of the role of Mardi Gras in maintaining racial divisions in New Orleans, beginning with carnival's earliest days and closing with detailed accounts of the furious city council debates around desegregation of the krewes in the early 1990s.

Reid Mitchell, *All on a Mardi Gras Day* (Harvard). Another great cultural study of New Orleans carnival, tracing its long history as a political battleground. Well-written, vivid and accessible, with chapters covering race, gender, class and sexuality.

Al Rose, *Storyville* (University of Alabama). Sizeable volume on New Orleans' notorious late nineteenth-century red-light district, packed full of photographs, newspaper reports and extracts from the famed "blue book", and scattered with oral accounts. Informative and fun, though the tone, at once prurient *and* puritanical, can jar.

Lyle Saxon, *Fabulous New Orleans* (Pelican). Compelling, evocative historical vignettes by one of the major lights in the renewal of the French Quarter in the 1930s. The account of a late nineteenth-century Mardi Gras, as seen through the eyes of the author as a young boy, is as fresh today as when it was written. Other works by Saxon include *Lafitte the Pirate* (Pelican), an enjoyable, rollicking biography of the much mythologized buccaneer, and *Gumbo Ya-Ya* (Pelican), a collection of Louisiana folk tales.

Michael P. Smith, *Mardi Gras Indians* (Pelican). Coffee-table book detailing the history and cultural significance of New Orleans' unique Mardi Gras Indians. Their lavish, breathtaking costumes, paraded on Mardi Gras morning, are captured in the book's fabulous photographs.

Christina Vella, *Intimate Enemies: the two Worlds of the Baroness Pontalba* (Louisiana State University Press). Detailed, sprightly biography of one of the colonial city's most fascinating figures. The saga of the baroness' eventful life, divided between New Orleans and France, makes gripping reading.

Architecture

Randolph Delehanty, *Ultimate Guide to New Orleans* (Chronicle). A dozen architectural tours of the city, written in a lively and personal style by the curator of the Ogden Museum of Southern Art.

Malcolm Heard, *French Quarter Manual* (University of Mississippi). Outstanding volume, filled with old photos, plans and literary extracts. Not only an illuminating guide to the baffling array of styles that make up the French Quarter's vernacular architecture, but also a lively read.

Richard Sexton and Randolph Delehanty, *New Orleans: Elegance and Decadence* (Chronicle). Luxurious coffee-table book filled with fabulous photographs and intelligent captions detailing the city's distinctive aesthetic style.

S. Frederick Starr, *Southern Comfort* (Princeton). Beautifully illustrated coffee-table book, surveying the development of the Garden District in the nineteenth century, telling the stories of its developers, architects, craftsmen and residents.

Music

Danny Barker and Allyn Shipton, *Buddy Bolden and the Last Days of Storyville* (Cassell). Highly entertaining, anecdotal stories of New Orleans' early jazz scene by one of its leading lights. The much-loved Barker, who died in 1994, was well known for his chatty style, which perfectly encapsulates the spirit of the music he played.

Jason Berry, Jonathan Foose and Tad Jones, *Up from the Cradle of Jazz* (Da Capo). Copious, fascinating account of the genesis and the heyday of New Orleans r'n'b; written in the 1980s, the tone is a little dated now, but it's a compelling read all the same.

Mac Rebennack (Dr John) with Jack Rummel, *Under a Hoodoo Moon* (St Martin's Press). Addled but very readable autobiography from New Orleans' inimitable "Night Tripper", maestro of the city's distinctive piano funk style. His prelude, which calls the book "a testament to funksterators, tricknologists, mu-jicians, who got music burning in their brains and no holes in their souls", sets the tone.

A history of New Orleans music

The exuberant, soulful **music** of New Orleans has had an impact on North America and the world out of all proportion to the city's size. Though no single reason can explain why New Orleans gave birth to jazz a century ago, no other city was so ideally situated to synthesize the traditions of the Old World and the New. Not only did it pass from French, to Spanish and into American hands, but it was home from its earliest years to large populations both of African slaves and free people of color. As an international port, it was also exposed to the manifold rhythms of Latin America and the Caribbean.

For details on where to hear the best
New Orleans music, turn to the Live Music chapter,
which starts on p.191.

Thanks to the Code Noir, adopted in Louisiana in 1724 (see p.261), New Orleans was the only city in the United States in which slaves, including first-generation arrivals from Africa and Haiti, congregated freely together. Right up until the mid-1800s, at weekly gatherings in **Congo Square** (see p.261), the slaves sang in African languages, played African instruments and performed African dances. As well as being joined by free people of color and local Houmas tribes, they became a tourist attraction for whites, watched by crowds of Anglo-American New Orleanians and visitors from further afield. The Yankee architect Benjamin Latrobe, for example, in 1819 commented on the dancing, the drums and a "curious . . . stringed instrument which no doubt was imported from Africa", which sounds like a forerunner of the banjo.

An even more direct influence on the emergence of jazz, however, was **brass band** music. New Orlean's first brass parade took place in 1787, to celebrate a meeting between Governor Miro and the Houmas. By 1820, each ethnic group had its favorite ensembles, who competed in occasional "battles of the bands". In 1838, the *Picayune* referred to "a real mania in this city for horn and trumpet playing". That mania only increased thereafter, with marching bands featuring prominently in **Mardi Gras parades** and being hired for public occasions of all kinds – including, famously, funerals.

Meanwhile, from the early nineteenth century onward, formal, classically trained orchestras would play the latest European dance tunes in the ballrooms, and the city also boasted a thriving opera house. The cultural links between Louisiana and France remained strong, and many musicians completed their schooling in Europe.

After the **Civil War**, brass band music grew ever more popular throughout the United States, given impetus by a craze for the rousing tunes of bandmaster John Philip Sousa. The voices of newly freed slaves were now also being heard, albeit largely at first in bowdlerized minstrel and vaudeville shows. In New Orleans, the merging of musical traditions was hastened by an influx of ex-slaves from rural Louisiana, as well as migrants from the North, and even from Germany and Italy. In addition, in the bitter aftermath of **Reconstruction**, the city's extraordinarily complex system of social and racial gradations, based on subtle differences in skin tone and degrees of European, Caribbean or African ancestry, became eroded. As a result of the Supreme Court ruling in the *Plessy vs Ferguson* case (see p.269), which led to the legal categorization of all people of color as "negroes", mixed-race Creoles and black musicians found themselves competing for work and, inevitably, playing together.

Jazz

Toward the end of the nineteenth century, the music that became known as "**jazz**" developed out of the incorporation of African and Caribbean rhythms into both brass band and popular dance music. This was often a very literal process, as young, unschooled musicians from the "spasm" bands who played home-made instruments for tips on the streets would graduate into membership of formally constituted brass bands. Increasingly, in turn, brass band musicians joined the ad-hoc groups who were now providing the entertainment in the clubs and dance halls. In part because they supplied the sheer volume essential in crowded indoor venues, trumpets, cornets, trombones and clarinets swiftly replaced the violin as lead instruments, playing above a rhythm section of perhaps guitar, bass, drums and piano.

Legend has it that the defining moment in jazz history came when the smooth, sophisticated band led from 1893 onward by the Creole multi-instrumentalist **John Robichaux** was rendered passé by the "hot" new sounds of the anarchic, flamboyant cornet player **Buddy Bolden**, who founded his own band in 1897. In fact there's no evidence that Robichaux, whose band thrived for at least two decades more and featured many of the seminal figures of early jazz, was any less talented or popular than Bolden. Bolden did, however, provide the archetype of the tortured jazz genius: he was declared insane following his erratic behavior during a Labor Day parade in 1906 and never played again.

Few early jazz groups seem to have played in the brothels of **Storyville**, New Orleans' red-light district, which flourished between 1897 and 1917 (see p.111). Most brothels employed solo pianists, often known as "professors". Storyville was not so much the "birthplace of jazz" as the incubator for a particular kind of jazz – piano-based, ragtime-derived and Caribbean-influenced. Its most famous exponent, **Jelly Roll Morton**, was later to claim, "I myself happened to be the creator of jazz in 1902".

In the absence of the fabled Edison cylinder said to have been cut by Buddy Bolden around 1900, no one now knows what the first jazz bands sounded like. New Orleans musicians were responsible for the earliest **recordings** of jazz, twenty years later, but by then the music had expanded far beyond the city. Following the closure of Storyville, which coincided with a clampdown on live entertainment throughout the city, there was a mass exodus of musicians to Chicago and then New York, where they helped to trigger the start of the worldwide Jazz Age of the 1920s.

Freddie Keppard, whose band took Chicago by storm in 1914, refused to be recorded on the grounds that other musicians would copy his style. As a result, the first jazz band to make a record, in New York in 1917, was a group of white New Orleanians called the **Original Dixieland Jazz Band**. Their million-selling *Dixie Jass Band One-Step* inspired black New Orleans bands such as those of **Edward "Kid" Ory** (in California) and **Joe "King" Oliver** (in Chicago) to try their hands. Oliver's Creole Jazz Band cut the first definitive jazz classics in 1923, then broke up acrimoniously, but his second trumpeter, **Louis Armstrong**, went on to form the Hot Fives – which occasionally grew to become the Hot Sevens – in New York. Jelly Roll Morton was also in Chicago by 1923 and reached his creative peak recording there with the Red Hot Peppers in 1926.

New Orleans itself soon came to be seen as a backwater, far from the cutting edge of jazz, and even those New Orleans musicians who had achieved success elsewhere found it hard to adapt to the advent of Big Band and swing music during the 1930s. Several jazz pioneers dropped into obscurity and despair – Oliver, for example, died as a janitor in Savannah in 1938 – while those who managed to crest the incoming wave, such as Armstrong and the saxophonist Sidney Bechet, displayed a marked reluctance to return home to the South.

As academic interest in jazz grew, however, New Orleans

came to be seen as a repository of "authentic" jazz. Hence the excitement over the "rediscovery" of a former Oliver and Armstrong sideman, trumpeter **Bunk Johnson**, in the early 1940s. Dental problems had precluded Johnson from playing for ten years, so the well-wishers who paid for his teeth to be fixed felt that he could not have been corrupted by modern styles. His re-emergence did him little long-term good, but the jazz revival continues to this day, with the New Orleans, or **Dixieland**, style being regarded as "traditional".

Rhythm and blues

In the late 1940s, New Orleans once again spearheaded the creation of a radical new form of popular music. While the blues had never been a major force in the city, its electrified cousin, **rhythm and blues**, certainly was. In collaboration with the bandleader and producer **Dave Bartholomew**, a shy young bar-room pianist, **Antoine "Fats" Domino**, announced himself as *The Fat Man* in 1949. Together they went on to sell a hundred million records worldwide, with hits including *Ain't It a Shame* and *Blueberry Hill*. Domino's sound changed little over the years, but its crossover appeal with young white audiences meant that he became regarded as a rock'n'roll rather than an r'n'b star.

Thanks to Fats Domino's huge international success, New Orleans became a major **recording center** for the first time. Cosimo Matassa's studio at Rampart and Dumaine churned out a stream of hits, not only from Domino himself but by emulators such as Lloyd *Lawdy Miss Clawdy* Price, and even Little Richard from Georgia, all of whose greatest material was recorded in New Orleans. However, the most influential figure within the city itself was Henry Roeland Byrd. A former tapdancer and boxer who reinvented himself in 1949 as pianist **Professor Longhair**, "Fess" was a one-man synthesis of all that made

New Orleans funky. One bandmate defined his style as "a Caribbean left hand and a boogie woogie right hand", Jerry Wexler of Atlantic Records hailed him as "the Picasso of keyboard funk" and he himself said his music consisted of "offbeat Spanish beats and Calypso downbeats". His genius remained unrecognized and unrewarded for most of his life, but his legacy includes three of New Orleans' greatest party records: *Tipitina*, which gave its name to the uptown club where he gave his final performances before his death in 1980, the carnival anthem *Go to the Mardi Gras*, and the extraordinary, intoxicating *Big Chief*.

During the early 1960s, New Orleans churned out an almost inexhaustible stream of r'n'b and pop hits, thanks largely to composer-producer-pianist **Allen Toussaint**. He was responsible for Jessie Hill's *Ooh Poo Pah Doo*, Ernie K-Doe's *Mother-in-Law*, former boxing champion Lee Dorsey's *Working In a Coalmine* and *Holy Cow*, and the young Irma Thomas' *It's Raining* and *Ruler of My Heart*. The much-loved Toussaint later achieved fame as a solo artist and continues to work in the city, promoting new talent both on his NYNO record label and in showcase concerts.

The 1960s to the present

The city's music scene all but collapsed in the mid-1960s, however, as recording studios went broke and clubs closed down. Some blame a "clean-up" operation by district attorney Jim Garrison, of *JFK* fame; others say it was the advent of rock music that delivered the hammer blow. Among musicians who left town was session man Mac Rebennack, who, while working for Sonny and Cher in California, developed a musical persona based on the nineteenth-century voodoo man **Dr John**. Failing to find anyone willing to play the part, he took on the role of the "Night-Tripper" himself. Though albums from 1967's *Gris-Gris* onward may have gone overboard on depicting New

Orleans as a mysterious, voodoo-riddled and otherworldly realm, he was scrupulous about honoring the city's musical heritage, working with Professor Longhair and employing such prime talent as keyboard wizard **James Booker**.

Over the last twenty years, three major factors have restored New Orleans music to its current comparatively healthy state. The first was the success of the Neville brothers. The eldest, Art Neville, recorded *Mardi Gras Mambo* with the Hawkettes in 1954 and was also (as he remains) a member of the Meters – nowadays known as the funky Meters – while the pure-voiced man-mountain Aaron cut an all-time **soul** classic in 1967's *Tell It Like It Is*. They only came together as a group with brothers Charles and Cyril for the *Wild Tchoupitoulas* album in 1976. A critical if not a financial triumph, that superb tribute to the music of the **Mardi Gras Indians** (see p.275) resulted in the formation of the **Neville Brothers**, still the city's best-known band.

In addition, New Orleans continues to produce major-league jazz stars, even if most of them swiftly move onto the international arena. The **Marsalis** family – especially trumpeter Wynton, the virtuoso classicist, and the funkier saxophonist Branford – were the great success story of the 1980s, while another young trumpeter, Nicholas Payton, was the discovery of the 1990s.

The final factor has been the emergence of new, young **brass bands** whose raw energy must surely be a match for the "spasm" bands of a century ago; New Orleans now boasts more of these rambunctious groups than ever before. Groups such as the Dirty Dozen, who started out in the 1970s as a kazoo band, paved the way for the revival, but the first of the new generation to achieve a commercial impact, with an exciting, raucous sound that extended from traditional standards to Michael Jackson covers, was the ReBirth Brass Band in the 1980s. In their wake came the

New Birth, the Lil Rascals, the Soul Rebels, Coolbone and others, from whose ranks charismatic performers such as the ubiquitous **Kermit Ruffins** and James Andrews have justifiably become solo stars.

Discography

Various Artists, *Crescent City Soul: The Sound of New Orleans 1947–1974* (EMI). None of the dozens of compilations of New Orleans r'n'b is perfect – there's just too much material to choose from – but this four-CD set is as close as any, including essentials such as *The Fat Man* (Fats Domino), *Mother-in-Law* (Ernie K-Doe) and *Ooh Poo Pah Do* (Jessie Hill), plus another 116 cuts besides.

Louis Armstrong, *The Hot Fives (and Sevens) Volumes 1–3* (Columbia). Definitive collection of the 1925–28 recordings whereby New Orleans' greatest son brought jazz onto the world stage.

Coolbone *Brass-Hop* (Hollywood Records). This funky, hard-hitting 1997 experiment in rap-brass fusion benefits from a slick LA production job; if you prefer a rougher sound, try the Soul Rebels' *Let Your Mind be Free* (Mardi Gras Records).

Doc Cheatham and Nicholas Payton, *Doc Cheatham and Nicholas Payton* (Verve). Two great trumpeters breathe fresh life into jazz standards, in a gloriously elegiac meeting that was recorded in 1996 when Cheatham, who has since died, was 91 and Payton was just 23.

Dr John, *Goin' Back To New Orleans* (Warner Brothers). Accompanied by a fabulous roster of postwar greats, Dr John takes a vibrant, inspirational journey through a century of New Orleans music.

Fats Domino, *My Blue Heaven: The Best of Fats Domino* (EMI). You'd need a box set to do Fats full justice, but this twenty-track anthology has the major hits.

Jelly Roll Morton, *The Chicago Years* (Louisiana Red Hot Records). The Red Hot Peppers' finest moments, recorded between 1926 and 1928, and lovingly restored to near-pristine condition.

The Neville Brothers *Treacherous: A History of the Neville Brothers* (Rhino). This exciting, eclectic compilation of Nevilles' highlights stops in 1985, but it takes in Art's 1954 *Mardi Gras Mambo*, Aaron's sweet soul ballad *Tell It Like It Is* from 1967 and two stand-out tracks from *The Wild Tchoupitoulas* album of Mardi Gras Indian music (see p.275).

Professor Longhair, *Fess: The Professor Longhair Story* (Rhino). Sumptuous two-CD selection of the best of Fess, worth the price for 1964's *Big Chief – Part 2* alone.

ReBirth Brass Band, *We Come To Party* (Shanachie). And party they surely do, with raucous, uplifting brass rearrangements of Michael Jackson and Marvin Gaye hits plus their own second-line stomps.

Kermit Ruffins, *The Barbecue Swingers Live* (Basin Street Records). The hardest-working musician in New Orleans, versatile trumpeter Kermit Ruffins is on peak, convivial form in this 1998 live CD, which ranges from traditional brass to exuberant rap.

Irma Thomas, *Time Is On My Side: The Best of Irma Thomas* (EMI). The young Irma Thomas sings her heart out on stunning songs like *Time Is On My Side*, *Ruler of My Heart*, and *It's Raining*, recorded in collaboration with producer Allen Toussaint in the 1960s.

Greg Ward

DISCOGRAPHY

New Orleans on film

New Orleans has captured the imagination of filmmakers since 1918, when the first Tarzan movie, *Tarzan of the Apes*, was filmed in the nearby swamps, with members of the New Orleans Athletic Club swinging through the trees in ape costumes. It's a supremely photogenic city, particularly in the crumbling old streets of the French Quarter, which lend themselves perfectly to steamy, noirish visions and haunting Gothic nightmares. On top of that, its countless romantic associations, swathed in myth – Mardi Gras, the Mississippi River, the lost culture of the Creoles, the pirates, the prostitutes, the voodoo queens – are rich pickings for storytellers.

All the King's Men (Robert Rossen, 1949). Thinly veiled biopic of 1930s State Governor Huey Long – popularly known as the "Kingfish" for his catchphrase "Every man a king" – whose hard-nosed combination of radical politics, bully-boy tactics, and blatant corruption led to his assassination in 1936. A gripping tale, offering a perceptive insight into Louisiana's notoriously corrupt political system.

Always for Pleasure (Les Blank, 1978). Outstanding music documentary, composed from an impressionistic whirl through New Orleans' street parades, jazz funerals and Mardi Gras festivities. Performances include superb turns by Professor Longhair and the Wild Tchoupitoulas Mardi Gras Indians.

Angel Heart (Alan Parker, 1987). Heavy-handed, portentous thriller, set in the 1950s, in which Mickey Rourke's New York private eye, Harry Angel, meets his nemesis in the demonic Louis Cyphre (Robert de Niro). New Orleans is shown at its darkest, a murky netherworld of Faustian pacts and perverse voodoo rituals.

The Big Easy (Jim McBride, 1986). Dennis Quaid shot to fame as the easy-going, maverick New Orleans cop who plays cat-and-mouse with uptight assistant DA Ellen Barkin. Barkin, of course, is eventually won over by the dissolute charms of the French Quarter, and Quaid, of course, straightens up his act. Great fun, not least for Quaid's preposterous Cajun accent.

The Buccaneer (Cecil B. De Mille,1938). Riproaring swashbuckler, romanticizing the role of pirate Jean Lafitte in Andrew Jackson's victory against the British in the 1815 Battle of New Orleans.

Down by Law (Jim Jarmusch, 1986). From its moody opening shots, panning across decrepit, hauntingly beautiful streetscapes, to the stylish soundtrack from Tom Waits and John Lurie, Jarmusch's low-key, monochrome hymn to New Orleans low life is a treat. Waits and Lurie are the jaded jailbirds making a bid for freedom, led by their *faux naif* cellmate, Roberto Benigni in an early American role. New Orleans at its dissipated best, populated by pimps, corrupt policemen and tear-stained lushes.

Easy Rider (Dennis Hopper, 1969). Hippy anthem to life on the road, full of scenes of hirsute bikers Dennis Hopper and Peter Fonda riding their Harleys cross-country in search of freedom. New Orleans, where they pick up a couple of hookers and suffer a bad trip in St Louis No. 1 Cemetery, represents the final death blow to their dreams and propels them toward a tragic demise. For all their hazy acid-trip posturing, the New Orleans scenes do evoke an oddly true-to-life impression of the city's decadence and decay, and, in particular, the bizarre spectacle of Mardi Gras.

The Flame of New Orleans (René Clair, 1941). Marlene Dietrich is fabulous as a Russian emigré posing as an heiress in this romantic drama set on the Mississippi steamboats and in the gambling dens and barrelhouses of nineteenth-century New Orleans.

Hard Target (John Woo, 1993). Noisy, explosion-filled action movie in which Jean-Claude Van Damme's unfortunately coiffed kick-boxing Cajun is tracked by bow-and-arrow wielding baddies through the city and into the swamps, with a fast and furious finale in a Mardi Gras den. Woo's Hong Kong aesthetic is strangely captivating, all freeze frames, slow motion and gratuitous violence, and despite its absurdities, the movie does a good job of representing New Orleans' rough-around-the-edges glamor.

Interview with the Vampire (Neil Jordan, 1994). Movie version of Anne Rice's first vampire novel, with Tom Cruise surprisingly effective as the malevolent Lestat, and the puffy-faced Brad Pitt less convincing as his victim/consort Louis. The complexities of the novel don't quite make it onto the screen, though Kirsten Dunst as the tragic child vampire Claudia casts a chilling presence.

Jezebel (William Wyler, 1938). Classic melodrama set in antebellum New Orleans. Bette Davis shines as the stubborn, rebellious heroine – turning up at a society ball in a scarlet dress, that kind of thing – whose ultimate punishment is to lose the man she loves (Henry Fonda, suitably lily-livered in the role) to yellow fever.

JFK (Oliver Stone, 1991). A relentless three hours' worth of Stone's conspiracy theory paranoia can be a bit much, and Kevin Costner is dull as New Orleans DA Jim Garrison, investigating the Kennedy assassination, but the supporting cast – including Gary Oldman as Oswald – put in some great performances, and there are some great location shots of the city.

King Creole (Michael Curtiz, 1958). Elvis, at his darkest, pouting best, turns out an accomplished performance as a street hustler in this drama of gangsters, sleazy nightclubs and doomed love. The black-and-white city looks wonderfully dissolute, and the songs, including the title number, *I'm Evil*, and *Crawfish*, are among the King's finest.

My Forbidden Past (Robert Stevenson, 1951). Passions run high in 1890s New Orleans, when bad-to-the-bone heiress Ava Gardner steams and schemes, hoping to seduce a lazily sexy Robert Mitchum away from his wife.

Panic in the Streets (Elia Kazan, 1950). Pacy film noir, in which
bubonic plague-carrying murderer Jack Palance is hunted down
along New Orleans' seedy waterfront.

Piano Players Rarely Ever Play Together (J. Palfi Stevenson,
1982). Magnificent documentary, which brings three generations
of piano maestros – Tuts Washington, Professor Longhair and
Allen Toussaint – to play together for the first time. Their personal
interaction in the build-up to the performance, and the interplay
of their different musical styles, are fascinating in themselves, but
Longhair's sudden death during filming, and the footage of his
jazz funeral, serve to make it an even more poignant document.
And the music, of course, is fantastic.

Pretty Baby (Louis Malle, 1977). Seductive portrayal of the Storyville
bordellos of the early 1900s, seen through the eyes of a virgin
prostitute (Brooke Shields) and tortured photographer E.J.
Bellocq (Keith Carradine), and filmed on location at the *Columns
Hotel* in the Garden District (see p.141). Bellocq's real-life
portraits of New Orleans' prostitutes provided much of the
inspiration for the movie.

A Streetcar Named Desire (Elia Kazan, 1951). In a tortuous attempt
to comply with the Production Code, which controlled censorship
in Hollywood, Tennessee Williams' drama about nymphomania,
hysteria and homosexuality loses something in the film version.
Still hugely atmospheric, though, with great performances from
Method actors Marlon Brando and Kim Hunter as Stanley and
Stella; Hunter won an Academy Award, as did Vivien Leigh, all
rolling eyes and wilting feather boas as the troubled Blanche
Dubois. New Orleans – the little you see of it outside Stanley and
Stella's shabby apartment – is suitably steamy.

Wild at Heart (David Lynch, 1990). At the time of its release, Lynch's
surreal, dark style was all the rage; a decade later, however, the
movie's self-conscious bizarreness palls somewhat, especially in
comparison with the director's earlier works, *Eraserhead* and

Blue Velvet. Nicolas Cage and Laura Dern ham it up as the passion-crazy lovers fleeing Dern's evil mother; New Orleans, a nightmare of violet shadows and lacy iron balconies, is just one stop on their crazy roadtrip through the Deep South.

INDEX

Stay in touch with us!

ROUGH*NEWS* is Rough Guides' free newsletter.
In three issues a year we give you news, travel issues, music reviews, readers' letters and the latest dispatches from authors on the road.

I would like to receive ROUGH*NEWS*: please put me on your free mailing list.

NAME . . . .

ADDRESS . . . .

Please clip or photocopy and send to: Rough Guides, 1 Mercer Street, London WC2H 9QJ, England

or Rough Guides, 375 Hudson Street, New York, NY 10014, USA.

ROUGH GUIDES: Travel

ROUGH GUIDES: Mini Guides, Travel Specials and Phrasebooks

MINI GUIDES

Antigua
Bangkok
Barbados
Big Island of Hawaii
Boston
Brussels
Budapest
Dublin
Edinburgh
Florence
Honolulu
Lisbon
London Restaurants
Madrid
Maui
Melbourne
New Orleans
St Lucia

Seattle
Sydney
Tokyo
Toronto

TRAVEL SPECIALS

First-Time Asia
First-Time Europe
More Women Travel

PHRASEBOOKS

Czech
Dutch
Egyptian Arabic
European
French

German
Greek
Hindi & Urdu
Hungarian
Indonesian
Italian
Japanese
Mandarin
  Chinese
Mexican
  Spanish
Polish
Portuguese
Russian
Spanish
Swahili
Thai
Turkish
Vietnamese

AVAILABLE AT ALL GOOD BOOKSHOPS

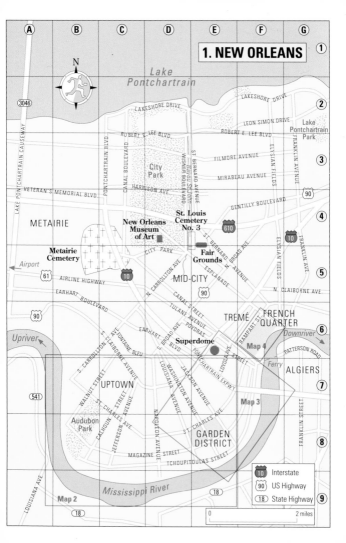

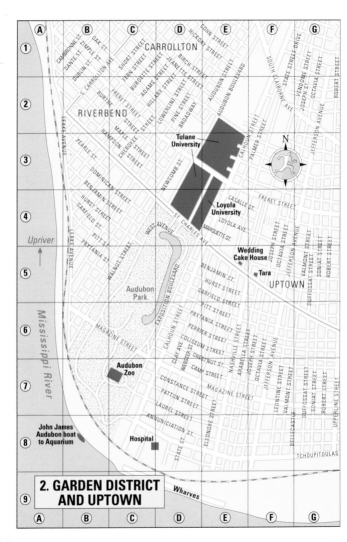

2. GARDEN DISTRICT AND UPTOWN